Keto Crock Pot Cookbook

600 Easy & Delicious Crock Pot Recipes for Rapid Weight Loss & Burn

Fat Forever (Crock Pot Cookbook for Beginners and Pros)

Rondan Jasmin

Table of contents

Introduction

What is the Keto Diet?

The ketogenic diet plan has surfaced as an efficient culinary approach to avoid and treat all health problems. It offers low carb and high-fat meals, which is not only invigorating but also super healthy. As people mistakenly assume that a high-fat diet is a root cause of all health issues, it is not entirely true. In the absence of carbohydrates, good fat can prove to be advantageous for our health, which is the real objective of a ketogenic diet. It is responsible for accelerating the body's natural metabolic process called Ketosis, by keeping the carb intake down to 50 grams per day or less. To harness its true benefits, it requires a good and deep understanding of the diet, its Dos and Don'ts just to get started with it, that is why the content of this cookbook will help you explore the basics of a ketogenic diet along with the recipes. These recipes are created with the consideration of the latest slow cooking innovation Crock-Pot so you can cook and enjoy with complete ease and convenience.

Perks of going, Keto

The following list includes the most prominent advantages of a ketogenic diet. With years of research, even professionals of the field have proven these health advantages:

1. Removal of Excess Fat

When the aim of a diet is solely to consume fat and procure energy for the body, then consequently, it will burn all the excess fats. The ketogenic meal is, therefore, great to reduce fat deposits in any part of the body and renders it more light and active.

2. Controlling of Cholesterol

As the ketogenic diet put fat into good use, all the good and bad cholesterols are processed out of the body. The blood cholesterol levels, therefore, drop to a desirable state. Lesser cholesterol in the blood means, no accumulation in the vessels and no obstruction in the cardiovascular system.

3. Maintained Blood Sugar

As all diabetic patients suffer from high blood sugar levels due to low production of insulin, they can gain maximum benefit out of the ketogenic diet as it provides better low carb alternatives. They can live a pro-active and healthy life without using any forms of sugar at all.

4. High Energy Diet

We all know that a single fat molecule produces twice the amount of energy produced by the breakdown of the same amount of carbohydrates. That is why the ketogenic diet being rich in fat gives a big boost of energy after every single meal. Such energy is enough to spend the day with good zeal.

5. Active Life with Greater Vitality

Scientific researches have also recently discovered a direct relation between vitality and ketogenic life by observing people, been having keto meals for years. It can be all true as a balanced diet is a key to longevity, and keto diet ensures that balance.

6. Healthy Mind

As discussed earlier, this diet itself surfaced as a non-medicinal treatment of epilepsy, which proves its effectiveness in improving mental health. Doctors are now even prescribing it to Alzheimer's patients as a long-lasting treatment. Both energy and fat from the keto diet are responsible for strengthening our brain cells.

7. Weight Loss

We have already established the fact that ketogenic diet help to remove fat deposits from the body. Eventually, it reduces obesity. Within two to three weeks of keto lifestyle, a person can lose about 2 to 3 lbs.

A Closer Look into the Ketogenic Lifestyle

What to Enjoy on this Diet?

- Keto-Friendly Animal Produce

Meat in any of its forms doesn't contain carbohydrates, so it is completely allowed on a ketogenic diet. It includes seafood, poultry: chicken, turkey, duck, beef, mutton, lamb, pork, etc.

- Low Carb Vegetables

To identify vegetables as ketogenic, one simple rule should be kept in mind that those grown mostly below the ground are rich in carbohydrates and are not keto-friendly, especially underground tubers. Whereas all the vegetables above the ground are keto-friendly, these include green leafy vegetables, tomatoes, cucumber, asparagus, broccoli, cabbage, cauliflower, etc.

- Keto Seeds and Nuts

Seeds and dry nuts do not contain excessive carbohydrates, and a balanced amount of them can be taken on a keto diet. Pumpkin seeds, pistachio, almonds, etc. are all allowed.

- Limited Dairy Items

For dairy products, we need to be a bit more careful as not all of them are prohibited on a keto diet. Milk contains more carbohydrates; therefore, it should be avoided. Whereas cheese, yogurt, cream, cream cheese, butter, eggs are all keto-friendly.

Animal milk can be substituted with:

1. Soy milk
2. Almond milk
3. Coconut milk
4. Macadamia milk
5. Hemp milk

- Keto-Friendly Fruits

Like veggies, not all fruits are good for the ketogenic diet. Some are high in carbs like apple, pineapple, banana, etc. However, you can enjoy blackberries, cranberries, avocado, coconut, blueberries, strawberries, as they have low carb content.

- Healthy Fats and Oils

When it comes to fat, there is no compulsion or reservations for a ketogenic diet. You can use all plant oils, and animal fat, including olive oil, butter, canola oil, etc.

- Low Carb-Sweeteners

1. Stevia
2. Erythritol
3. Swerve
4. Monk fruit sweetener
5. Natvia

What Should you be Avoiding?

1. Say No to Grains

Edible grains are a great source of carbohydrates, whether its wheat, rice, barley, millet, etc. So, these all are strictly forbidden on a keto-friendly diet. Products obtained from these grains are also not allowed, including wheat flour, all-purpose flour, rice flours, etc. Flour of such sort can be replaced with:

- Almond flour
- Coconut flour
2. Animal Milk

All dairy items are allowed on a ketogenic diet except for animal milk.

3. NO Legumes

All legumes are grown underground, and they are high carb food items. Legumes include all lentils, beans, and chickpeas. None of them are keto-friendly and should be completely avoided.

4. Avoid all Sugars

Sugar is nothing but the purest form of carbohydrates. Hence it should be avoided completely, whether its white sugar, confectionary, granulated, brown, baking sugar, etc. Products containing a high level of sugar are also prohibited like molasses, honey, dates, processed food, and beverages.

5. High Glycaemic Fruits

Fruits like banana, oranges, apples, pomegranate, pineapple, pears, watermelon are all very rich in sugar. Avoid using these fruits, especially on a ketogenic diet. Extract and juices obtained from these fruits should be avoided.

6. Underground Tubers and Starchy Vegetables

Tubers are underground vegetables, and they basically store food for plants in the form of carbohydrates. These include potatoes, beetroots, and yams. They all are not good for a ketogenic diet.

Chapter 1: Breakfast and Brunch

Zucchini Bread

Prep Time: 10 minutes; Cooking Time: 3 hours; Serving: 6
Ingredients:

- 1 cup of almond flour
- 1/3 cup of coconut flour
- 2 teaspoons of cinnamon
- 1 1/2 teaspoon of baking powder
- 1/2 teaspoon of baking soda
- 1/2 teaspoon of salt
- 1/2 teaspoon of xanthan gum optional
- 3 eggs
- 1/3 cup of coconut oil softened, or butter
- 1/2 cup of swerve
- 2 teaspoons of vanilla
- 2 cups of zucchini, shredded
- 1/2 cup of walnuts or pecans, diced

Method:

1. Start by beating all the wet Ingredients: in an electric mixer.
2. Whisk the dry Ingredients: separately in a bowl.
3. Add this flour mixture to the prepared wet mixture and beat well until smooth.
4. Fold in walnut and shredded zucchini, then mix roughly.
5. Spread this zucchini batter into a greased loaf pan (suitable to the size of the crockpot)
6. Place this pan in the crockpot.
7. Cover your Crockpot and select the high settings for 3 hours.
8. Remove the crockpot's lid.
9. Slice and serve warm.

Nutritional Information per Serving:

- Calories 108
- Total Fat 9 g
- Saturated Fat 4.3 g
- Cholesterol 180 mg
- Sugar 0.5 g
- Fiber 0.1 g
- Sodium 146 mg
- Protein 6 g

Cheesy Cauliflower Garlic Bread

Prep Time: 10 minutes; Cooking Time: 3 hours; Serving: 4
Ingredients:

- 12 oz. cauliflower florets, diced
- 2 large eggs
- 2 cups of mozzarella, shredded
- 3 tablespoons of coconut flour
- 1/2 teaspoon of salt
- 1/2 teaspoon of pepper
- 2 cloves garlic, minced
- 1/4 cup of fresh basil diced

Method:

1. Start by greasing the base of your Crockpot.
2. Mix and whisk all the Ingredients: together in a bowl except 1 cup of cheese
3. Pour this mixture into the pot and top with reserved these
4. Cover your crockpot and select the Low settings for 3 hours.
5. Remove the crockpot's lid.
6. Serve warm.

Nutritional Information per Serving:

- Calories 112
- Total Fat 4.9 g
- Saturated Fat 1.9 g
- Cholesterol 10 mg

- Sugar 0.8 g
- Fiber 0.4 g
- Sodium 355 mg
- Protein 3 g

Bell Pepper Hash

Prep Time: 10 minutes; Cooking Time: 3 hours; Serving: 4

Ingredients:
- 2 tablespoon of olive oil
- 3 eggplant, cubed
- 1 yellow onion, diced
- 1 red bell pepper, diced
- 1 teaspoon of garlic powder
- 1 teaspoon of sweet paprika
- 1 teaspoon of onion powder
- Salt and black pepper- to taste
- ½ cup of vegetable stock

Method:
1. Start by throwing all the Ingredients: into the Crockpot.
2. Cover your Crockpot and select the high settings for 3 hours.
3. Remove the crockpot's lid.
4. Check if the eggplants are al dente else cook for another 30 minutes or more.
5. Mix gently and serve warm.

Nutritional Information per Serving:
- Calories 132
- Total Fat 10.9 g
- Saturated Fat 2.7 g
- Cholesterol 164 mg
- Sugar 0.5 g
- Fiber 2.3 g
- Sodium 65 mg
- Protein 6.3 g

Ham Frittata

Prep Time: 10 minutes; Cooking Time: 3 hours; Serving: 6

Ingredients:
- 6 cups of keto bread, cubed
- 4 oz. green chilies, diced
- 2 cups of almond milk
- 5 eggs, room temperature
- 1 tablespoon of mustard
- 10 oz. ham, cubed
- 4 oz. cheddar cheese, shredded
- Salt and black pepper- to taste
- Cooking spray

Method:
1. Start by greasing the base of your Crockpot.
2. Whisk the egg with all other Ingredients: and pour into crockpot.
3. Cover your crockpot and select the Low settings for 3 hours.
4. Remove the crockpot's lid.
5. Slice and serve warm.

Nutritional Information per Serving:
- Calories 204
- Total Fat 15.7 g
- Saturated Fat 9.7 g
- Cholesterol 49 mg
- Sugar 3.4 g
- Fiber 1.5 g
- Sodium 141 mg
- Protein 26.3 g

Cheesy Sausage Quiche

Prep Time: 10 minutes; Cooking Time: 4 hours; Serving: 4

Ingredients:

- 4 bacon strips, cooked and crumbled
- 2 cups of almond milk
- 1 lb. sausage, diced
- 2 eggs, room temperature
- 2 ½ cups of cheddar cheese, shredded
- 1/2 teaspoon of onion powder
- 3 tablespoons of parsley, chopped
- Salt and black pepper- to taste
- Cooking spray

Method:
1. Start by greasing the base of your Crockpot.
2. Whisk the egg with all other Ingredients: and pour into crockpot.
3. Cover your crockpot and select the Low settings for 4 hours.
4. Remove the crockpot's lid.
5. Slice and serve warm.

Nutritional Information per Serving:
- Calories 356
- Total Fat 11.7 g
- Saturated Fat 1.8 g
- Cholesterol 5 mg
- Sugar 0.1 g
- Fiber 2.3 g
- Sodium 323 mg
- Protein 18.1 g

Mushroom Casserole

Prep Time: 10 minutes; Cooking Time: 3 hours 5 minutes; Serving: 3
Ingredients:
- 3 eggs
- 2 ½ oz. cremini mushrooms, diced
- 5 oz. cauliflower florets, diced
- ½ leek, sliced
- 1/4 teaspoon of salt
- Black pepper to taste
- 6 sausage links, cooked and sliced
- ½ (8 oz.) package cheddar cheese

Method:
1. Start by greasing the base of your Crockpot.
2. Spread all the veggies, sausages, and mushrooms.
3. Whisk the egg with remaining Ingredients: except for cheese and pour them over the veggies.
4. Cover your Crockpot and select the medium settings for 3 hours.
5. Remove the crockpot's lid.
6. Drizzle the reserved cheese on top and then cover again.
7. Cook for another 5 minutes on High setting.
8. Serve warm.

Nutritional Information per Serving:
- Calories 244
- Total Fat 11.5 g
- Saturated Fat 1.5 g
- Cholesterol 61 mg
- Sugar 0.4 g
- Fiber 0.2 g
- Sodium 246 mg
- Protein 12.5 g

Breakfast Frittata

Prep Time: 10 minutes; Cooking Time: 3 hours; Serving: 8
Ingredients:
- ¾ cups of spinach, frozen
- 1 ½ cups of red bell pepper, diced
- ¼ cups of red onion, diced
- 8 eggs
- ½ teaspoons of black pepper
- 1 teaspoon of salt

- 1 ⅓ cups of sausages, cooked and diced

Method:
1. Start by greasing the base of your Crockpot.
2. Whisk the egg with remaining Ingredients: and pour into crockpot.
3. Cover your crockpot and select the Low settings for 3 hours.
4. Remove the crockpot's lid.
5. Slice and serve warm.

Nutritional Information per Serving:
- Calories 131
- Total Fat 8.5 g
- Saturated Fat 11.5 g
- Cholesterol 51 mg
- Sugar 0.5 g
- Fiber 0.4 g
- Sodium 346 mg
- Protein 2.5 g

Mexican Casserole

Prep Time: 10 minutes; Cooking Time: 3 hours; Serving: 10
Ingredients:
- 12 oz. Jones Dairy Farm Pork Sausage Roll
- 1/2 teaspoon of garlic powder
- 1/2 teaspoon of coriander
- 1 teaspoon of cumin
- 1 teaspoon of chili powder
- 1/4 teaspoon of salt
- 1/4 teaspoon of pepper
- 1 cup of salsa
- 10 eggs
- 1 cup of almond milk
- 1 cup of Pepper Jack cheese

Method:
1. First, sauté the sausages in a greased pan until brown and keep them aside.
2. Now begin by greasing the base of your Crockpot.
3. Whisk the egg with remaining Ingredients: and pour into crockpot.
4. Spread the sautéed and crumbled sausages on top.
5. Cover your crockpot and select the Low settings for 3 hours.
6. Remove the crockpot's lid.
7. Slice and serve warm.

Nutritional Information per Serving:
- Calories 231
- Total Fat 18.5 g
- Saturated Fat 11.5 g
- Cholesterol 51 mg
- Sugar 0.5 g
- Fiber 0.4 g
- Sodium 346 mg
- Protein 12.5 g

Morning Quiche

Prep Time: 10 minutes; Cooking Time: 4 hours; Serving: 10
Ingredients:
- 1 tablespoon of butter
- 10 eggs, beaten
- 1 cup of light cream or half & half
- 8 oz. shredded cheddar cheese
- 1/2 teaspoon of black pepper
- 10 pieces cooked bacon, diced
- 1/2 cup of diced spinach

Method:
1. Start by greasing the base of your Crockpot.

2. Whisk the egg with remaining Ingredients: except for bacon and pour into crockpot.
3. Crumble and spread the bacon over the mixture.
4. Cover your crockpot and select the Low settings for 4 hours.
5. Remove the crockpot's lid.
6. Slice and serve warm.

Nutritional Information per Serving:
- Calories 211
- Total Fat 18.5 g
- Saturated Fat 11.5 g
- Cholesterol 51 mg
- Sugar 0.5 g
- Fiber 0.4 g
- Sodium 346 mg
- Protein 11.5 g

Sweet Pepper Hash

Prep Time: 10 minutes; Cooking Time: 3 hours; Serving: 10
Ingredients:
- 12-ounce smoked chicken sausage, cooked
- 1 teaspoon of olive oil
- 1 ½ cups of sweet onion, sliced
- 2 teaspoons of fresh thyme
- ½ teaspoon of black pepper
- 10 eggs, beaten
- ¼ cup of chicken broth
- 1 ½ cups of diced green, red, and yellow sweet peppers
- ½ cup of Swiss cheese, shredded
- 2 teaspoons of fresh tarragon
- ¼ cup of cheddar cheese, shredded

Method:
1. First, start by sautéing onion, and sausages separately in a greased skillet for 5 minutes.
2. Now begin by greasing the base of your Crockpot.
3. Add the sautéed onion, sausages, and other veggies to the Crockpot.
4. Whisk the egg with remaining Ingredients: except for cheese and pour into crockpot.
5. Sprinkle the cheese on top of this mixture.
6. Cover your Crockpot and select the high settings for 3 hours.
7. Remove the crockpot's lid.
8. Slice and serve warm.

Nutritional Information per Serving:
- Calories 184
- Total Fat 12.7 g
- Saturated Fat 7.3 g
- Cholesterol 35 mg
- Sugar 2.7 g
- Fiber 1.6 g
- Sodium 222 mg
- Protein 12.2 g

Grain-Free Granola with Orange Zest

Prep Time: 10 minutes; Cooking Time: 4 hours; Serving: 4
Ingredients:
- 2 cups of shredded coconut unsweetened
- 1/4 cup of sunflower seeds
- 1/4 cup of pumpkin seeds
- 2/3 cup of almonds diced
- 2 tablespoons of cacao nibs
- 3 tablespoons of coconut oil
- 2 tablespoons of granulated Swerve
- 4 tablespoons of cocoa powder unsweetened

- 2 tablespoons of orange zest

Method:
1. Start by throwing all the Ingredients: into the Crockpot.
2. Cover your Crockpot and select the high settings for 4 hours.
3. Remove the crockpot's lid.
4. Serve.

Nutritional Information per Serving:
- Calories 188
- Total Fat 12.5 g
- Saturated Fat 4.4 g
- Cholesterol 53 mg
- Sugar 0.3 g
- Fiber 2 g
- Sodium 1098 mg
- Protein 14.6 g

Egg Cauliflower Casserole

Prep Time: 10 minutes; Cooking Time: 3 hours 5 minutes; Serving: 6

Ingredients:
- 10 oz. cauliflower florets, diced
- 6 eggs
- 1/2 teaspoon of salt
- Black pepper to taste
- 12 sausage, cooked and sliced
- 1 leek, sliced
- 1 (8 oz.) package cheddar cheese

Method:
1. Start by greasing the base of your Crockpot.
2. Spread all the veggies, sausages, and mushrooms.
3. Whisk the egg with remaining Ingredients: except for cheese and pour them over the veggies.
4. Cover your Crockpot and select the medium settings for 3 hours.
5. Remove the crockpot's lid.
6. Drizzle the reserved cheese on top and then cover again.
7. Cook for another 5 minutes on High setting.
8. Serve warm.

Nutritional Information per Serving:
- Calories 244
- Total Fat 11.5 g
- Saturated Fat 1.5 g
- Cholesterol 61 mg
- Sugar 0.4 g
- Fiber 0.2 g
- Sodium 246 mg
- Protein 12.5 g

Arugula Frittata

Prep Time: 10 minutes; Cooking Time: 3 hours; Serving: 4

Ingredients:
- 2 cups of baby arugula
- ¼ cup of red onion, sliced
- ¼ cup of feta cheese, crumbled
- Salt and black pepper, to taste
- ¼ cup of almond milk
- ½ teaspoon of oregano, dried
- 4 eggs
- ¾ cups of red peppers, roasted, diced

Method:
1. Start by greasing the base of your Crockpot.
2. Spread the arugula and peppers at the base of the pot.
3. Whisk the egg with remaining Ingredients: and pour into crockpot.

4. Cover your crockpot and select the Low settings for 3 hours.
5. Remove the crockpot's lid.
6. Slice and serve warm.

Nutritional Information per Serving:
- Calories 260
- Total Fat 22.9 g
- Saturated Fat 7.3 g
- Cholesterol 0 mg
- Sugar 1.8 g
- Fiber 1.4 g
- Sodium 9 mg
- Protein 5.6 g

Minced Turkey Egg Casserole

Prep Time: 10 minutes; Cooking Time: 4 hours; Serving: 12
Ingredients:
- 1 zucchini, cubed
- 12 eggs, room temperature
- 1 lb. turkey, ground
- 1 cup of baby spinach
- 1 tablespoon of olive oil
- 1/2 teaspoon of chili powder
- 2 tomatoes, diced
- Salt and black pepper- to taste

Method:
1. Start by greasing the base of your Crockpot.
2. Spread the zucchini and turkey ground at the base of the pot.
3. Whisk the egg with all other Ingredients: and pour into crockpot.
4. Cover your Crockpot and select the medium settings for 4 hours.
5. Remove the crockpot's lid.
6. Slice and serve warm.

Nutritional Information per Serving:
- Calories 238
- Total Fat 16.9 g
- Saturated Fat 16.9 g
- Cholesterol 32 mg
- Sugar 0.1 g
- Fiber 7.2 g
- Sodium 469 mg
- Protein 10.8 g

Egg Hash Browns

Prep Time: 10 minutes; Cooking Time: 3 hours; Serving: 4
Ingredients:
- 2 tablespoons of chives, diced
- 1 egg, whisked
- 16 oz. hash browns
- 1/2 teaspoon of paprika
- 1/2 teaspoon of garlic powder
- 1/4 cup of olive oil
- 1 cup of cheddar, shredded
- Salt and black pepper- to taste

Method:
1. Start by greasing the base of your Crockpot.
2. Spread the hash browns at the base of the pot.
3. Whisk the egg with all other Ingredients: and pour into crockpot.
4. Cover your crockpot and select the Low settings for 3 hours.
5. Remove the crockpot's lid.
6. Slice and serve warm.

Nutritional Information per Serving:
- Calories 228
- Total Fat 20.2 g
- Saturated Fat 12.5 g
- Cholesterol 54 mg
- Sugar 2.3 g
- Fiber 2.4 g

- Sodium 250 mg
- Protein 23.7 g

Mushroom Spinach Breakfast

Prep Time: 10 minutes; Cooking Time: 3 hours; Serving: 4

Ingredients:
- 4 chipolatas
- 7 oz. baby spinach
- 8 chestnuts mushrooms, halved
- 8 tomatoes, halved
- 1 garlic clove, minced
- 4 eggs, room temperature
- 4 bacon strips, diced
- Salt and black pepper- to taste
- Cooking spray

Method:
1. Start by greasing the base of your Crockpot.
2. Whisk spinach with all other Ingredients: and spread into the crockpot.
3. Make four wells into this mixture and crack on egg into each well.
4. Cover your crockpot and select the Low settings for 3 hours.
5. Remove the crockpot's lid.
6. Serve.

Nutritional Information per Serving:
- Calories 393
- Total Fat 15.8 g
- Saturated Fat 10.3 g
- Cholesterol 47 mg
- Sugar 0.4 g
- Fiber 0.4 g
- Sodium 421 mg
- Protein 12.6 g

Bacon Topped Hash Browns

Prep Time: 10 minutes; Cooking Time: 3 hours; Serving: 4

Ingredients:
- 2 lbs. hash browns
- 1 cup of milk
- 1 cup of cheddar cheese, shredded
- 6 green onions, diced
- 8 bacon strips, diced
- 6 eggs, room temperature
- 9 oz. cream cheese
- 1 yellow onion, diced
- Salt and black pepper- to taste
- Cooking spray

Method:
1. Start by greasing the base of your Crockpot.
2. Spread the hash brown at the base of the pot.
3. Whisk the egg with all other Ingredients: and pour into crockpot.
4. Cover your crockpot and select the Low settings for 3 hours.
5. Remove the crockpot's lid.
6. Slice and serve warm.

Nutritional Information per Serving:
- Calories 382
- Total Fat 36.5 g
- Saturated Fat 5.5 g
- Cholesterol 0 mg
- Sugar 3.4 g
- Fiber 5.5 g
- Sodium 73 mg
- Protein 6.3 g

Italian Chicken Frittata

Prep Time: 10 minutes; Cooking Time: 3 hours; Serving: 8

Ingredients:

- 1/2 lbs. chicken sausage, casings removed and diced
- 1 sweet onion, diced
- 1 red bell pepper, diced
- 2 tablespoon of olive oil
- 1 orange bell pepper, diced
- 1 green bell pepper, diced
- 8 eggs, whisked
- 1/2 cup of mozzarella cheese, shredded
- 2 teaspoons of oregano, diced
- Salt and black pepper- to taste

Method:
1. Start by greasing the base of your Crockpot.
2. Spread the sausage and veggies at the base of the pot.
3. Whisk the egg with all other Ingredients: except cheese and pour into crockpot.
4. Cover your crockpot and select the Low settings for 3 hours.
5. Remove the crockpot's lid.
6. Drizzle the cheese on top and serve warm.

Nutritional Information per Serving:
- Calories 345
- Total Fat 31.4 g
- Saturated Fat 12.7 g
- Cholesterol 64 mg
- Sugar 0.8 g
- Fiber 1.9 g
- Sodium 4.2 mg
- Protein 14.8 g

Creamy Egg and Ham Delight

Prep Time: 10 minutes; Cooking Time: 3 hours; Serving: 4
Ingredients:
- 4 eggs, room temperature
- 2 teaspoons of butter, soft
- 2 ham slices
- 3 tablespoons of parmesan, grated
- 2 teaspoons of chives, diced
- 2 tablespoons of heavy cream
- Salt and black pepper- to taste
- A pinch Smoked paprika

Method:
1. Start by greasing the base of your Crockpot.
2. Spread the ham at the base of the pot.
3. Whisk the egg with all other Ingredients: and pour into crockpot.
4. Cover your crockpot and select the Low settings for 3 hours.
5. Remove the crockpot's lid.
6. Slice and serve warm.

Nutritional Information per Serving:
- Calories 284
- Total Fat 26.4 g
- Saturated Fat 15.6 g
- Cholesterol 184 mg
- Sugar 3.6 g
- Fiber 3.1 g
- Sodium 244 mg
- Protein 16.8 g

Kale with Eggs

Prep Time: 10 minutes; Cooking Time: 3 hours; Serving: 4
Ingredients:
- 7 oz. Kale, chopped
- 1 garlic clove, minced
- 4 eggs, room temperature
- 4 bacon strips, diced
- Salt and black pepper- to taste
- Cooking spray

Method:
1. Start by greasing the base of your Crockpot.

2. Whisk kale with all other Ingredients: and spread into the crockpot.
3. Make four wells into this mixture and crack on egg into each well.
4. Cover your crockpot and select the Low settings for 3 hours.
5. Remove the crockpot's lid.
6. Serve.

Nutritional Information per Serving:
- Calories 393
- Total Fat 15.8 g
- Saturated Fat 10.3 g
- Cholesterol 47 mg
- Sugar 0.4 g
- Fiber 0.4 g
- Sodium 421 mg
- Protein 12.6 g

Asparagus Parmesan Frittata

Prep Time: 10 minutes; Cooking Time: 4 hours; Serving: 6
Ingredients:
- 4 eggs, whisked
- 2 tablespoons of parmesan, grated
- 4 tablespoons of almond milk
- 10 asparagus tips, steamed
- Salt and black pepper- to taste
- Cooking spray

Method:
1. Start by greasing the base of your Crockpot.
2. Spread the asparagus at the base of the pot.
3. Whisk the egg with all other Ingredients: and pour into crockpot.
4. Cover your crockpot and select the Low settings for 3 hours.
5. Remove the crockpot's lid.
6. Slice and serve warm.

Nutritional Information per Serving:
- Calories 278
- Total Fat 20.7 g
- Saturated Fat 5.7 g
- Cholesterol 44 mg
- Sugar 3.1 g
- Fiber 1.5 g
- Sodium 232 mg
- Protein 16.4 g

Ricotta Frittata

Prep Time: 10 minutes; Cooking Time: 5 hours; Serving: 12
Ingredients:
- 6 oz. jarred roasted red bell peppers, diced
- 12 eggs, whisked
- 2 tablespoons of chives, diced
- 6 tablespoon of ricotta cheese
- 1/2 cup of parmesan, grated
- 3 garlic cloves, minced
- 2 tablespoons of parsley, chopped
- Salt and black pepper- to taste
- Cooking spray

Method:
1. Start by greasing the base of your Crockpot.
2. Spread the peppers at the base of the pot.
3. Whisk the egg with remaining Ingredients: and pour into crockpot.
4. Cover your crockpot and select the Low settings for 5 hours.
5. Remove the crockpot's lid.
6. Slice and serve warm.

Nutritional Information per Serving:
- Calories 337
- Total Fat 34.5 g

- Saturated Fat 20 g
- Cholesterol 90 mg
- Sugar2.9 g
- Fiber 3 g
- Sodium 206 mg
- Protein 23 g

Smoked Sausages with Grits

Prep Time: 10 minutes; Cooking Time: 4 hours; Serving: 4
Ingredients:
- 1 ½ lb. Smoked sausage, diced and browned
- A pinch of salt and black pepper
- 1 ½ cups of keto grits
- 1 ½ teaspoon of thyme, diced
- 1/4 teaspoon of garlic powder
- 4 ½ cups of water
- 16 oz. Cheddar cheese, shredded
- 1 cup of almond milk
- Cooking spray
- 4 eggs, whisked

Method:
1. Boil water in a suitable cooking pot after placing it over medium heat.
2. Add grits to the water and cover them for 5 minutes, then take them off from the heat.
3. Stir cheese and mix well until it melts.
4. Stir in almond milk, salt, pepper, garlic powder, eggs, and thyme.
5. Add the grits mixture and all other Ingredients: to the Crockpot.
6. Cover your crockpot and select the Low settings for 4 hours.
7. Remove the crockpot's lid.
8. Serve.

Nutritional Information per Serving:
- Calories 226
- Total Fat 17.1 g
- Saturated Fat 10.6 g
- Cholesterol 56 mg
- Sugar 2.9 g
- Fiber 2.4 g
- Sodium 88 mg
- Protein 14.1 g

Coconut Chip Rice Pudding

Prep Time: 10 minutes; Cooking Time: 2.5 hours; Serving: 2
Ingredients:
- 1 cup of cauliflower rice
- 1/2 cup of coconut chips
- 1 cup of almond milk
- 2 cups of water
- 1/2 cup of maple syrup
- 1/4 cup of raisins
- 1/4 cup of almonds
- A pinch Cinnamon powders

Method:
1. Start by throwing all the Ingredients: into the Crockpot.
2. Cover your crockpot and select the Low settings for 2 1/2 hours.
3. Remove the crockpot's lid.
4. Serve fresh.

Nutritional Information per Serving:
- Calories 432
- Total Fat 42.3 g
- Saturated Fat 26.7 g
- Cholesterol 144 mg
- Sugar 5.6 g
- Fiber 4.5 g
- Sodium 148 mg
- Protein 4.2 g

Blanc Leeks Frittata

Prep Time: 10 minutes; Cooking Time: 3 hours; Serving: 10

Ingredients:
- 1/4 cup of almond milk
- 10 eggs, whisked
- 5 oz. fromage blanc, crumbled
- 2 tablespoons of butter, melted
- 2 leeks, sliced
- Salt and black pepper- to taste

Method:
1. Start by greasing the base of your Crockpot with cooking spray.
2. Whisk the egg with all other Ingredients: and pour into crockpot.
3. Cover your crockpot and select the Low settings for 3 hours.
4. Remove the crockpot's lid.
5. Serve warm.

Nutritional Information per Serving:
- Calories 244
- Total Fat 20.4 g
- Saturated Fat 67 g
- Cholesterol 130 mg
- Sugar 1 g
- Fiber 0.8 g
- Sodium 506 mg
- Protein 12.3 g

Cherry Rice Pudding

Prep Time: 10 minutes; Cooking Time: 2.5 hours; Serving: 4

Ingredients:
- 1 ½ cups of cauliflower rice
- 1 ½ teaspoon of cinnamon powder
- 1 cup of water
- 3 cups of almond milk
- 1 cup of cherries, dried
- 1/3 cup of brown swerve
- A pinch of salt
- 2 tablespoons of butter

Method:
1. Start by throwing all the Ingredients: into the base of your Crockpot.
2. Cover your crockpot and select the Low settings for 2 ½ hours.
3. Remove the crockpot's lid.
4. Serve fresh.

Nutritional Information per Serving:
- Calories 214
- Total Fat 19.4 g
- Saturated Fat 57 g
- Cholesterol 120 mg
- Sugar 0.8 g
- Fiber 0.3 g
- Sodium 343 mg
- Protein 8.3 g

Butter Omelette

Prep Time: 10 minutes; Cooking Time: 3 hours; Serving: 10

Ingredients:
- 1/4 cup of almond milk
- 10 eggs, whisked
- 2 tablespoons of butter, melted
- Salt and black pepper- to taste

Method:
1. Start by greasing the base of your Crockpot with cooking spray.
2. Whisk the egg with all other Ingredients: and pour into crockpot.
3. Cover your crockpot and select the Low settings for 3 hours.
4. Remove the crockpot's lid.

5. Serve warm.

Nutritional Information per Serving:
- Calories 244
- Total Fat 20.4 g
- Saturated Fat 67 g
- Cholesterol 130 mg
- Sodium 506 mg
- Protein 12.3 g

Onion Zucchini Hash

Prep Time: 10 minutes; Cooking Time: 3 hours; Serving: 2

Ingredients:
- 1 ½ zucchini, cubed
- 1 yellow onion, diced
- 2 teaspoon of olive oil
- 2 eggs, room temperature
- 1/2 teaspoon of thyme, dried
- 1 green bell pepper, diced
- Salt and black pepper- to taste

Method:
1. Start by greasing the base of your Crockpot with cooking spray.
2. Whisk the egg with all other Ingredients: and pour into crockpot.
3. Cover your crockpot and select the Low settings for 3 hours.
4. Remove the crockpot's lid.
5. Serve warm.

Nutritional Information per Serving:
- Calories 212
- Total Fat 15.7 g
- Saturated Fat 9.7 g
- Cholesterol 49 mg
- Sodium 141 mg
- Protein 8.5 g

Cheesy Vegan Mix

Prep Time: 10 minutes; Cooking Time: 4 hours; Serving: 8

Ingredients:
- 1 yellow onion, sliced
- 2 red bell pepper, diced
- 2 tablespoon of olive oil
- 8 eggs, room temperature
- 2 tablespoons of mustard
- 3 cups of almond milk
- 8 oz. Brie, trimmed and cubed
- 12 oz. Keto bread, cubed
- 4 oz. Parmesan, grated
- Salt and black pepper- to taste

Method:
1. Start by greasing the base of your Crockpot.
2. Spread the bread, brie, and bell pepper at the base of the pot.
3. Whisk the egg with remaining Ingredients: and pour into crockpot.
4. Cover your crockpot and select the Low settings for 4 hours.
5. Remove the crockpot's lid.
6. Serve warm.

Nutritional Information per Serving:
- Calories 135
- Total Fat 9.9 g
- Saturated Fat 3.2 g
- Cholesterol 34 mg
- Sodium 10 mg
- Protein 28.6 g

Broccoli Egg Casserole

Prep Time: 10 minutes; Cooking Time: 3 hours; Serving: 4

Ingredients:

- 1 broccoli head, florets separated and steamed
- 1 tomato, diced
- 1 teaspoon of thyme, diced
- 3 carrots, diced and steamed
- 2 oz. Cheddar cheese, grated
- 2 oz. Almond milk
- 1 teaspoon of parsley, chopped
- 2 eggs, room temperature
- Salt and black pepper- to taste

Method:
1. Start by greasing the base of your Crockpot.
2. Spread the broccoli and carrots at the base of the pot.
3. Whisk the egg with remaining Ingredients: and pour into crockpot.
4. Cover your crockpot and select the Low settings for 3 hours.
5. Remove the crockpot's lid.
6. Serve warm.

Nutritional Information per Serving:
- Calories 254
- Total Fat 10.4 g
- Saturated Fat 57 g
- Cholesterol 110 mg
- Sodium 156 mg
- Protein 16.7 g

Rice & Shrimp Frittata

Prep Time: 10 minutes; Cooking Time: 2 hours; Serving: 4
Ingredients:
- 4 eggs, room temperature
- 1/2 cup of shrimp, cooked, peeled, deveined and diced
- 1/2 cup of baby spinach, chopped
- 1/2 teaspoon of basil, dried
- Cooking spray
- Salt and black pepper- to taste
- 1/2 cup of cauliflower rice, cooked
- 1/2 cup of Monterey jack cheese, grated

Method:
1. Start by greasing the base of your Crockpot.
2. Spread the shrimp and spinach at the base of the pot.
3. Whisk the egg with remaining Ingredients: and pour into crockpot.
4. Cover your crockpot and select the Low settings for 2 hours.
5. Remove the crockpot's lid.
6. Serve warm.

Nutritional Information per Serving:
- Calories 399
- Total Fat 17.4 g
- Saturated Fat 11.3 g
- Cholesterol 47 mg
- Sodium 192 mg
- Protein 12.4 g

Chive and Mushroom Omelette

Prep Time: 10 minutes; Cooking Time: 2 hours; Serving: 1
Ingredients:
- 1 cup of egg whites
- 1/4 cup of mushrooms, diced
- 2 tablespoons of chives, diced
- 1/4 cup of tomato, diced
- 2 tablespoon of skim almond milk
- Salt and black pepper- to taste

Method:
1. Start by greasing the base of your Crockpot.
2. Whisk the egg with all other Ingredients: and pour into crockpot.
3. Cover your crockpot and select the Low settings for 2 hours.

4. Remove the crockpot's lid.
5. Slice and serve warm.

Nutritional Information per Serving:
- Calories 267
- Total Fat 28.5 g
- Saturated Fat 2.7 g
- Cholesterol 0 mg
- Sodium 320 mg
- Protein 15.9 g

Leeks Parsley Quiche

Prep Time: 10 minutes; Cooking Time: 3 hours; Serving: 10
Ingredients:
- 1/4 cup of almond milk
- 10 eggs, whisked
- ¼ cup of parsley, chopped
- ½ cup of mushrooms, diced
- 2 tablespoons of butter, melted
- 2 leeks, sliced
- Salt and black pepper- to taste

Method:
1. Start by greasing the base of your Crockpot with cooking spray.
2. Whisk the egg with all other Ingredients: and pour into crockpot.
3. Cover your crockpot and select the Low settings for 3 hours.
4. Remove the crockpot's lid.
5. Serve warm.

Nutritional Information per Serving:
- Calories 244
- Total Fat 20.4 g
- Saturated Fat 67 g
- Cholesterol 130 mg
- Sodium 506 mg
- Protein 12.3 g

Breakfast Cream and Egg Soufflé

Prep Time: 10 minutes; Cooking Time: 2 hours; Serving: 4
Ingredients:
- 4 eggs, whisked
- 4 tablespoons of heavy cream
- 2 tablespoons of parsley, chopped
- 2 tablespoons of chives, diced
- A pinch of red chili pepper, crushed
- Salt and black pepper- to taste

Method:
1. Start by adding and whisking all the Ingredients: in a mixing bowl.
2. Divide the souffle mixture into four ramekins.
3. Place these ramekins in the Crockpot and pour ¼ cup of water into its base.
4. Cover your Crockpot and select the high settings for 2 hours.
5. Remove the crockpot's lid.
6. Serve fresh.

Nutritional Information per Serving:
- Calories 224
- Total Fat 22.4 g
- Saturated Fat 17 g
- Cholesterol 30 mg
- Sodium 206 mg
- Protein 14.3 g

Long Beans, Egg Omelette

Prep Time: 10 minutes; Cooking Time: 3 hours; Serving: 4
Ingredients:

- 4 long beans, trimmed and sliced
- 1/2 teaspoon of soy sauce
- 1 tablespoon of olive oil
- 3 eggs, whisked
- 4 garlic cloves, minced
- A pinch of salt and black pepper

Method:
1. Start by greasing the base of your Crockpot.
2. Whisk the egg with all other Ingredients: and pour into crockpot.
3. Cover your crockpot and select the Low settings for 3 hours.
4. Remove the crockpot's lid.
5. Serve warm.

Nutritional Information per Serving:
- Calories 296
- Total Fat 10.4 g
- Saturated Fat 1.5 g
- Cholesterol 8 mg
- Sodium 226 mg
- Protein 14.3 g

Tapioca Chocolate Pudding

Prep Time: 10 minutes; Cooking Time: 2 hours; Serving: 1
Ingredients:
- 14 oz. almond milk
- 7 oz. water
- ¼ cup of sugar-free chocolate chips
- ⅔ cup of tapioca pearls

Method:
1. Start by throwing all the pudding Ingredients: into the Crockpot.
2. Cover your crockpot and select the Low settings for 2 hours.
3. Remove the crockpot's lid.
4. Serve fresh.

Nutritional Information per Serving:
- Calories 266
- Total Fat 26.4 g
- Saturated Fat 4 g
- Cholesterol 13 mg
- Sodium 455 mg
- Protein 10.6 g

Cinnamon Cheese Flaxseed meal

Prep Time: 10 minutes; Cooking Time: 2 hours; Serving: 2
Ingredients:
- 1 cup of steel flaxseed meal
- 3 cups of almond milk
- 1 tablespoon of butter
- 2 tablespoons of swerves
- 2 oz. cream cheese, soft
- 3/4 cup of raisins
- 1 teaspoon of cinnamon powder
- 1/4 cup of brown swerve

Method:
1. Start by whisking cream cheese and cinnamon in a bowl.
2. Refrigerate this mixture until the flaxseed meal is ready.
3. Now start throwing all other Ingredients: into the Crockpot
4. Cover your crockpot and select the Low settings for 2 hours.
5. Remove the crockpot's lid.
6. Serve with cream cheese mixture on top.
7. Enjoy.

Nutritional Information per Serving:
- Calories 306
- Total Fat 10.4 g
- Saturated Fat 6.1 g
- Cholesterol 20 mg

- Sodium 406 mg
- Protein 12.2 g

Rosemary Egg Hash

Prep Time: 10 minutes; Cooking Time: 4 hours; Serving: 4
Ingredients:
- 4 carrots, peeled and sliced
- 6 garlic cloves, minced
- 2 eggs, whisked
- 4 bacon strips, diced
- 2 rosemary springs, diced
- 1 tablespoon of olive oil
- Salt and black pepper- to taste
- ¼ cup of almond milk

Method:
1. Start by throwing all the Ingredients: into the Crockpot.
2. Cover your crockpot and select the Low settings for 4 hours.
3. Remove the crockpot's lid.
4. Slice and serve warm.

Nutritional Information per Serving:
- Calories 213
- Total Fat 23.4 g
- Saturated Fat 6.1 g
- Cholesterol 102 mg
- Sodium 86 mg
- Protein 11.2 g

French Beans Omelette

Prep Time: 10 minutes; Cooking Time: 2.5 hours; Serving: 2
Ingredients:
- 3 oz. French beans, trimmed and sliced diagonally
- 2 eggs, whisked
- 1/2 teaspoon of soy sauce
- 1 tablespoon of olive oil
- 4 garlic cloves, minced
- salt and white pepper to taste

Method:
1. Start by greasing the base of your Crockpot.
2. Whisk the egg with all other Ingredients: and pour into crockpot.
3. Cover your crockpot and select the Low settings for 2 1/2 hours.
4. Remove the crockpot's lid.
5. Slice and serve warm.

Nutritional Information per Serving:
- Calories 392
- Total Fat 40.4 g
- Saturated Fat 6 g
- Cholesterol 20 mg
- Sodium 423 mg
- Protein 12 g

Bread Pudding

Prep Time: 10 minutes; Cooking Time: 5 hours; Serving: 4
Ingredients:
- 1/2 lb. keto bread, cubed
- 3/4 cup of almond milk
- 1 cup of water
- 2 teaspoons of cinnamon powder
- 1 ⅓ cup of almond flour
- 3/5 cup of brown swerve
- 2 teaspoon of xanthan gum
- 1 teaspoon of vanilla extract
- 3 oz. soft butter, melted

Method:
1. Start by throwing all the Ingredients: into the base of your Crockpot.

2. Cover your crockpot and select the Low settings for 5 hours.
3. Remove the crockpot's lid.
4. Serve Fresh.

Nutritional Information per Serving:
- Calories 274
- Total Fat 40.8 g
- Saturated Fat 25.5 g
- Cholesterol 105 mg
- Sodium 345 mg
- Protein 14.5 g

Onion Spinach Frittata

Prep Time: 10 minutes; Cooking Time: 3 hours; Serving: 10
Ingredients:
- 10 eggs, whisked
- 1 tablespoon of olive oil
- 1 cup of spinach, chopped
- 1 oz. cheddar cheese, grated
- 1/2 cup of sour cream
- 2 yellow onions, diced
- Salt and black pepper- to taste

Method:
1. Start by greasing the base of your Crockpot.
2. Whisk the egg with all other Ingredients: and pour into crockpot.
3. Cover your crockpot and select the Low settings for 3 hours.
4. Remove the crockpot's lid.
5. Serve.

Nutritional Information per Serving:
- Calories 349
- Total Fat 31.9 g
- Saturated Fat 15 g
- Cholesterol 46 mg
- Sodium 237 mg
- Protein 11 g

Delectable Breakfast Meal

Prep Time: 10 minutes; Cooking Time: 1.5 hours; Serving: 1
Ingredients:
- 1 tablespoon of butter, soft
- 1/4 cups of brown swerve
- 1 cup of water
- 1/2 cup of raisins
- 1/2 teaspoon of cinnamon powder
- 1 cup of flaxseed meal
- 1/2 cup of walnuts, diced

Method:
1. Start by throwing all the Ingredients: into the Crockpot.
2. Cover your crockpot and select the Low settings for 1 1/2 hours.
3. Remove the crockpot's lid.
4. Serve fresh.

Nutritional Information per Serving:
- Calories 238
- Total Fat 23.2 g
- Saturated Fat 13 g
- Cholesterol 61 mg
- Sodium 115 mg
- Protein 13.3 g

Chapter 2: Soups and Stews

Chicken Cordon Bleu Soup

Prep Time: 10 minutes; Cooking Time: 6 hours; Serving: 8
Ingredients:

- 6 cups of chicken stock
- 12 oz. diced ham
- 5 oz. mushrooms, diced
- 4 oz. onion, diced
- 2 teaspoons of dried tarragon
- 1 teaspoon of salt, more to taste
- 1 teaspoon of black pepper
- 1 lb. chicken breast, cubed
- 4 cloves garlic, minced
- 3 tablespoons of salted butter
- 1 1/2 cups of heavy cream
- 1/2 cup of sour cream
- 1/2 cup of grated Parmesan cheese
- 4 oz. Swiss cheese

Method:

1. Start by throwing all the Ingredients: into your Crockpot.
2. Mix well and cover the Crockpot with its lid.
3. Select the Low settings for 6 hours.
4. Serve warm.

Nutritional Information per Serving:

- Calories 266
- Total Fat 26.4 g
- Saturated Fat 4 g
- Cholesterol 13 mg
- Sugar 2 g
- Fiber 1.6 g
- Sodium 455 mg
- Protein 20.6 g

No Noodle Chicken Soup

Prep Time: 10 minutes; Cooking Time: 8 hours; Serving: 8
Ingredients:

- 1 whole chicken
- 2 bunches celery, diced into 4-inch pieces
- 3 tablespoons of salt
- 1 teaspoon of black pepper
- 6 cups of water
- 4 cups of mixed frozen vegetables

Method:

1. Start by throwing all the Ingredients: into your Crockpot.
2. Mix well and cover the Crockpot with its lid.
3. Select the Low settings for 8 hours.
4. Serve warm.

Nutritional Information per Serving:

- Calories 406
- Total Fat 40.4 g
- Saturated Fat 6.1 g
- Cholesterol 20 mg
- Sugar 5.1 g
- Fiber 4.4 g
- Sodium 406 mg
- Protein 22.2 g

White Chicken Chili Soup

Prep Time: 10 minutes; Cooking Time: 4 hours; Serving: 8
Ingredients:

- 2 lbs. boneless, skinless chicken breasts
- 2 onions, diced
- 4 cups of chicken broth
- 1 teaspoon of coriander powder
- 4 stalks celery, diced

- 1 tablespoon of salt
- 1 2 jalapeño pepper, minced
- 10 cloves garlic, smashed
- 1 tablespoon of chili powder
- 1 teaspoon of cumin
- 1 teaspoon of oregano
- ½ teaspoon of black pepper
- Serve with cilantro

Method:
1. Start by throwing all the Ingredients: into your Crockpot.
2. Mix well and cover the Crockpot with its lid.
3. Select the High settings for 4 hours.
4. Serve warm.

Nutritional Information per Serving:
- Calories 313
- Total Fat 23.4 g
- Saturated Fat 6.1 g
- Cholesterol 102 mg
- Sugar 2.1 g
- Fiber 1.5 g
- Sodium 86 mg
- Protein 31.2 g

Creamy Lemon Chicken Kale Soup

Prep Time: 10 minutes; Cooking Time: 6 hours; Serving: 8
Ingredients:
- 4 cups of shredded chicken
- 6 cups of bone broth
- 1 bunch of kale, rinsed, drained and sliced into 1/2-inch strips
- 3 lemons
- 2 tablespoons of fresh lemon juice
- 1 cup of onions, diced
- 1/2 cup of olive oil
- salt to taste

Method:
1. Start by throwing all the Ingredients: into your Crockpot.
2. Mix well and cover the Crockpot with its lid.
3. Select the Low settings for 6 hours.
4. Serve warm.

Nutritional Information per Serving:
- Calories 392
- Total Fat 40.4 g
- Saturated Fat 6 g
- Cholesterol 20 mg
- Sugar 3 g
- Fiber 4.2 g
- Sodium 423 mg
- Protein 22 g

Mexican Chicken Low Carb Soup

Prep Time: 10 minutes; Cooking Time: 4 hours; Serving: 4
Ingredients:
- 1 1/2 lbs. chicken pieces boneless/skinless
- 15.5 oz. chunky salsa
- 15 oz. chicken broth
- 8 oz. Monterey, shredded

Method:
1. Start by throwing all the Ingredients: into your Crockpot.
2. Mix well and cover the Crockpot with its lid.
3. Select the High settings for 4 hours.
4. Serve warm.

Nutritional Information per Serving:
- Calories 474
- Total Fat 40.8 g

- Saturated Fat 25.5 g
- Cholesterol 105 mg
- Sugar 1.8 g
- Fiber 0.8 g
- Sodium 345 mg
- Protein 24.5 g

Low Carb Taco Soup

Prep Time: 10 minutes; Cooking Time: 2 hours; Serving: 6
Ingredients:
- 2 lbs. ground pork beef or sausage
- 2, 8-ounce packages of cream cheese
- 2, 10-ounce cans of Rotel tomatoes
- 2 tablespoons of taco seasonings
- 4 cups of chicken broth
- 1 2 tablespoons of cilantro fresh or dried optional
- 1/2 cup of shredded cheese for garnish optional

Method:
1. Start by throwing all the Ingredients: into your Crockpot.
2. Mix well and cover the Crockpot with its lid.
3. Select the High settings for 2 hours.
4. Serve warm.

Nutritional Information per Serving:
- Calories 538
- Total Fat 23.2 g
- Saturated Fat 13 g
- Cholesterol 61 mg
- Sugar 0 g
- Fiber 0.9 g
- Sodium 115 mg
- Protein 21.3 g

Vegetable Beef Soup

Prep Time: 10 minutes; Cooking Time: 12 hours; Serving: 6
Ingredients:
- 4 slices bacon sliced into 1/2-inch chunks
- 2 lbs. stew meat, diced
- 2 tablespoons of red wine vinegar
- 32 oz. beef broth
- 1 medium yellow onion diced
- 1/4 cup of green beans, diced
- 1 small celeriac (about 6 oz.) diced
- 1/4 cup of carrots diced
- 2 tablespoons of tomato paste
- 1 28 oz. can tomato, diced
- 2 cloves garlic, smashed
- 1/2 teaspoon of rosemary, dried
- 1/2 teaspoon of thyme, dried
- 1/2 teaspoon of black pepper
- 1 teaspoon of salt

Method:
1. Start by throwing all the Ingredients: into your Crockpot.
2. Mix well and cover the Crockpot with its lid.
3. Select the Low settings for 12 hours.
4. Serve warm.

Nutritional Information per Serving:
- Calories 349
- Total Fat 31.9 g
- Saturated Fat 15 g
- Cholesterol 46 mg
- Sugar 1.4 g
- Fiber 3.4 g
- Sodium 237 mg
- Protein 11 g

Cream & Cheese Broccoli Soup

Prep Time: 10 minutes; Cooking Time: 3 hours; Serving: 4

Ingredients:

- ½ cup of fresh diced scallions
- 4 cups of vegetable broth
- ½ cup of heavy cream
- ⅓ cup of butter
- 2 cloves garlic, minced
- 1 onion, diced
- cheddar cheese, grated – for garnish
- 1 head broccoli, cut into florets
- salt and black pepper to taste

Method:

1. Start by throwing all the Ingredients: into your Crockpot.
2. Mix well and cover the Crockpot with its lid.
3. Select the High settings for 3 hours.
4. Serve warm.

Nutritional Information per Serving:

- Calories 287
- Total Fat 29.5 g
- Saturated Fat 3 g
- Cholesterol 0 mg
- Sugar 1.4g
- Fiber 4.3 g
- Sodium 388 mg
- Protein 14.2 g

Minestrone Kale Soup

Prep Time: 10 minutes; Cooking Time: 4 hours; Serving: 4

Ingredients:

- 1 yellow onion, diced
- 1 (28 oz.) can diced tomatoes
- 1 (6 oz.) can tomato paste
- 2 cloves garlic, minced
- 2 carrot, peeled and diced
- 2 bay leaves
- 1 green bell pepper, diced
- 3 cups of chicken broth
- 1 cup of celery, diced
- 2 cups of kale
- ½ cup of cauliflower rice
- ¼ cup of parmesan cheese
- 2 tablespoon of olive oil
- ½ teaspoon of oregano, dried
- ½ teaspoon of parsley, dried
- ½ teaspoon of thyme, dried
- ½ teaspoon of salt
- ¼ teaspoon of black pepper

Method:

1. Start by throwing all the Ingredients: except beans and cheese into your Crockpot.
2. Mix well and cover the Crockpot with its lid.
3. Select the Low settings for 4 hours.
4. Discard the bay leaves and add cheese along with beans
5. Serve warm.

Nutritional Information per Serving:

- Calories 324
- Total Fat 20.7 g
- Saturated Fat 6.7 g
- Cholesterol 45 mg
- Sugar 1.4 g
- Fiber 0.5 g
- Sodium 241 mg
- Protein 25.3 g

Cauliflower Bean Soup

Prep Time: 10 minutes; Cooking Time: 4 hours; Serving: 6

Ingredients:

- ½ Red bell pepper, diced
- ¼ head green cabbage, diced
- 2 cloves garlic, minced
- 1 carrot, diced
- 1 parsnip, diced
- 1 celery stalk, diced

- 4 cups of vegetable stock
- 1 cup of leeks, diced
- 1 cup of sliced mushrooms
- 1 cup of broccoli florets
- 1 cup of cauliflower florets
- ½ cup of fresh parsley, chopped
- ½ cup of green beans
- 2 tablespoon of olive oil
- 2 tablespoons of nutritional yeast
- ½ teaspoon of thyme, dried
- ½ teaspoon of black pepper
- Salt - to taste

Method:
1. Start by throwing all the Ingredients: into your Crockpot.
2. Mix well and cover the Crockpot with its lid.
3. Select the Low settings for 4 hours.
4. Serve warm.

Nutritional Information per Serving:
- Calories 384
- Total Fat 19.1 g
- Saturated Fat 7.7 g
- Cholesterol 35 mg
- Sugar 1.8 g
- Fiber 5.3 g
- Sodium 141 mg
- Protein 12.6 g

Chicken Soup

Prep Time: 10 minutes; Cooking Time: 6 hours; Serving: 8
Ingredients:
- 5 boneless, skinless chicken thighs
- 14 oz. canned whole tomatoes, diced
- 5 cups of chicken broth
- ¼ cup of cheddar cheese, shredded
- 2 jalapeno peppers stemmed, cored, and diced
- 3 cloves garlic, minced
- 2 tablespoon of tomato puree
- 1 tablespoon of chili powder
- 1 tablespoon of cumin, ground
- ½ teaspoon of oregano, dried
- fresh cilantro, diced for garnish

Method:
1. Start by throwing all the Ingredients: into your Crockpot.
2. Mix well and cover the Crockpot with its lid.
3. Select the Low settings for 6 hours.
4. Garnish with cilantro, and cheese
5. Serve warm.

Nutritional Information per Serving:
- Calories 215
- Total Fat 21.4 g
- Saturated Fat 67 g
- Cholesterol 123 mg
- Sugar 0.3 g
- Fiber 2.8 g
- Sodium 156 mg
- Protein 3.5 g

Bacon Beef Bolognese

Prep Time: 10 minutes; Cooking Time: 4 hours; Serving: 4
Ingredients:
- 2 lbs. ground beef
- 4 oz. bacon, diced
- 2 (28 oz.) cans crushed tomatoes
- 3 bay leaves
- 1 large onion, minced
- 2 celery stalks, minced
- 2 large carrots, minced
- ½ cup of yogurt
- 1/4 cup of diced fresh basil
- 1 tablespoon of butter, melted

- 3 tablespoons of dry white wine
- 1 teaspoon of salt
- ½ teaspoon of black pepper

Method:
1. Start by throwing all the Ingredients: into your Crockpot.
2. Mix well and cover the Crockpot with its lid.
3. Select the Low settings for 4 hours.
4. Serve warm.

Nutritional Information per Serving:
- Calories 191
- Total Fat 8.4 g
- Saturated Fat 0.7 g
- Cholesterol 0 mg
- Sugar 0.1 g
- Fiber 1.4 g
- Sodium 226 mg
- Protein 26.3 g

Sour Cream Soup

Prep Time: 10 minutes; Cooking Time: 5 hours; Serving: 6

Ingredients:
- 3 cauliflower head, diced
- 3 leeks, white part only, sliced
- 2 bay leaves
- 2 cloves garlic, minced
- ½ cup of sour cream
- 4 cups of vegetable broth
- 2 tablespoons of butter
- 2 tablespoons of rosemary
- 2 tablespoons of fresh chives
- salt and black pepper to taste

Method:
1. Start by throwing all the Ingredients: into your Crockpot.
2. Mix well and cover the Crockpot with its lid.
3. Select the Low settings for 5 hours.
4. Serve warm.

Nutritional Information per Serving:
- Calories 324
- Total Fat 13.4 g
- Saturated Fat 7 g
- Cholesterol 20 mg
- Sugar 2.1 g
- Fiber 4.8 g
- Sodium 136 mg
- Protein 24.2 g

Kale and Celery Stock

Prep Time: 10 minutes; Cooking Time: 5 hours; Serving: 8

Ingredients:
- 2 onions, diced
- 2 carrots, diced
- 4 garlic cloves
- 10 peppercorns
- 2 bay leaves
- 8 cups of cold water, filtered
- 1 cup of bell pepper, diced
- 2 cups of celery, diced
- 1 cup of kale
- a handful rosemary
- a handful parsley
- salt to taste

Method:
1. Start by throwing all the Ingredients: into your Crockpot.
2. Mix well and cover the Crockpot with its lid.
3. Select the Low settings for 5 hours.
4. Strain the cooked soup and add it to a jar.
5. Serve warm.

Nutritional Information per Serving:
- Calories 143
- Total Fat 16.7 g
- Saturated Fat 9.7 g
- Cholesterol 32 mg
- Sugar 2.4 g
- Fiber 5.7 g
- Sodium 141 mg
- Protein 3.4 g

Butternut Pumpkin Soup

Prep Time: 10 minutes; Cooking Time: 6 hours; Serving: 4
Ingredients:
- 1 large butternut pumpkin, cut into small pieces
- 1 onion, diced
- 2 chipotle peppers, seeded and minced
- 1 pinch cinnamon, ground
- 1 cup of half and half cream
- 4 cups of vegetable broth
- 1 tablespoon of olive oil
- ¼ teaspoon of nutmeg, grated
- ¼ teaspoon of cloves, ground
- 1 teaspoon of black pepper
- 1 teaspoon of salt

Method:
1. Start by throwing all the Ingredients: except half and half cream into your Crockpot.
2. Mix well and cover the Crockpot with its lid.
3. Select the Low settings for 6 hours.
4. Stir in half, and half cream then blend using a hand blender until smooth.
5. Serve warm.

Nutritional Information per Serving:
- Calories 334
- Total Fat 11.4 g
- Saturated Fat 1.2 g
- Cholesterol 0 mg
- Sugar 2.7 g
- Fiber 5.2 g
- Sodium 10 mg
- Protein 21.3 g

Italian Chicken Broth

Prep Time: 10 minutes; Cooking Time: 8 hours; Serving: 6
Ingredients:
- 2 lbs. of chicken wings
- 2 large carrots, diced
- 1 small handful fresh parsley
- 1 small handful fresh thyme
- 4 cloves garlic
- 4 spring onions, diced
- 1 bay leaf
- 6 cups of water

Method:
1. Start by throwing all the Ingredients: into your Crockpot.
2. Mix well and cover the Crockpot with its lid.
3. Select the Low settings for 8 hours.
4. Strain the cooked soup and pour it into a glass jar.
5. Serve warm.

Nutritional Information per Serving:
- Calories 204
- Saturated Fat 9.7 g
- Cholesterol 49 mg
- Total Carbs 2.6 g
- Sugar 3.4 g
- Fiber 1.5 g
- Sodium 141 mg
- Protein 6.3 g

Beef & Vegetable Stock

Prep Time: 10 minutes; Cooking Time: 12 hours; Serving: 12

Ingredients:

- 2 lbs. beef neck bones
- 2 onions, diced
- 1 carrot, diced
- 2 bay leaves
- 10 peppercorns
- 2 cups of celery, diced
- 12 cups of water
- 1 teaspoon of cider vinegar
- salt to taste

Method:

1. Start by throwing all the Ingredients: into your Crockpot.
2. Mix well and cover the Crockpot with its lid.
3. Select the Low settings for 12 hours.
4. Strain the cooked soup then pour it into a glass jar.
5. Serve warm.

Nutritional Information per Serving:

- Calories 331
- Total Fat 10.4 g
- Saturated Fat 9.5 g
- Cholesterol 10 mg
- Sugar 0.5 g
- Fiber 3.4 g
- Sodium 106 mg
- Protein 21.3 g

Blue Cheese Cauliflower Soup

Prep Time: 10 minutes; Cooking Time: 8 hours; Serving: 6

Ingredients:

- 1 large head cauliflower, cut into florets
- 4 oz. blue cheese
- 1 bay leaf
- 1 onion, diced
- 2 stalks celery, diced
- 3 cups of vegetable broth
- 2 cups of almond milk
- 2 tablespoons of butter
- ½ tablespoon of olive oil

Method:

1. Start by throwing all the Ingredients: except milk and cheese into your Crockpot.
2. Mix well and cover the Crockpot with its lid.
3. Select the Low settings for 8 hours.
4. Stir in milk and puree the soup using a handheld blender until smooth.
5. Add the blue cheese and mix well gently.
6. Serve warm.

Nutritional Information per Serving:

- Calories 479
- Total Fat 51.5 g
- Saturated Fat 29.7 g
- Cholesterol 106 mg
- Sugar 1.4 g
- Fiber 2.7 g
- Sodium 69 mg
- Protein 5.2 g

Eggplant Mushroom Soup

Prep Time: 10 minutes; Cooking Time: 6 hours; Serving: 6

Ingredients:

- 8 button mushrooms, sliced
- 2 eggplant, peeled and diced
- 1 red onion, diced
- 1 cup of creme fraiche

- 4 cups of vegetable stock
- 1 cup of spinach, chopped
- 2 tablespoons of white wine
- 1 tablespoon of olive oil
- 1 tablespoon of dry porcini mushrooms, soaked and drained
- ½ teaspoon of salt
- ½ teaspoon of black pepper

Method:
1. Start by throwing all the Ingredients: except crème Fraiche and slice mushrooms into your Crockpot.
2. Mix well and cover the Crockpot with its lid.
3. Select the Low settings for 6 hours.
4. Stir in crème Fraiche and puree the soup until smooth.
5. Garnish with sliced mushrooms.
6. Serve warm.

Nutritional Information per Serving:
- Calories 266
- Total Fat 26.9 g
- Saturated Fat 15.8 g
- Cholesterol 184 mg
- Sugar 0.4 g
- Fiber 0 g
- Sodium 218 mg
- Protein 4.5 g

Buttermilk Curry

Prep Time: 10 minutes; Cooking Time: 8 hours; Serving: 6
Ingredients:
- 1½ lbs. carrot, roughly diced
- 4 spring onions, diced into lengths
- 4 cups of chicken stock
- ½ cup of buttermilk
- 1½ teaspoon of cumin, ground
- ¼ teaspoon of cayenne pepper
- 1½ teaspoon of ground turmeric
- 2 tablespoon of curry powder
- 2 bay leaves
- 1 bunch cilantro leaves, diced
- salt and black pepper to taste

Method:
1. Start by throwing all the Ingredients: except cilantro into your Crockpot.
2. Mix well and cover the Crockpot with its lid.
3. Select the Low settings for 8 hours.
4. First, discard the bay leaves then puree the soup.
5. Pass this soup through a fine sieve.
6. Garnish with cilantro.
7. Serve warm.

Nutritional Information per Serving:
- Calories 149
- Total Fat 14.5 g
- Saturated Fat 8.1 g
- Cholesterol 56 mg
- Sugar 0.3 g
- Fiber 0 g
- Sodium 56 mg
- Protein 2.6 g

Swiss Cheese Onion Soup

Prep Time: 10 minutes; Cooking Time: 3 hours 4 minutes; Serving: 8
Ingredients:
- 8 cups of onion, sliced
- ½ cup of dry white wine
- 4 cups of beef stock
- 1 cup of swiss cheese, shredded
- ½ cup of water
- 2 sprigs fresh thyme

- 2 bay leaves
- 2 tablespoons of butter, melted
- 2 teaspoons of swerves
- 1 teaspoon of salt
- ½ teaspoon of black pepper

Method:
1. Start by throwing all the Ingredients: except cheese into your Crockpot.
2. Mix well and cover the Crockpot with its lid.
3. Select the Low settings for 3 hours.
4. Divide the cooked soups into servings bowl.
5. Top each bowl with ¼ of the cheese.
6. Place these bowls in the baking sheet.
7. Broil the soup for 4 minutes in the oven at 350 degrees F.
8. Serve warm.

Nutritional Information per Serving:
- Calories 345
- Total Fat 23.1 g
- Saturated Fat 9.1 g
- Cholesterol 96 mg
- Sugar 1.2 g
- Fiber 1.5 g
- Sodium 35 mg
- Protein 13.5 g

Spicy Mushroom Soup

Prep Time: 10 minutes; Cooking Time: 6 hours; Serving: 8
Ingredients:
- 1 (1 lb.) package fresh collard greens, trimmed
- 1 red chili, sliced
- 10 oz. ramen noodles
- 6 cups of chicken broth stock
- 1 cup of mushrooms, sliced
- 1 bunch fresh cilantro, diced
- 2 tablespoon of soy sauce
- 1 tablespoon of olive oil
- 2 tablespoons of garlic, minced
- 1 tablespoon of chili powder
- ½ teaspoon of ground ginger

Method:
1. Start by throwing all the Ingredients: except cilantro and red chili into your Crockpot.
2. Mix well and cover the Crockpot with its lid.
3. Select the Low settings for 6 hours.
4. Garnish with red chili and cilantro.
5. Serve warm.

Nutritional Information per Serving:
- Calories 305
- Total Fat 31 g
- Saturated Fat 19.5 g
- Cholesterol 103 mg
- Sugar 0.5 g
- Fiber 0.1 g
- Sodium 299 mg
- Protein 25 g

Tomato Cheese Soup

Prep Time: 10 minutes; Cooking Time: 6 hours; Serving: 2
Ingredients:
- 28 oz. canned tomatoes
- 1 onion, diced
- 1 carrot, peeled and diced
- 1 garlic clove, minced
- 1 cup of vegetable stock
- 1 cup of heavy cream
- 4 tablespoons of butter, at room temperature

- 2 tablespoon of olive oil
- 2 tablespoons of parsley, a diced
- salt and black pepper to taste

Method:
1. Start by throwing all the Ingredients: into your Crockpot.
2. Mix well and cover the Crockpot with its lid.
3. Select the Low settings for 6 hours.
4. Serve warm.

Nutritional Information per Serving:
- Calories 244
- Total Fat 24.8 g
- Saturated Fat 15.6 g
- Cholesterol 32 mg
- Sugar 0.4 g
- Fiber 0.1 g
- Sodium 204 mg
- Protein 14 g

Salsa Verde Soup

Prep Time: 10 minutes; Cooking Time: 10 hours; Serving: 4
Ingredients:
- 1 onion, diced
- 2 garlic cloves, minced
- 1 cup of wild rice
- ½ cup of prepared salsa Verde
- 2 ½ cups of vegetable broth
- 1 ½ cups of sugar-free tomato sauce
- 1 tablespoon of smoked paprika
- 2 teaspoons of cumin, ground
- 1 teaspoon of chili powder
- ¼ teaspoon of cayenne pepper
- Salt and black pepper to taste
- Crushed tortilla chips for garnish

Method:
1. Start by throwing all the Ingredients: into your Crockpot.
2. Mix well and cover the Crockpot with its lid.
3. Select the Low settings for 10 hours.
4. Garnish with tortilla chips.
5. Serve.

Nutritional Information per Serving:
- Calories 244
- Total Fat 24.8 g
- Saturated Fat 15.6 g
- Cholesterol 32 mg
- Sugar 0.4 g
- Fiber 0.1 g
- Sodium 204 mg
- Protein 24 g

Faro Mixed Chicken Soup

Prep Time: 10 minutes; Cooking Time: 8 hours; Serving: 6
Ingredients:
- 4 boneless, skinless chicken thighs
- 1 large onion, sliced
- 2 celery stalks, cut into squares
- 1 bay leaf
- 3 large carrots, sliced
- 6 cups of chicken broth
- ¼ cup of white wine
- 1 cup of faro
- 1 tablespoon of olive oil
- 1 teaspoon of garlic powder
- 1 teaspoon of cumin, ground
- 2 teaspoon of fresh parsley leaves

Method:
1. Start by throwing all the Ingredients: into your Crockpot.
2. Mix well and cover the Crockpot with its lid.
3. Select the Low settings for 8 hours.

4. Garnish with parsley.
5. Devour.

Nutritional Information per Serving:
- Calories 292
- Total Fat 26.2 g
- Saturated Fat 16.3 g
- Cholesterol 100 mg
- Sugar 6.6 g
- Fiber 0 g
- Sodium 86 mg
- Protein 15.2 g

Vegetable Bean Soup

Prep Time: 10 minutes; Cooking Time: 3 hours; Serving: 6
Ingredients:
- 30 oz. canned diced tomatoes
- 14 oz. French beans, sliced
- 2 serrano peppers, deseeded and diced
- 1 onion, diced
- 2 celery stalks, diced
- 3 carrots, diced
- 5 cups of vegetable broth
- ¼ cup of diced fresh cilantro
- 1 teaspoon of olive oil
- 2 teaspoons of cumin, ground
- 1 teaspoon of fine salt
- black pepper - to taste

Method:
1. Start by throwing all the Ingredients: into your Crockpot.
2. Mix well and cover the Crockpot with its lid.
3. Select the Low settings for 3 hours.
4. Serve warm.

Nutritional Information per Serving:
- Calories 211
- Total Fat 18.5 g
- Saturated Fat 11.5 g
- Cholesterol 51 mg
- Sugar 0.5 g
- Fiber 0.4 g
- Sodium 346 mg
- Protein 11.5 g

Minced Beef Coriander Chili

Prep Time: 10 minutes; Cooking Time: 5 hours; Serving: 2
Ingredients:
- 1 lb. beef, minced
- 2 tablespoon of tomato paste
- 1 tablespoon of cumin, ground
- 1 teaspoon of coriander, ground
- 1 yellow onion, diced
- 1 cup of beef stock
- 1 tablespoon of olive oil

Method:
1. Start by throwing all the Ingredients: into your Crockpot.
2. Mix well and cover the Crockpot with its lid.
3. Select the Low settings for 5 hours.
4. Serve warm.

Nutritional Information per Serving:
- Calories 384
- Total Fat 12.7 g
- Saturated Fat 7.3 g
- Cholesterol 35 mg
- Sugar 2.7 g
- Fiber 1.6 g
- Sodium 222 mg
- Protein 12.2 g

Jalapeno Pork Tenderloin Soup

Prep Time: 10 minutes; Cooking Time: 8 hours; Serving: 4
Ingredients:

- 1 cup of yellow onion, diced
- cooking spray
- 2/3 cup of green bell pepper, diced
- 1 tablespoon of garlic, minced
- 1 jalapeno pepper, diced
- 1 lb. pork tenderloin, cubed
- 2 cups of chicken stock
- 2 teaspoon of chili powder
- 1 teaspoon of cumin, ground
- Salt, and black pepper   to taste
- 14 oz. canned tomatoes, diced
- 2 tablespoons of cilantro, diced

Method:

1. Start by throwing all the Ingredients: except cilantro into your Crockpot.
2. Mix well and cover the Crockpot with its lid.
3. Select the Low settings for 8 hours.
4. Garnish with cilantro.
5. Serve warm.

Nutritional Information per Serving:

- Calories 388
- Total Fat 12.5 g
- Saturated Fat 4.4 g
- Cholesterol 53 mg
- Sugar 0.3 g
- Fiber 2 g
- Sodium 1098 mg
- Protein 24.6 g

Meatball Spinach Soup

Prep Time: 10 minutes; Cooking Time: 12 hours; Serving: 4
Ingredients:

- 1 lb. pork, ground
- 3 garlic cloves, minced
- 2 green onions, diced
- 1-inch ginger, grated
- 1-quart chicken stock
- 1 cup of spinach, torn
- Salt and black pepper- to taste

Method:

1. Start by mixing pork with garlic, green onions, ginger, pepper, and salt in a large bowl.
2. Make medium meatballs out of this mixture.
3. Now place the meatballs in the crockpot along with other Ingredients:.
4. Cover the crockpot with its lid.
5. Select the Low settings for 12 hours.
6. Garnish with cilantro.
7. Serve warm.

Nutritional Information per Serving:

- Calories 341
- Total Fat 11.3 g
- Saturated Fat 3.8 g
- Cholesterol 181 mg
- Sugar 0.5 g
- Fiber 0 g
- Sodium 334 mg
- Protein 18.9 g

Creamy Turkey Spinach Medley

Prep Time: 10 minutes; Cooking Time: 8 hours 5 minutes; Serving: 6
Ingredients:

- 18 oz. of turkey meat, minced
- 3 oz. spinach
- 20 oz. canned tomatoes, diced
- 2 tablespoon of olive oil
- 2 tablespoon of coconut cream
- 2 garlic cloves, minced
- 2 yellow onions, sliced
- 2 tablespoons of ginger, grated
- 1 tablespoon of turmeric powder
- 2 tablespoon of chili powder
- Salt and black pepper- to taste

Method:
1. Start by throwing all the Ingredients: except spinach into your Crockpot.
2. Mix well and cover the Crockpot with its lid.
3. Select the Low settings for 8 hours.
4. Stir in spinach and cover again, then leave it for 5 minutes.
5. Serve warm.

Nutritional Information per Serving:
- Calories 341
- Total Fat 11.3 g
- Saturated Fat 3.8 g
- Cholesterol 181 mg
- Sugar 0.5 g
- Fiber 0 g
- Sodium 334 mg
- Protein 12.9 g

Turkey Squash Stew

Prep Time: 10 minutes; Cooking Time: 8 hours; Serving: 4

Ingredients:
- 4 cups of turkey meat, cooked and shredded 4 cups of
- 2 cups of zucchini squash, diced
- 1 cup of chicken stock
- Salt and black pepper- to taste
- 1 teaspoon of garlic, minced
- ½ cup of sugar-free Salsa Verde
- 1 teaspoon of coriander, ground
- 2 teaspoons of cumin, ground
- ¼ cup of tomato, diced
- 1 tablespoon of parsley, chopped

Method:
1. Start by throwing all the Ingredients: except cilantro into your Crockpot.
2. Mix well and cover the Crockpot with its lid.
3. Select the Low settings for 8 hours.
4. Garnish with cilantro.
5. Serve warm.

Nutritional Information per Serving:
- Calories 260
- Total Fat 22.9 g
- Saturated Fat 7.3 g
- Cholesterol 0 mg
- Sugar 1.8 g
- Fiber 1.4 g
- Sodium 9 mg
- Protein 35.6 g

Flavoursome Turkey Stew

Prep Time: 10 minutes; Cooking Time: 5 hours; Serving: 4

Ingredients:
- 3 teaspoon of olive oil
- 1 green bell pepper, diced
- 1 lb. turkey meat, ground
- 1 tablespoon of garlic, minced
- 1 yellow onion, diced
- 1 teaspoon of ancho chilies, ground
- 1 tablespoon of chili powder
- 8 oz. canned green chilies and juice, diced
- 8 oz. tomato paste

- 15 oz. canned tomatoes, diced
- 2 cups of beef stock
- salt and black pepper - to taste

Method:
1. Start by throwing all the Ingredients: except cilantro into your Crockpot.
2. Mix well and cover the Crockpot with its lid.
3. Select the Low settings for 5 hours.
4. Garnish with cilantro.
5. Serve warm.

Nutritional Information per Serving:
- Calories 408
- Total Fat 9 g
- Saturated Fat 4.3 g
- Cholesterol 180 mg
- Sugar 0.5 g
- Fiber 0.1 g
- Sodium 146 mg
- Protein 26 g

Cauliflower Turkey Soup

Prep Time: 10 minutes; Cooking Time: 5 hours; Serving: 6
Ingredients:
- 4 shallots, diced
- 1 lb. turkey, ground
- Salt and black pepper - to taste
- 1 red bell pepper, diced
- 5 cups of chicken stock
- 1 and ½ cups of cauliflower florets, diced
- 2 tablespoon of olive oil
- 15 oz. canned tomatoes, diced

Method:
1. Start by throwing all the Ingredients: except cilantro into your Crockpot.
2. Mix well and cover the Crockpot with its lid.
3. Select the Low settings for 5 hours.
4. Garnish with cilantro.
5. Serve warm.

Nutritional Information per Serving:
- Calories 312
- Total Fat 4.9 g
- Saturated Fat 1.9 g
- Cholesterol 10 mg
- Sugar 0.8 g
- Fiber 0.4 g
- Sodium 355 mg
- Protein 23 g

Creamy Eggplant Soup

Prep Time: 10 minutes; Cooking Time: 8 hours; Serving: 4
Ingredients:
- 1 eggplant, diced
- 4 tomatoes
- 1 teaspoon of garlic, minced
- 1/4 yellow onion, diced
- 2 tablespoons of basil, diced
- 4 tablespoons of parmesan, grated
- 1 tablespoon of olive oil
- 2 cups of chicken stock
- 1 bay leaf
- 1/2 cup of heavy cream
- salt and black pepper - to taste

Method:
1. Start by throwing all the Ingredients: except cilantro into your Crockpot.
2. Mix well and cover the Crockpot with its lid.
3. Select the Low settings for 8 hours.

4. Garnish with cilantro.
5. Serve warm.

Nutritional Information per Serving:
- Calories 304
- Total Fat 15.7 g
- Saturated Fat 9.7 g
- Cholesterol 49 mg
- Sugar 3.4 g
- Fiber 1.5 g
- Sodium 141 mg
- Protein 6.3 g

Chard Chicken Soup

Prep Time: 10 minutes; Cooking Time: 5 hours; Serving: 8

Ingredients:
- 4 cups of swiss chard, diced
- 4 cups of chicken breast, cooked and shredded
- 2 cups of water
- 1 cup of mushrooms, sliced
- 1/4 cup of onion, diced
- 8 cups of chicken stock
- 2 tablespoons of vinegar
- 1/4 cup of basil, diced
- 1 tablespoon of garlic, minced
- 4 bacon strips, diced
- 1/4 cup of sundried tomatoes, diced
- 1 cup of green beans, cut into medium pieces
- 1 tablespoon of coconut oil, melted
- Salt and black pepper- to taste

Method:
1. Start by throwing all the Ingredients: except cilantro into your Crockpot.
2. Mix well and cover the Crockpot with its lid.
3. Select the Low settings for 5 hours.
4. Garnish with cilantro.
5. Serve warm.

Nutritional Information per Serving:
- Calories 238
- Total Fat 16.9 g
- Saturated Fat 16.9 g
- Cholesterol 32 mg
- Sugar 0.1 g
- Fiber 7.2 g
- Sodium 469 mg
- Protein 10.8 g

Capers Eggplant Stew

Prep Time: 10 minutes; Cooking Time: 6 hours; Serving: 4

Ingredients:
- 2 eggplants, cut into medium chunks
- 1 red onion, diced
- 1 teaspoon of oregano, dried
- 2 tablespoons of olive oil
- 2 tablespoons of capers, diced
- 2 garlic cloves, diced
- 1 bunch parsley, a diced
- 1 handful green olives, pitted and sliced
- 5 tomatoes, diced
- ½ cup of vegetable stock
- 3 tablespoons of herb vinegar
- Salt and black pepper- to taste

Method:
1. Start by throwing all the Ingredients: except cilantro into your Crockpot.
2. Mix well and cover the Crockpot with its lid.
3. Select the Low settings for 6 hours.
4. Garnish with cilantro.

5. Serve warm.

Nutritional Information per Serving:
- Calories 228
- Total Fat 20.2 g
- Saturated Fat 12.5 g
- Cholesterol 54 mg
- Sugar 2.3 g
- Fiber 2.4 g
- Sodium 250 mg
- Protein 3.7 g

Swiss Vegetable Soup

Prep Time: 10 minutes; Cooking Time: 6 hours; Serving: 8

Ingredients:
- 1 red onion, diced
- 1 bunch swiss chard, a diced
- 2 zucchinis, diced
- 1 green bell pepper, diced
- 1 lb. sausage, diced
- 2 garlic cloves, minced
- 1 cup of cauliflower florets, diced
- 1 cup of green beans, diced
- 6 cups of chicken stock
- 7 oz. canned tomato paste
- 2 cups of water
- 2 teaspoons of thyme, diced
- 1 teaspoon of rosemary, dried
- 1 tablespoon of fennel, minced
- 1/2 teaspoon of red pepper flakes
- Grated parmesan for serving
- 6 carrots, diced
- 4 cups of tomatoes, diced
- Salt and black pepper- to taste

Method:
1. Start by throwing all the Ingredients: into your Crockpot.
2. Mix well and cover the Crockpot with its lid.
3. Select the Low settings for 6 hours.
4. Serve warm.

Nutritional Information per Serving:
- Calories 382
- Total Fat 36.5 g
- Saturated Fat 5.5 g
- Cholesterol 0 mg
- Sugar 3.4 g
- Fiber 5.5 g
- Sodium 73 mg
- Protein 6.3 g

Chapter 3: Poultry

Aromatic Jalapeno Wings

Prep Time: 10 minutes; Cooking Time: 3 hours; Servings: 4

Ingredients:
- 1 jalapeño pepper, diced
- ½ cup of fresh cilantro, diced
- 3 tablespoon of coconut oil
- Juice from 1 lime
- 2 garlic cloves, peeled and minced
- Salt and black pepper ground, to taste
- 2 lbs. chicken wings
- Lime wedges, to serve
- Mayonnaise, to serve

Method:
1. Start by throwing all the Ingredients: into the large bowl and mix well.
2. Cover the wings and marinate them in the refrigerator for 2 hours.
3. Now add the wings along with their marinade into the Crockpot.
4. Cover it and cook for 3 hours on Low Settings.
5. Garnish as desired.
6. Serve warm.

Nutritional Information per Serving:
- Calories 246
- Total Fat 7.4 g
- Saturated Fat 4.6 g
- Cholesterol 105 mg
- Sugar 6.5 g
- Fiber 2.7 g
- Sodium 353 mg
- Protein 37.2 g

Turkey Meatballs

Prep Time: 10 minutes; Cooking Time: 6 hours; Servings: 4

Ingredients:
- 1 lb. turkey meat, ground
- 1 yellow onion, minced
- 4 garlic cloves, minced
- ¼ cup of parsley, chopped
- salt, and black pepper to taste
- 1 teaspoon of oregano, dried
- 1 egg, whisked
- ¼ cup of almond milk
- 2 teaspoon of coconut aminos
- 12 mushrooms, diced
- 1 cup of chicken stock
- 2 tablespoon of olive oil
- 2 tablespoons of butter

Method:
1. Thoroughly mix turkey meat with onion, garlic, parsley, pepper, salt, egg, aminos, and oregano in a bowl.
2. Make 1-inch small meatballs out of this mixture.
3. Add these meatballs along with other Ingredients: into the Crockpot.
4. Cover it and cook for 6 hours on Low Settings.
5. Garnish as desired.
6. Serve warm.

Nutritional Information per Serving:
- Calories 293
- Total Fat 16 g
- Saturated Fat 2.3 g
- Cholesterol 75 mg
- Sugar 2.6 g
- Fiber 1.9 g
- Sodium 386 mg
- Protein 34.2 g

Barbeque Chicken Wings

Prep Time: 10 minutes; Cooking Time: 3 hours; Servings: 4

Ingredients:
- 2 lbs. chicken wings
- 1/2 cup of water
- 1/2 teaspoon of basil, dried
- 3/4 cup of BBQ sauce
- 1/2 cup of lime juice
- 1 teaspoon of red pepper, crushed
- 2 teaspoons of paprika
- 1/2 cup of swerve
- Salt and black pepper- to taste
- A pinch cayenne peppers

Method:
1. Start by throwing all the Ingredients: into the Crockpot and mix them well.
2. Cover it and cook for 3 hours on Low Settings.
3. Garnish as desired.
4. Serve warm.

Nutritional Information per Serving:
- Calories 457
- Total Fat 19.1 g
- Saturated Fat 11 g
- Cholesterol 262 mg
- Sugar 1.2 g
- Fiber 1.7 g
- Sodium 557 mg
- Protein 32.5 g

Saucy Duck

Prep Time: 10 minutes; Cooking Time: 6 hours; Servings: 4

Ingredients:
- 1 duck, cut into small chunks
- 4 garlic cloves, minced
- 4 tablespoons of swerves
- 2 green onions, roughly diced
- 4 tablespoon of soy sauce
- 4 tablespoon of sherry wine
- 1/4 cup of water
- 1-inch ginger root, sliced
- A pinch salt
- black pepper to taste

Method:
1. Start by throwing all the Ingredients: into the Crockpot and mix them well.
2. Cover it and cook for 6 hours on Low Settings.
3. Garnish as desired.
4. Serve warm.

Nutritional Information per Serving:
- Calories 338
- Total Fat 3.8 g
- Saturated Fat 0.7 g
- Cholesterol 22 mg
- Fiber 2.4 g
- Sugar 1.2 g
- Sodium 620 mg
- Protein 15.4g

Chicken Roux Gumbo

Prep Time: 10 minutes; Cooking Time: 6 hours; Servings: 24

Ingredients:
- 1 lb. chicken thighs, cut into halves
- 1 tablespoon of vegetable oil

Aromatics:
- 1 bell pepper, diced
- 1 lb smoky sausage, sliced, crispy, and crumbled.
- Salt and black pepper- to taste
- 2 quarts' chicken stock

- 15 oz. canned tomatoes, diced
- 1 celery stalk, diced
- salt to taste
- 4 garlic cloves, minced
- 1/2 lbs. okra, sliced
- 1 yellow onion, diced
- a dash tabasco sauce

For the roux:
- 1/2 cup of almond flour
- 1/4 cup of vegetable oil
- 1 teaspoon of Cajun spice

Method:
1. Start by throwing all the Ingredients: except okra and roux Ingredients: into the Crockpot.
2. Cover it and cook for 5 hours on Low Settings.
3. Stir in okra and cook for another 1 hour on low heat.
4. Mix all the roux Ingredients: and add them to the Crockpot.
5. Stir cook on high heat until the sauce thickens.
6. Garnish as desired.
7. Serve warm.

Nutritional Information per Serving:
- Calories 604
- Total Fat 30.6 g
- Saturated Fat 13.1 g
- Cholesterol 131 mg
- Fiber 0.2 g
- Sugar 20.3 g
- Sodium 834 mg
- Protein 54.6 g

Cider-Braised Chicken

Prep Time: 10 minutes; Cooking Time: 5 hours; Servings: 2
Ingredients:
- 4 chicken drumsticks
- 2 tablespoon of olive oil
- ½ cup of apple cider vinegar
- 1 tablespoon of balsamic vinegar
- 1 chili pepper, diced
- 1 yellow onion, minced
- Salt and black pepper- to taste

Method:
1. Start by throwing all the Ingredients: into a bowl and mix them well.
2. Marinate this chicken for 2 hours in the refrigerator.
3. Spread the chicken along with its marinade in the Crockpot.
4. Cover it and cook for 5 hours on Low Settings.
5. Garnish as desired.
6. Serve warm.

Nutritional Information per Serving:
- Calories 311
- Total Fat 25.5 g
- Saturated Fat 12.4 g
- Cholesterol 69 mg
- Fiber 0.7 g
- Sugar 0.3 g
- Sodium 58 mg
- Protein 18.4 g

Chunky Chicken Salsa

Prep Time: 10 minutes; Cooking Time: 6 hours; Servings: 2
Ingredients:
- 1 lb. chicken breast, skinless and boneless
- 1 cup of chunky salsa
- 3/4 teaspoon of cumin

- A pinch oregano
- Salt and black pepper- to taste

Method:
1. Start by throwing all the Ingredients: into the Crockpot and mix them well.
2. Cover it and cook for 6 hours on Low Settings.
3. Garnish as desired.
4. Serve warm.

Nutritional Information per Serving:
- Calories 541
- Total Fat 34 g
- Saturated Fat 8.5 g
- Cholesterol 69 mg
- Fiber 1.2 g
- Sugar 1 g
- Sodium 547 mg
- Protein 20.3 g

Dijon Chicken

Prep Time: 10 minutes; Cooking Time: 6 hours; Servings: 4
Ingredients:
- 2 lbs. chicken thighs, skinless and boneless
- 3/4 cup of chicken stock
- 1/4 cup of lemon juice
- 2 tablespoon of extra virgin olive oil
- 3 tablespoon of Dijon mustard
- 2 tablespoons of Italian seasoning
- Salt and black pepper- to taste

Method:
1. Start by throwing all the Ingredients: into the Crockpot and mix them well.
2. Cover it and cook for 6 hours on Low Settings.
3. Garnish as desired.
4. Serve warm.

Nutritional Information per Serving:
- Calories 398
- Total Fat 13.8 g
- Saturated Fat 5.1 g
- Cholesterol 200 mg
- Fiber 1 g
- Sugar 1.3 g
- Sodium 272 mg
- Protein 51.8 g

Chicken Thighs with Vegetables

Prep Time: 10 minutes; Cooking Time: 6 hours; Servings: 6
Ingredients:
- 6 chicken thighs
- 1 teaspoon of vegetable oil
- 15 oz. canned tomatoes, diced
- 1 yellow onion, diced
- 2 tablespoon of tomato paste
- 1/2 cup of white wine
- 2 cups of chicken stock
- 1 celery stalk, diced
- 1/4 lb. baby carrots, cut into halves
- 1/2 teaspoon of thyme, dried
- Salt and black pepper- to taste

Method:
1. Start by throwing all the Ingredients: into the Crockpot and mix them well.
2. Cover it and cook for 6 hours on Low Settings.
3. Shred the slow-cooked chicken using a fork and return to the pot.
4. Mix well and garnish as desired.
5. Serve warm.

Nutritional Information per Serving:

- Calories 372
- Total Fat 11.8 g
- Saturated Fat 4.4 g
- Cholesterol 62 mg
- Fiber 0.6 g
- Sugar 27.3 g
- Sodium 871 mg
- Protein 34 g

Chicken Dipped in tomatillo Sauce

Prep Time: 10 minutes; Cooking Time: 6 hours; Servings: 4
Ingredients:
- 1 lb. chicken thighs, skinless and boneless
- 2 tablespoon of extra virgin olive oil
- 1 yellow onion, sliced
- 1 garlic clove, crushed
- 4 oz. canned green chilies, diced
- 1 handful cilantro, diced
- 15 oz. cauliflower rice, already cooked
- 5 oz. tomatoes, diced
- 15 oz. cheddar cheese, grated
- 4 oz. black olives, pitted and diced
- Salt and black pepper- to taste
- 15 oz canned tomatillos, diced

Method:
1. Start by throwing all the Ingredients: into the Crockpot and mix them well.
2. Cover it and cook for 5 6 hours on Low Settings.
3. Shred the slow-cooked chicken and return to the pot.
4. Mix well and garnish as desired.
5. Serve warm.

Nutritional Information per Serving:
- Calories 427
- Total Fat 31.1 g
- Saturated Fat 4.2 g
- Cholesterol 0 mg
- Sugar 12.4 g
- Fiber 19.8 g
- Sodium 86 mg
- Protein 23.5 g

Chicken with Lemon Parsley Butter

Prep Time: 10 minutes; Cooking Time: 3 hours; Servings: 10
Ingredients:
- 1 (5 – 6lbs) whole roasting chicken, rinsed
- 1 cup of water
- 1/2 teaspoon of kosher salt
- 1/4 teaspoon of black pepper
- 1 whole lemon, sliced
- 4 tablespoons of butter
- 2 tablespoons of fresh parsley, chopped

Method:
1. Start by seasoning the chicken with all the herbs and spices.
2. Place this chicken in the Crockpot.
3. Cover it and cook for 3 hours on High Settings.
4. Meanwhile, melt butter with lemon slices and parsley in a saucepan.
5. Drizzle the butter over the Crockpot chicken.
6. Serve warm.

Nutritional Information per Serving:
- Calories 379
- Saturated Fat 18.6 g
- Cholesterol 141 mg
- Total Carbs 9.7g
- Fiber 0.9 g
- Sugar 1.3 g

- Sodium 193 mg
- Protein 25.2 g

Paprika Chicken

Prep Time: 10 minutes; Cooking Time: 8 hours; Servings: 8
Ingredients:
- 1 free-range whole chicken
- 1 tablespoon of olive oil
- 1 tablespoon of dried paprika
- 1 tablespoon of curry powder
- 1 teaspoon of dried turmeric
- 1 teaspoon of salt

Method:
1. Start by mixing all the spices and oil in a bowl except chicken.
2. Now season the chicken with these spices liberally.
3. Add the chicken and spices to your Crockpot.
4. Cover the lid of the crockpot and cook for 8 hours on Low.
5. Serve warm.

Nutritional Information per Serving:
- Calories 313
- Total Fat 134g
- Saturated Fat 78 g
- Cholesterol 861 mg
- Fiber 0.7 g
- Sugar 19 g
- Sodium 62 mg
- Protein 24.6 g

Rotisserie Chicken

Prep Time: 10 minutes; Cooking Time: 8 hours 5 minutes; Servings: 10
Ingredients:
- 1 organic whole chicken
- 1 tablespoon of olive oil
- 1 teaspoon of thyme
- 1 teaspoon of rosemary
- 1 teaspoon of garlic, granulated
- salt and pepper

Method:
1. Start by seasoning the chicken with all the herbs and spices.
2. Broil this seasoned chicken for 5 minutes in the oven until golden brown.
3. Place this chicken in the Crockpot.
4. Cover it and cook for 8 hours on Low Settings.
5. Serve warm.

Nutritional Information per Serving:
- Calories 301
- Total Fat 12.2 g
- Saturated Fat 2.4 g
- Cholesterol 110 mg
- Fiber 0.9 g
- Sugar 1.4 g
- Sodium 276 mg
- Protein 28.8 g

Crockpot Chicken Adobo

Prep Time: 10 minutes; Cooking Time: 8 hours; Servings: 6
Ingredients:
- 1/4 cup of apple cider vinegar
- 12 chicken drumsticks
- 1 onion, diced into slices
- 2 tablespoons of olive oil
- 10 cloves garlic, smashed
- 1 cup of gluten-free tamari
- 1/4 cup of diced green onion

Method:

1. Place the drumsticks in the Crockpot and then add the remaining Ingredients: on top.
2. Cover it and cook for 8 hours on Low Settings.
3. Mix gently, then serve warm.

Nutritional Information per Serving:
- Calories 249
- Total Fat 11.9 g
- Saturated Fat 1.7 g
- Cholesterol 78 mg
- Fiber 1.1 g
- Sugar 0.3 g
- Sodium 79 mg
- Protein 25 g

Chicken Ginger Curry

Prep Time: 10 minutes; Cooking Time: 6 hours; Servings: 4

Ingredients:
- 1 ½ lbs. chicken drumsticks (approx. 5 drumsticks), skin removed
- 1 (13.5 oz.) can coconut milk
- 1 onion, diced
- 4 cloves garlic, minced
- 1-inch knob fresh ginger, minced
- 1 Serrano pepper, minced
- 1 tablespoon of Garam Masala
- ½ teaspoon of cayenne
- ½ teaspoon of paprika
- ½ teaspoon of turmeric
- salt and pepper, adjust to taste

Method:
1. Start by throwing all the Ingredients: into the Crockpot.
2. Cover it and cook for 6 hours on Low Settings.
3. Garnish as desired.
4. Serve warm.

Nutritional Information per Serving:
- Calories 248
- Total Fat 15.7 g
- Saturated Fat 2.7 g
- Cholesterol 75 mg
- Fiber 0g
- Sugar 1.1 g
- Sodium 94 mg
- Protein 14.1 g

Thai Chicken Curry

Prep Time: 10 minutes; Cooking Time: 2.5 hours; Servings: 2

Ingredients:
- 1 can coconut milk
- 1/2 cup of chicken stock
- 1 lb. boneless, skinless chicken thighs, diced
- 1 2 tablespoons of red curry paste
- 1 tablespoon of coconut aminos
- 1 tablespoon of fish sauce
- 2 3 garlic cloves, minced
- Salt and black pepper-to taste
- red pepper flakes as desired
- 1 bag frozen mixed veggies

Method:
1. Start by throwing all the Ingredients: except vegetables into the Crockpot.
2. Cover it and cook for 2 hours on Low Settings.
3. Remove its lid and thawed veggies.
4. Cover the crockpot again then continue cooking for another 30 minutes on Low settings.
5. Garnish as desired.

6. Serve warm.

Nutritional Information per Serving:
- Calories 327
- Total Fat 3.5 g
- Saturated Fat 0.5 g
- Cholesterol 162 mg
- Fiber 0.4 g
- Sugar 0.5 g
- Sodium 142 mg
- Protein 21.5 g

Lemongrass and Coconut Chicken Drumsticks

Prep Time: 10 minutes; Cooking Time: 5 hours; Servings: 5

Ingredients:
- 10 drumsticks, skin removed
- 1 thick stalk fresh lemongrass
- 4 cloves garlic, minced
- 1 thumb-size piece of ginger
- 1 cup of coconut milk
- 2 tablespoons of Red Boat fish sauce
- 3 tablespoons of coconut aminos
- 1 teaspoon of five-spice powder
- 1 large onion, sliced
- ¼ cup of fresh scallions, diced
- Kosher salt
- Black pepper

Method:
1. Start by throwing all the Ingredients: into the Crockpot.
2. Cover it and cook for 5 hours on Low Settings.
3. Garnish as desired.
4. Serve warm.

Nutritional Information per Serving:
- Calories 372
- Total Fat 11.1 g
- Saturated Fat 5.8 g
- Cholesterol 610 mg
- Fiber 0.2 g
- Sugar 0.2 g
- Sodium 749 mg
- Protein 63.5 g

Green Chile Chicken

Prep Time: 10 minutes; Cooking Time: 6 hours; Servings: 6

Ingredients:
- 8 chicken thighs, thawed, boneless and skinless
- 1 (4 oz.) can green chilis
- 2 teaspoons of garlic salt
- optional: add in ½ cup of diced onions

Method:
1. Start by throwing all the Ingredients: into the Crockpot.
2. Cover it and cook for 6 hours on Low Settings.
3. Garnish as desired.
4. Serve warm.

Nutritional Information per Serving:
- Calories 248
- Total Fat 2.4 g
- Saturated Fat 0.1 g
- Cholesterol 320 mg
- Fiber 0.7 g
- Sugar 0.7 g
- Sodium 350 mg
- Protein 44.3 g

Garlic Butter Chicken with Cream Cheese Sauce

Prep Time: 10 minutes; Cooking Time: 6 hours; Servings: 4

Ingredients:

For the garlic chicken:
- 8 garlic cloves, sliced
- 1.5 teaspoons of salt
- 1 stick of butter

For the cream cheese sauce:
- 8 oz. of cream cheese
- 1 cup of chicken stock

- 2 2.5 lbs. of chicken breasts
- Optional 1 onion, sliced

- salt to taste

Method:
1. Start by throwing all the Ingredients: for garlic chicken into the Crockpot.
2. Cover it and cook for 6 hours on Low Settings.
3. Now stir cook all the Ingredients: for cream cheese sauce in a saucepan.
4. Once heated, pour this sauce over the cooked chicken.
5. Garnish as desired.
6. Serve warm.

Nutritional Information per Serving:
- Calories 301
- Total Fat 12.2 g
- Saturated Fat 2.4 g
- Cholesterol 110 mg
- Fiber 0.9 g
- Sugar 1.4 g
- Sodium 276 mg
- Protein 28.8 g

Jerk chicken

Prep Time: 10 minutes; Cooking Time: 6 hours; Servings: 5

Ingredients:
- 5 drumsticks and 5 wings
- 4 teaspoons of salt
- 4 teaspoons of paprika
- 1 teaspoon of cayenne pepper
- 2 teaspoons of onion powder
- 2 teaspoons of thyme
- 2 teaspoons of white pepper
- 2 teaspoons of garlic powder
- 1 teaspoon of black pepper

Method:
1. Start by throwing all the Ingredients: into the Crockpot.
2. Cover it and cook for 6 hours on Low Settings.
3. Garnish as desired.
4. Serve warm.

Nutritional Information per Serving:
- Calories 249
- Total Fat 11.9 g
- Saturated Fat 1.7 g
- Cholesterol 78 mg
- Fiber 1.1 g
- Sugar 0.3 g
- Sodium 79 mg
- Protein 35 g

Spicy Wings with Mint Sauce

Prep Time: 10 minutes; Cooking Time: 6 hours; Servings: 6

Ingredients:
- 1 tablespoon of cumin
- 18 chicken wings, cut in half
- 1 tablespoon of turmeric
- 1 tablespoon of coriander
- 1 tablespoon of fresh ginger, finely grated
- 2 tablespoon of olive oil
- 1 tablespoon of paprika

- A pinch of cayenne pepper
- ¼ cup of chicken stock

Chutney/ Sauce:
- 1 cup of fresh mint leaves
- Juice of ½ lime
- ¾ cup of cilantro
- 1 Serrano pepper
- 1 tablespoon of water

- Salt and black pepper ground, to taste

- 1 small ginger piece, peeled and diced
- 1 tablespoon of olive oil
- Salt and black pepper ground, to taste

Method:
1. Start by throwing all the Ingredients: for wings into the Crockpot.
2. Cover it and cook for 6 hours on Low Settings.
3. Meanwhile, blend all the mint sauce Ingredients: in a blender jug.
4. Serve the cooked wings with mint sauce.
5. Garnish as desired.
6. Serve warm.

Nutritional Information per Serving:
- Calories 248
- Total Fat 15.7 g
- Saturated Fat 2.7 g
- Cholesterol 75 mg

- Fiber 0g
- Sugar 0 g
- Sodium 94 mg
- Protein 24.9 g

Cacciatore Olive Chicken

Prep Time: 10 minutes; Cooking Time: 6 hours; Servings: 4

Ingredients:
- 28 oz. canned tomatoes and juice, crushed
- 8 chicken drumsticks, bone-in
- 1 cup of chicken stock
- 1 bay leaf

- 1 teaspoon of garlic powder
- 1 yellow onion, diced
- 1 teaspoon of oregano, dried
- salt to taste

Method:
1. Start by throwing all the Ingredients: into the Crockpot and mix them well.
2. Cover it and cook for 6 hours on Low Settings.
3. Garnish as desired.
4. Serve warm.

Nutritional Information per Serving:
- Calories 297
- Total Fat 16.2 g
- Saturated Fat 6.5 g
- Cholesterol 35 mg

- Sugar 3.3 g
- Fiber 1.9 g
- Sodium 575 mg
- Protein 8.9 g

Duck and Vegetable Stew

Prep Time: 10 minutes; Cooking Time: 5 hours; Servings: 4

Ingredients:
- 1 duck, diced into medium pieces
- 1 tablespoon of wine
- 2 carrots, diced
- 2 cups of water

- 1 cucumber, diced
- 1-inch ginger pieces, diced
- Salt and black pepper- to taste

Method:
1. Start by throwing all the Ingredients: except into the Crockpot and mix them well.
2. Cover it and cook for 5 hours on Low Settings.
3. Garnish with cucumber.
4. Serve warm.

Nutritional Information per Serving:
- Calories 449
- Total Fat 23.4 g
- Saturated Fat 1.5 g
- Cholesterol 210 mg
- Fiber 1.3 g
- Sugar 22g
- Sodium 838 mg
- Protein 28.5g

Chicken Eggplant Curry

Prep Time: 10 minutes; Cooking Time: 6 hours; Servings: 6

Ingredients:
- 8 chicken pieces
- 1 eggplant, cubed
- 3 garlic cloves, crushed
- 2 tablespoon of vegetable oil
- 1/8 teaspoon of cumin, ground
- 1/4 teaspoon of coriander, ground
- 14 oz. canned coconut milk
- 3 bird's eye chilies, cut into halves
- 1-inch piece ginger, sliced
- 1/2 cup of cilantro, diced
- 1/2 cup of basil, diced
- cooked barley for serving
- 1 tablespoon of fish sauce
- 4 cups of spinach, chopped
- lime wedges for serving
- 2 tablespoon of green curry paste
- 6 cups of quash, cubed
- Salt and black pepper- to taste

Method:
1. Start by throwing all the Ingredients: into the Crockpot and mix them well.
2. Cover it and cook for 6 hours on Low Settings.
3. Garnish as desired.
4. Serve warm.

Nutritional Information per Serving:
- Calories 383
- Total Fat 36.3 g
- Saturated Fat 5.5 g
- Cholesterol 112 mg
- Fiber 1.3 g
- Sugar 1.7 g
- Sodium 444 mg
- Protein 7.3 g

Mushroom Cream Goose Curry

Prep Time: 10 minutes; Cooking Time: 6.5 hours; Servings: 6

Ingredients:
- 12 oz. canned mushroom cream
- 1 goose breast, fat: trimmed off and cut into pieces
- 1 goose leg, skinless
- 1 yellow onion, diced
- 3 ½ cups of water
- 2 teaspoons of garlic, minced
- 1 goose thigh, skinless
- Salt and black pepper- to taste

Method:
1. Start by throwing all the Ingredients: into the Crockpot except cream and mix them well.
2. Cover it and cook for 6 hours on Low Settings.
3. Stir in mushroom cream and cook for another 30 minutes on low heat.

4. Give it a stir and garnish as desired.
5. Serve warm.

Nutritional Information per Serving:
- Calories 288
- Total Fat 5.7g
- Saturated Fat 1.8 g
- Cholesterol 60 mg
- Fiber 0.2 g
- Sugar 0.1 g
- Sodium 554 mg
- Protein 25.6g

Colombian Chicken

Prep Time: 10 minutes; Cooking Time: 6 hours; Servings: 4
Ingredients:
- 1 chicken, cut into 8 pieces
- 2 bay leaves
- 4 big tomatoes, cut into medium chunks
- 1 yellow onion, sliced
- Salt and black pepper- to taste

Method:
1. Start by throwing all the Ingredients: into the Crockpot and mix them well.
2. Cover it and cook for 6 hours on Low Settings.
3. Garnish as desired.
4. Serve warm.

Nutritional Information per Serving:
- Calories 481
- Total Fat 11.1 g
- Saturated Fat 0.1 g
- Cholesterol 320 mg
- Fiber 1.7 g
- Sugar 3 g
- Sodium 203 mg
- Protein 7 g

Chicken Curry

Prep Time: 10 minutes; Cooking Time: 6 hours; Servings: 6
Ingredients:
- 3 lb. chicken drumsticks and thighs
- 1 yellow onion, diced
- 2 tablespoons of butter, melted
- 1/2 cup of chicken stock
- 15 oz. canned tomatoes, crushed
- 1/4 cup of lemon juice
- 4 garlic cloves, minced
- 1 lb. spinach, chopped
- 1/2 cup of heavy cream
- 1 tablespoon of ginger, grated
- 1/2 cup of cilantro, diced
- 1 ½ teaspoon of paprika
- 1 tablespoon of cumin, ground
- 1 ½ teaspoon of coriander, ground
- 1 teaspoon of turmeric, ground
- Salt and black pepper- to taste
- A pinch cayenne peppers

Method:
1. Start by throwing all the Ingredients: into the Crockpot except lemon juice, cream, and cilantro, then mix them well.
2. Cover it and cook for 6 hours on Low Settings.
3. Stir in remaining Ingredients: and cook again for 1 hour on low heat.
4. Garnish as desired.
5. Serve warm.

Nutritional Information per Serving:
- Calories 537
- Total Fat 19.8 g

- Saturated Fat 1.4 g
- Cholesterol 10 mg
- Fiber 0.9 g
- Sugar 1.4 g
- Sodium 719 mg
- Protein 37.6.8 g

Saucy Teriyaki Chicken

Prep Time: 10 minutes; Cooking Time: 6 hours; Servings: 4
Ingredients:
- 2 lbs. chicken breasts, skinless and boneless
- 2/3 cup of teriyaki sauce
- 1 tablespoon of honey
- 1/2 cup of chicken stock
- a handful green onions, diced
- salt and black pepper - to taste

Method:
1. Start by throwing all the Ingredients: into the Crockpot and mix them well.
2. Cover it and cook for 6 hours on Low Settings.
3. Garnish as desired.
4. Serve warm.

Nutritional Information per Serving:
- Calories 609
- Total Fat 50.5 g
- Saturated Fat 11.7 g
- Cholesterol 58 mg
- Fiber 1.5 g
- Sugar 0.3 g
- Sodium 463 mg
- Protein 29.3 g

Chicken Shrimp Curry

Prep Time: 10 minutes; Cooking Time: 6 hours; Servings: 6
Ingredients:
- 8 oz. shrimp, peeled and deveined
- 8 oz. sausages, sliced
- 8 oz. chicken breasts, skinless, boneless and diced
- 2 tablespoon of extra virgin olive oil
- 1 teaspoon of creole seasoning
- 3 garlic cloves, minced
- 1 yellow onion, diced
- 1 green bell pepper, diced
- 3 celery stalks, diced
- 1 cup of cauliflower rice
- 1 cup of chicken stock
- 2 cups of canned tomatoes, diced
- 3 tablespoons of parsley, chopped
- 2 teaspoons of thyme, dried
- A pinch cayenne peppers
- 2 teaspoon of Worcestershire sauce
- 1 dash tabasco sauce

Method:
1. Start by throwing all the Ingredients: into the Crockpot except shrimp and mix them well.
2. Cover it and cook for 5 hours on Low Settings.
3. Stir in shrimp and cook for another 1 hour on low heat.
4. Garnish as desired.
5. Serve warm.

Nutritional Information per Serving:
- Calories 240
- Saturated Fat 2.7 g
- Cholesterol 15 mg
- Total Carbs 7.1 g
- Fiber 0g
- Sugar 0 g
- Sodium 474 mg
- Protein 14.9 g

Ground Duck Chili

Prep Time: 10 minutes; Cooking Time: 6 hours; Servings: 8

Ingredients:

- 1 yellow onion, cut into half
- 1 garlic heat, top trimmed off
- 2 cloves
- 1 bay leaf
- 6 cups of water
- Salt- to taste

For the duck:

- 1 lb. Duck, ground
- 15 oz. Canned tomatoes and their juices, diced
- 4 oz. Canned green chilies and their juice
- 1 teaspoon of Swerve
- 1 tablespoon of Vegetable oil
- 1 yellow onion, minced
- 2 carrots, diced
- Salt and black pepper- to taste
- Handful cilantro, diced

Method:

1. Start by throwing all other Ingredients: into the Crockpot and mix them well.
2. Cover it and cook for 6 hours on Low Settings.
3. Garnish as desired.
4. Serve warm.

Nutritional Information per Serving:

- Calories 548
- Total Fat 22.9 g
- Saturated Fat 9 g
- Cholesterol 105 mg
- Sugar 10.9 g
- Fiber 6.3 g
- Sodium 350 mg
- Protein 40.1 g

Chicken Stew

Prep Time: 10 minutes; Cooking Time: 10 hours; Servings: 4

Ingredients:

- 2 ½ lb. Chicken pieces
- 8 oz. Bacon, diced
- 1 cup of Yellow onion, diced
- 8 oz. wild rice
- 2 Carrots, diced
- 12 Parsley springs, diced
- 2 tablespoon of Extra virgin olive oil
- A drizzle of olive oil for serving
- 2 Bay leaves
- 1-quart Chicken stock
- 2 teaspoon of Sherry vinegar
- Salt and black pepper- to taste

Method:

1. Start by throwing all the Ingredients: into the Crockpot and mix them well.
2. Cover it and cook for 10 hours on Low Settings.
3. Remove the cooked chicken and shred its meat.
4. Return the chicken meat to the stew and mix well.
5. Garnish as desired.
6. Serve warm.

Nutritional Information per Serving:

- Calories 201
- Saturated Fat 4.5 g
- Cholesterol 57 mg
- Total Carbs 4.7 g
- Fiber 1.2 g
- Sugar 1.3 g
- Sodium 340 mg
- Protein 15.3g

Turkey Chili

Prep Time: 10 minutes; Cooking Time: 5 hours; Servings: 4

Ingredients:
- 1 lb. turkey meat, ground
- 1 ½ teaspoon of cumin
- 5 oz. water
- 1 yellow onion, diced
- 1 yellow bell pepper, diced
- 3 garlic cloves, diced
- 2 ½ tablespoon of chili powder
- A pinch of cayenne pepper
- 12 oz. veggies stock
- Salt and black pepper- to taste

Method:
1. Start by throwing all the Ingredients: into the Crockpot and mix them well.
2. Cover it and cook for 5 hours on Low Settings.
3. Garnish as desired.
4. Serve warm.

Nutritional Information per Serving:
- Calories 695
- Total Fat 17.5 g
- Saturated Fat 4.8 g
- Cholesterol 283 mg
- Fiber 1.8 g
- Sugar 0.8 g
- Sodium 355 mg
- Protein 117.4 g

Saucy Goose Satay

Prep Time: 10 minutes; Cooking Time: 6 hours; Servings: 4

Ingredients:
- 1 goose breast half, skinless, boneless and sliced
- 1/4 cup of sweet chili sauce
- 1 sweet onion, diced
- 2 teaspoons of garlic, diced
- 1/4 cup of extra virgin olive oil
- Salt and black pepper- to taste

Method:
1. Start by throwing all the Ingredients: into the Crockpot and mix them well.
2. Cover it and cook for 5-6 hours on Low Settings.
3. Garnish as desired.
4. Serve warm.

Nutritional Information per Serving:
- Calories 545
- Total Fat 36.4 g
- Saturated Fat 10.1 g
- Cholesterol 200 mg
- Fiber 0.2 g
- Sugar 0 g
- Sodium 272 mg
- Protein 42.5 g

Lemongrass Chicken Curry

Prep Time: 10 minutes; Cooking Time: 6 hours; Servings: 5

Ingredients:
- 1 bunch lemongrass, rough bottom removed and trimmed
- 1-inch piece ginger root, diced
- 4 garlic cloves, crushed
- 3 tablespoon of coconut aminos
- 1 teaspoon of Chinese five-spice
- 10 chicken drumsticks
- 1 cup of coconut milk
- 1/4 cup of cilantro, diced
- 1 yellow onion, diced
- 1 tablespoon of lime juice
- 2 tablespoon of fish sauce

- 1 teaspoon of butter
- Salt and black pepper- to taste

Method:
1. First blend lemongrass with garlic, ginger, five-spice, fish sauce, and aminos in a food processor.
2. Now start by throwing all the Ingredients:, including the lemongrass mixture into the Crockpot, and mix them well.
3. Cover it and cook for 6 hours on Low Settings.
4. Garnish as desired.
5. Serve warm.

Nutritional Information per Serving:
- Calories 405
- Total Fat 22.7 g
- Saturated Fat 6.1 g
- Cholesterol 4 mg
- Fiber 1.4 g
- Sugar 0.9 g
- Sodium 227 mg
- Protein 45.2 g

Sesame Chicken Satay

Prep Time: 10 minutes; Cooking Time: 6 hours; Servings: 4
Ingredients:
- 2 lbs. chicken breasts, skinless, boneless and diced
- 1/2 cup of yellow onion, diced
- 1 tablespoon of vegetable oil
- 6 tablespoons of water
- 2 teaspoon of sesame oil
- 1/2 cup of honey
- 2 tablespoon of xanthan gum
- 1/4 teaspoon of red pepper flakes
- 2 green onions, diced
- 1 tablespoon of sesame seeds, toasted
- 2 garlic cloves, minced
- 1/2 cup of soy sauce
- 1/4 cup of ketchup
- Salt and black pepper- to taste

Method:
1. Start by throwing all the Ingredients: into the Crockpot except green onions, sesame seeds, and xanthan gum and mix them well.
2. Cover it and cook for 6 hours on Low Settings.
3. Mix xanthan gum with a tablespoon of water and add to the chicken.
4. Stir cook on High heat until the mixture thickens.
5. Garnish with sesame seeds and green onions.
6. Serve warm.

Nutritional Information per Serving:
- Calories 545
- Total Fat 36.4 g
- Saturated Fat 10.1 g
- Cholesterol 200 mg
- Fiber 0.2 g
- Sugar 0 g
- Sodium 272 mg
- Protein 42.5 g

Moroccan Cranberry Chicken

Prep Time: 10 minutes; Cooking Time: 6.5 hours; Servings: 6
Ingredients:
- 6 chicken thighs
- 1 teaspoon of cloves
- 2 tablespoon of extra virgin olive oil
- 10 cardamom pods
- 1/2 teaspoon of cumin
- 1/2 teaspoon of ginger
- 1/2 cup of parsley, diced

- 1/2 teaspoon of turmeric
- 1/2 teaspoon of cinnamon, ground
- 2 bay leaves
- 1/2 teaspoon of coriander
- 2 yellow onions, diced
- 2 tablespoon of tomato paste
- 5 garlic cloves, diced
- 1/4 cup of cranberries, dried
- 1 juice of a lemon
- 1 cup of green olives
- 1 cup of chicken stock
- 1 teaspoon of paprika
- 1/4 cup of white wine

Method:
1. Start by throwing all the Ingredients: into the Crockpot except cranberries and mix them well.
2. Cover it and cook for 6 hours on Low Settings.
3. Remove and discard the cloves, cardamom, and bay leaves.
4. Stir in cranberries and cook for another 30 minutes on low heat.
5. Garnish as desired.
6. Serve warm.

Nutritional Information per Serving:
- Calories 405
- Total Fat 22.7 g
- Saturated Fat 6.1 g
- Cholesterol 4 mg
- Fiber 1.4 g
- Sugar 0.9 g
- Sodium 227 mg
- Protein 45.2 g

Chicken with Romano Cheese

Prep Time: 10 minutes; Cooking Time: 6 hours; Servings: 6
Ingredients:
- 6 chicken things, boneless and skinless and cut into medium chunks
- 1 teaspoon of chicken bouillon granules
- 1 cup of Romano cheese, grated
- 1 yellow onion, diced
- 4 oz. mushrooms, sliced
- 1 teaspoon of garlic, minced
- 1/2 cup of white almond flour
- 2 tablespoon of vegetable oil
- 10 oz. sugar-free tomato sauce
- 1 teaspoon of basil, dried
- 1 teaspoon of white wine vinegar
- 1 tablespoon of swerve
- 1 tablespoon of oregano, dried
- Salt and black pepper- to taste

Method:
1. Start by throwing all the Ingredients: into the Crockpot except cheese and mix them well.
2. Cover it and cook for 6 hours on Low Settings.
3. Garnish with cheese.
4. Serve warm.

Nutritional Information per Serving:
- Calories 361
- Total Fat 16.3 g
- Saturated Fat 4.9 g
- Cholesterol 114 mg
- Fiber 0.1 g
- Sugar 18.2 g
- Sodium 515 mg
- Protein 33.3 g

Chicken with Celery Stick

Prep Time: 10 minutes; Cooking Time: 6 hours; Servings: 4

Ingredients:
- 2 lbs. chicken breasts, skinless and bone-in
- 4 carrots, diced
- 1 yellow onion, diced
- 1/2 teaspoon of thyme, dried
- 1 tablespoon of chives
- 3 celery stalks, diced
- 3/4 cup of chicken stock
- Salt and black pepper- to taste

Method:
1. Start by throwing all the Ingredients: into the Crockpot except chives and mix them well.
2. Cover it and cook for 5 6 hours on Low Settings.
3. Garnish with chives.
4. Serve warm.

Nutritional Information per Serving:
- Calories 188
- Total Fat 6 g
- Saturated Fat 1 g
- Cholesterol 72 mg
- Fiber 1.6 g
- Sugar 2.3 g
- Sodium 472 mg
- Protein 25 g

Chicken Drumsticks

Prep Time: 10 minutes; Cooking Time: 6 hours; Servings: 6

Ingredients:
- 8 chicken drumsticks
- 8 oz. sugar-free tomato sauce
- 1 tablespoon of chicken bouillon
- 1/2 yellow onion, diced
- 1 tomato, diced
- 1/4 cup of cilantro, diced
- 1 garlic clove, minced
- 1 teaspoon of extra virgin olive oil
- 1/2 teaspoon of garlic powder
- 3 scallions, diced
- 2 cups of water
- 1/2 teaspoon of cumin, ground
- Salt and black pepper- to taste

Method:
1. Start by throwing all the Ingredients: into the Crockpot and mix them well.
2. Cover it and cook for 5 6 hours on Low Settings.
3. Garnish as desired.
4. Serve warm.

Nutritional Information per Serving:
- Calories 180
- Total Fat 20 g
- Saturated Fat 5 g
- Cholesterol 151 mg
- Fiber 1 g
- Sugar 1.2 g
- Sodium 686 mg
- Protein 21 g

Coconut Chicken Curry

Prep Time: 10 minutes; Cooking Time: 6 hours; Servings: 4

Ingredients:
- 15 oz. chicken breast, diced
- 5 oz. canned coconut cream
- 1 tablespoon of extra virgin olive oil
- 1 yellow onion, sliced
- 1 bag chicken curry base
- 1/2 bunch coriander, diced

Method:

1. Start by throwing all the Ingredients: into the Crockpot and mix them well.
2. Cover it and cook for 6 hours on Low Settings.
3. Garnish as desired.
4. Serve warm.

Nutritional Information per Serving:
- Calories 140
- Total Fat 7.9 g
- Saturated Fat 1.8 g
- Cholesterol 5 mg
- Sugar 7.1 g
- Fiber 2.6 g
- Sodium 581 mg
- Protein 7.2 g

Chicken Liver with Anchovies

Prep Time: 10 minutes; Cooking Time: 3 hours; Servings: 2

Ingredients:
- 1 teaspoon of extra virgin olive oil
- 3/4 lb. chicken liver
- 1 yellow onion, roughly diced
- 1 bay leaf
- 1/4 cup of red wine
- ¼ cup of vegetable stock
- 2 anchovies
- 1 tablespoon of capers, drained and diced
- 1 tablespoon of butter, melted
- Salt and black pepper- to taste

Method:
1. Start by throwing all the Ingredients: into the Crockpot and mix them well.
2. Cover it and cook for 3 hours on Low Settings.
3. Garnish as desired.
4. Serve warm.

Nutritional Information per Serving:
- Calories 541
- Total Fat 34 g
- Saturated Fat 8.5 g
- Cholesterol 69 mg
- Fiber 1.2 g
- Sugar 1 g
- Sodium 547 mg
- Protein 20.3 g

Chapter 4: Beef

Sweet Passata Dipped Steaks

Prep Time: 10 minutes; Cooking Time: 2 hours; Servings: 4
Ingredients:

- ¼ cup of Tomato passata
- 1 teaspoon of Ginger, grated
- 1 tablespoon of Mustard
- 1 Garlic clove, minced
- 1 teaspoon of Garlic, minced
- 1 tablespoon of Stevia
- 1 tablespoon of Olive oil
- 1 and ½ lbs. Beef steaks

Method:
1. Start by putting all the Ingredients: into your Crockpot.
2. Cover it and cook for 2 hours on High settings.
3. Once done, uncover the pot and mix well.
4. Garnish as desired.
5. Serve warm.

Nutritional Information per Serving:
- Calories 371
- Total Fat 17.2 g
- Saturated Fat 9.4 g
- Cholesterol 141 mg
- Sodium 153 mg
- Fiber 0.9 g
- Sugar 1.4 g
- Protein 32 g

Mushroom Beef Goulash

Prep Time: 10 minutes; Cooking Time: 8 hours; Servings: 3
Ingredients:

- 1 and ½ lbs. beef, cubed
- 1 red bell pepper, diced
- 1 yellow onion, diced
- 2 garlic cloves, minced
- 2 teaspoons of sweet paprika
- 3 oz. mushrooms halved
- 2 bay leaves
- a drizzle of olive oil
- ½ cup of beef stock
- ½ cup of coconut cream

Method:
1. Start by putting all the Ingredients: into your Crockpot.
2. Cover it and cook for 8 hours on Low settings.
3. Once done, uncover the pot and mix well.
4. Remove and discard the bay leaves.
5. Garnish as desired.
6. Serve warm.

Nutritional Information per Serving:
- Calories 291
- Total Fat 14.2 g
- Saturated Fat 4.4 g
- Cholesterol 180 mg
- Sodium 154 mg
- Fiber 3.1 g
- Sugar 3.6 g
- Protein 20.8 g

Beef Onion Stew

Prep Time: 10 minutes; Cooking Time: 4 hours; Servings: 2
Ingredients:

- 1 tablespoon of olive oil
- 1 yellow onion, diced
- 1 lb. beefsteak, cut into strips
- 2 springs onions, diced

- 1 cup of tomato passata
- Salt and black pepper- to taste

Method:
1. Start by putting all the Ingredients: into your Crockpot except the spring onions.
2. Cover it and cook for 4 hours on medium settings.
3. Once done, uncover the pot and mix well.
4. Garnish with spring onions.
5. Serve warm.

Nutritional Information per Serving:
- Calories 419
- Total Fat 13.2 g
- Saturated Fat 21.4 g
- Cholesterol 140 mg
- Sodium 161 mg
- Fiber 2.9 g
- Sugar 3.4 g
- Protein 36.2 g

Beef Steaks with Peppercorn Sauce

Prep Time: 10 minutes; Cooking Time: 8 hours; Servings: 2

Ingredients:
- 2 medium sirloin beef steaks
- 1 teaspoon of black peppercorns
- ¼ cup of sugar-free tomato sauce
- Salt and black pepper- to taste
- 1 tablespoon of olive oil

Method:
1. Start by putting all the Ingredients: into your Crockpot.
2. Cover it and cook for 8 hours on Low settings.
3. Once done, uncover the pot and mix well.
4. Garnish as desired.
5. Serve warm.

Nutritional Information per Serving:
- Calories 351
- Total Fat 12.2 g
- Saturated Fat 2.4 g
- Cholesterol 110 mg
- Sodium 276 mg
- Fiber 0.9 g
- Sugar 1.4 g
- Protein 15.8 g

Pumpkin Beef Chili

Prep Time: 10 minutes; Cooking Time: 3 hours; Servings: 6

Ingredients:
- 1 tablespoon of Olive oil
- 1 green bell pepper, diced
- 1 ½ lb. Beef, ground
- 6 garlic cloves, minced
- 28 oz. canned tomatoes, diced
- 14 oz. pumpkin puree
- 1 cup of chicken stock
- 2 tablespoon of Chili powder
- 1 ½ teaspoon of Cumin, ground
- 1 teaspoon of Cinnamon powder
- Salt and black pepper- to taste

Method:
1. Start by putting all the Ingredients: into your Crockpot.
2. Cover it and cook for 4 hours on Low settings.
3. Once done, uncover the pot and mix well.
4. Garnish as desired.
5. Serve warm.

Nutritional Information per Serving:

- Calories 238
- Total Fat 13.8 g
- Saturated Fat 1.7 g
- Cholesterol 221 mg
- Sodium 120 mg
- Fiber 2.4 g
- Sugar 11.2 g
- Protein 34.4g

Olives Beef Stew

Prep Time: 10 minutes; Cooking Time: 1o hours; Serving: 4
Ingredients:

- 28 oz. beefsteak, cubed
- 1 tablespoon of olive oil
- 1 tablespoon of parsley, chopped
- Salt and black pepper- to taste
- 8 oz. tomato passata
- 1 yellow onion, diced
- 1 cup of green olives pitted and sliced

Method:

1. Start by putting all the Ingredients: into your Crockpot.
2. Cover it and cook for 10 hours on Low settings.
3. Once done, uncover the pot and mix well.
4. Garnish as desired.
5. Serve warm.

Nutritional Information per Serving:

- Calories 359
- Total Fat 34 g
- Saturated Fat 10.3 g
- Cholesterol 112 mg
- Sugar 2 g
- Fiber 1.3 g
- Sodium 92 mg
- Protein 27.5 g

Beef Cabbage Casserole

Prep Time: 10 minutes; Cooking Time: 8 hours; Servings: 6
Ingredients:

- ½ cabbage head, shredded
- 1 yellow onion, diced
- 3 garlic cloves, minced
- 1 ½ lb. beef, ground
- 1 ½ cups of tomatoes, crushed
- 2 cups of cauliflower rice
- A drizzle of olive oil
- Salt and black pepper- to taste
- ½ teaspoon of Red pepper, crushed
- ½ cup of parsley, chopped

Method:

1. Start by putting all the Ingredients: into your Crockpot.
2. Cover it and cook for 8 hours on Low settings.
3. Once done, uncover the pot and mix well.
4. Garnish as desired.
5. Serve warm.

Nutritional Information per Serving:

- Calories 204
- Total Fat 10.6 g
- Saturated Fat 13.1 g
- Cholesterol 131 mg
- Sodium 141 mg
- Fiber 0.2 g
- Sugar 14.3 g
- Protein 12.6 g

Vegetable Beef Stew

Prep Time: 10 minutes; Cooking Time: 8 hours; Servings: 2
Ingredients:

- ½ lb. beef meat, cubed
- ½ yellow onion, diced
- 3 oz. tomato paste
- 1 garlic clove, minced
- ½ tablespoon of thyme, diced
- 1 carrot, diced
- 1.5 celery stalks, diced
- 1 tablespoon of parsley, chopped
- 1 tablespoon of white vinegar
- salt and black pepper to taste

Method:
1. Start by putting all the Ingredients: into your Crockpot.
2. Cover it and cook for 8 hours on Low settings.
3. Once done, uncover the pot and mix well.
4. Garnish as desired.
5. Serve warm.

Nutritional Information per Serving:
- Calories 311
- Total Fat 25.5 g
- Saturated Fat 12.4 g
- Cholesterol 69 mg
- Sodium 58 mg
- Fiber 0.7 g
- Sugar 7.3 g
- Protein 17.5 g

Spicy Mexican Luncheon

Prep Time: 10 minutes; Cooking Time: 8 hours; Servings: 4
Ingredients:
- 2 lbs. beef stew meat, cubed
- 6 tomatoes, diced
- 2 red onion, diced
- 10 oz. canned green chilies, diced
- 4 teaspoon of chili powder
- 2 teaspoon of cumin powder
- 2 teaspoons of oregano, dried
- 4 cups of vegetable broth
- salt and black pepper to taste

Method:
1. Start by putting all the Ingredients: into your Crockpot.
2. Cover it and cook for 8 hours on Low settings.
3. Once done, uncover the pot and mix well.
4. Garnish as desired.
5. Serve warm.

Nutritional Information per Serving:
- Calories 338
- Total Fat 34 g
- Saturated Fat 8.5 g
- Cholesterol 69 mg
- Sodium 217 mg
- Fiber 1.2 g
- Sugar 12 g
- Protein 30.3 g

Beef & Broccoli

Prep Time: 10 minutes; Cooking Time: 10 hours; Servings: 4
Ingredients:
- 2 lbs. flank steak, slice into 2" chunks
- 2/3 cup of liquid aminos
- 1 cup of beef broth
- 3 tablespoons of swerve
- 1 teaspoon of freshly grated ginger
- 3 garlic cloves, minced
- 1/4 1/2 teaspoons of red pepper flakes
- 1/2 teaspoons of salt
- 1 head broccoli, diced
- 1 red bell pepper, diced
- 1 teaspoon of sesame seeds

Method:
1. Start by putting all the Ingredients: into your Crockpot except the broccoli and bell pepper.
2. Cover it and cook for 10 hours on Low settings.
3. Once done, uncover the pot and mix well.
4. Stir in broccoli and bell pepper then continue cooking for 1 hour on low heat.
5. Serve warm.

Nutritional Information per Serving:
- Calories 527
- Total Fat 49 g
- Saturated Fat 14 g
- Cholesterol 83 mg
- Sodium 92 mg
- Sugar 1 g
- Fiber 1 g
- Protein 19 g

Beef Mushroom Stroganoff

Prep Time: 10 minutes; Cooking Time: 8 hours; Servings: 2
Ingredients:
- 1 brown onion sliced and quartered
- 2 cloves garlic, smashed
- 2 slices streaky bacon diced
- 1 lb. beef, stewing steak cubed
- 1 teaspoon of smoked paprika
- 3 tablespoons of tomato paste
- 1 cup of beef stock
- ½ cup of mushrooms quartered

Method:
1. Start by putting all the Ingredients: into your Crockpot.
2. Cover it and cook for 8 hours on Low settings.
3. Once done, uncover the pot and mix well.
4. Serve warm.

Nutritional Information per Serving:
- Calories 416
- Total Fat 19.2 g
- Saturated Fat 2.4 g
- Cholesterol 14 mg
- Sodium 261 mg
- Fiber 2.3 g
- Sugar 5.4 g
- Protein 41.1 g

Garlic Beef Stew with Olives, Capers, and Tomatoes

Prep Time: 10 minutes; Cooking Time: 4 hours; Servings: 6
Ingredients:
- 2 3 lb. beef chuck roast, cut into pieces
- 1 2 tablespoons of olive oil
- 1 can beef broth
- 1 cup of garlic cloves, peeled and cut into lengthwise slivers
- 1 cup of Kalamata Olives, cut in half lengthwise
- 2 tablespoons of capers, rinsed
- 3 bay leaves
- 1 teaspoon of dried Greek oregano
- 1 can (14.5 oz.) tomatoes with juice
- 1 small can (8 oz.) sugar-free tomato sauce
- 2 tablespoons of tomato paste
- 3 tablespoons of red wine vinegar
- fresh black pepper to taste

Method:
1. Start by putting all the Ingredients: into your Crockpot.
2. Cover it and cook for 4 hours on High settings.

3. Once done, uncover the pot and mix well.
4. Serve warm.

Nutritional Information per Serving:
- Calories 378
- Total Fat 18.2 g
- Saturated Fat 3.1 g
- Cholesterol 320 mg
- Sodium 130 mg
- Fiber 0.7 g
- Sugar 2.7 g
- Protein 34.3 g

Mexican Chili

Prep Time: 10 minutes; Cooking Time: 8 hours; Servings: 6
Ingredients:
- 2 1/2 lbs. ground beef
- 1 medium red onion, diced and divided
- 4 tablespoons of minced garlic
- 3 large ribs of celery, diced
- ¼ cup of pickled jalapeno slices
- 6 oz. can tomato paste
- 14.5 oz. can tomato and green chilies
- 14.5 oz. can stew tomatoes with Mexican seasoning
- 2 tablespoons of Worcestershire sauce or Coconut Aminos
- 4 tablespoons of chili powder
- 2 tablespoons of cumin, mounded
- 2 teaspoons of salt
- 1/2 teaspoons of cayenne
- 1 teaspoon of garlic powder
- 1 teaspoon of onion powder1 teaspoon of oregano
- 1 teaspoon of black pepper
- 1 bay leaf

Method:
1. Start by putting all the Ingredients: into your Crockpot.
2. Cover it and cook for 8 hours on Low settings.
3. Once done, uncover the pot and mix well.
4. Serve warm.

Nutritional Information per Serving:
- Calories 429
- Total Fat 15.1 g
- Saturated Fat 9.4 g
- Cholesterol 130 mg
- Sodium 132 mg
- Fiber 2.9 g
- Sugar 2.4 g
- Protein 33.1 g

Green Chile Shredded Beef Cabbage Bowl

Prep Time: 10 minutes; Cooking Time: 4 hours; Servings: 4
Ingredients:
For Crockpot Beef:
- 2 lb. beef chuck roast, well-trimmed and cut into thick strips
- 1 tablespoon of Kalyn's taco seasoning 2 3 teaspoons of olive oil

For Cabbage Slaw and Dressing:
- 1 small head green cabbage
- 1/2 small head red cabbage
- 1/2 cup of sliced green onion
- 6 tablespoons of mayo or light mayo
- 2 cans (4 oz. can) diced chilis with juice

- 4 teaspoons of fresh-squeezed lime juice
- 2 teaspoons of green tabasco sauce

Method:

1. Start by putting all the Ingredients: for beef into your Crockpot.
2. Cover it and cook for 4 hours on High settings.
3. Once done, uncover the pot and mix well.
4. Now toss all the coleslaw Ingredients: in a salad bowl.
5. Serve the beef with coleslaw.

Nutritional Information per Serving:

- Calories 429
- Total Fat 11.9 g
- Saturated Fat 1.7 g
- Cholesterol 78 mg
- Sodium 79 mg
- Fiber 1.1 g
- Sugar 0.3 g
- Protein 35 g

Chipotle Barbacoa Recipe

Prep Time: 10 minutes; Cooking Time: 10 hours; Servings: 6

Ingredients:

- 3 lb. beef brisket or chuck roast
- 1/2 cup of beef broth
- 2 medium chipotle chilis in adobo
- 5 cloves garlic
- 2 tablespoons of apple cider vinegar
- 2 tablespoons of lime juice
- 1 tablespoon of oregano, dried
- 2 teaspoons of cumin
- 2 teaspoons of salt
- 1 teaspoon of black pepper
- 1/2 teaspoons of cloves, ground
- 2 whole bay leaf

Method:

1. Start by putting all the Ingredients: into your Crockpot.
2. Cover it and cook for 10 hours on Low settings.
3. Once done, uncover the pot and mix well.
4. Shred the slow-cooked beef and return it to the pot.
5. Serve warm.

Nutritional Information per Serving:

- Calories 248
- Total Fat 15.7 g
- Saturated Fat 2.7 g
- Cholesterol 75 mg
- Sodium 94 mg
- Fiber 0.2 g
- Sugar 0.1 g
- Protein 43.2 g

Southwestern Pot Roast

Prep Time: 10 minutes; Cooking Time: 11 hours; Servings: 6

Ingredients:

- 3 lb. boneless chuck roast, trimmed of visible fat
- 1 can (14 oz.) beef broth
- 1 1/4 cup of your favorite salsa
- 1 2 teaspoons of olive oil for browning meat

Method:

1. Start by putting all the Ingredients: into your Crockpot.
2. Cover it and cook for 10 hours on Low settings.
3. Once done, uncover the pot and mix well.
4. Continue cooking for 1 hour on low heat until the sauce thickens.
5. Serve warm.

Nutritional Information per Serving:

- Calories 259
- Total Fat 9 g
- Saturated Fat 13 g
- Cholesterol 52 mg
- Sugar 1 g
- Fiber 1 g
- Sodium 992 mg
- Protein 20 g

Crockpot Chinese Beef

Prep Time: 10 minutes; Cooking Time: 7 hours; Servings: 4

Ingredients:
- Salt and black pepper
- 2 tablespoons of olive oil
- 1 cup of beef stock
- 2 lbs. stew beef
- 1/2 cup of cooking sherry
- 1/4 cup of coconut aminos
- 2 tablespoons of unseasoned rice wine vinegar
- 2 red bell peppers, seeded and sliced
- 1 tablespoon of 1 teaspoon of Chinese five-spice powder
- 1 teaspoon of red pepper flakes
- 8 oz. cremini mushrooms, quartered
- 2 large shallots, sliced
- 3 cloves garlic, minced
- 2 green onions, sliced
- 1 (2 inches) piece fresh ginger, grated
- 2 cups of snow peas
- 2 tablespoons of sesame seeds, for garnish

Method:
1. Start by putting all the Ingredients: into your Crockpot except the sesame seeds, peas, and green onions.
2. Cover it and cook for 6 hours on medium settings.
3. Once done, uncover the pot and mix well.
4. Stir in snow peas then continue cooking for 1 hour on low heat.
5. Garnish with sesame seeds and green onions.
6. Serve warm.

Nutritional Information per Serving:
- Calories 254
- Total Fat 15 g
- Saturated Fat 7 g
- Cholesterol 79 mg
- Sugar 3 g
- Fiber 1 g
- Sodium 812 mg
- Protein 21 g

Meatballs with Saucy Mushrooms

Prep Time: 10 minutes; Cooking Time: 6 hours; Servings: 4

Ingredients:
- 1 lb. beef meat, ground
- 1 yellow onion, minced
- 4 garlic cloves, minced
- ¼ cup of parsley, chopped
- salt, and black pepper to taste
- 1 teaspoon of oregano, dried
- 1 egg whisked
- ¼ cup of almond milk
- 2 teaspoon of coconut aminos
- 12 mushrooms, diced
- 1 cup of chicken stock
- 2 tablespoon of olive oil
- 2 tablespoons of butter

Method:
1. Thoroughly mix beef meat with garlic, onion, parsley, pepper, salt, egg, aminos, and oregano in a bowl.

2. Make 1-inch small meatballs out of this mixture.
3. Now start by putting all the Ingredients: into your Crockpot including the meatballs
4. Cover it and cook for 6 hours on medium settings.
5. Once done, uncover the pot and mix well.
6. Serve warm.

Nutritional Information per Serving:
- Calories 231
- Total Fat 17.8 g
- Saturated Fat 10.3 g
- Cholesterol 112 mg
- Sugar 0.2 g
- Fiber 0 g
- Sodium 92 mg
- Protein 16.4 g

Nutmeg Meatballs Curry

Prep Time: 10 minutes; Cooking Time: 8 hours; Servings: 4
Ingredients:
- 2/3 lbs. Beef meat, ground
- ½ egg
- 1 tablespoon of parsley, chopped
- 1 garlic clove, minced
- Salt and black pepper- to taste
- ¼ cup of vegetable broth
- ½ cup of tomato passata
- ¼ teaspoon of nutmeg, ground
- ¼ teaspoon of sweet paprika
- 1 tablespoon of olive oil
- 1 carrot, diced

Method:
1. Thoroughly mix the meat with egg, parsley, salt, pepper, garlic, nutmeg, and paprika in a suitable bowl.
2. Mix well and make small meatballs out of this mixture.
3. Now start by putting all the Ingredients: into your Crockpot.
4. Cover it and cook for 8 hours on Low settings.
5. Once done, uncover the pot and mix well.
6. Garnish as desired.
7. Serve warm.

Nutritional Information per Serving:
- Calories 328
- Total Fat 13.8 g
- Saturated Fat 5.1 g
- Cholesterol 200 mg
- Sodium 172 mg
- Fiber 1 g
- Sugar 3.3 g
- Protein 31.8 g

Barbecue Beef Short Ribs

Prep Time: 10 minutes; Cooking Time: 6 hours; Servings: 6
Ingredients:
- 3 lbs. short ribs
- 1 1/2 teaspoons of kosher salt
- 1/2 teaspoon of black pepper
- 2 tablespoons of olive oil
- 1/3 cup of beef stock
- 1/4 cup of red wine
- 1/2 cup of water
- 1/2 teaspoon of liquid smoke
- 1 cup of barbecue sauce
- 1 teaspoon of Worcestershire sauce
- 1/2 teaspoon of onion powder
- 1/2 teaspoon of chili powder
- 1/2 teaspoon of garlic powder

Method:

1. Start by putting all the Ingredients: into your Crockpot.
2. Cover it and cook for 6 hours on Low settings.
3. Once done, uncover the pot and mix well.
4. Garnish as desired.
5. Serve warm.

Nutritional Information per Serving:
- Calories 314
- Total Fat 18.2 g
- Saturated Fat 2.4 g
- Cholesterol 110 mg
- Sodium 231 mg
- Fiber 0.9 g
- Sugar 1.4 g
- Protein 26.3 g

Smothered Steak

Prep Time: 10 minutes; Cooking Time: 8 hours; Servings: 4
Ingredients:
- 1 1/2 lbs. sirloin tips, sliced
- 4 tablespoons of flour
- 2 tablespoons of vegetable oil
- 1 large green bell pepper, sliced
- 1 large onion, sliced
- 1 can (4 oz.) sliced mushrooms, drained
- 1 can (14.5 oz.) diced tomatoes
- 3 tablespoons of soy sauce
- 1/2 teaspoon of garlic powder
- 1/4 teaspoon of Black pepper
- 1/4 teaspoon of crushed red pepper

Method:
1. Start by putting all the Ingredients: into your Crockpot.
2. Cover it and cook for 8 hours on Low settings.
3. Once done, uncover the pot and mix well.
4. Garnish as desired.
5. Serve warm.

Nutritional Information per Serving:
- Calories 384
- Total Fat 8.9 g
- Saturated Fat 4.5 g
- Cholesterol 57 mg
- Sodium 340 mg
- Fiber 1.2 g
- Sugar 1.3 g
- Protein 43.3g

Garlic Creamy Beef Steak

Prep Time: 10 minutes; Cooking Time: 4 hours; Servings: 2
Ingredients:
- 1 lb. beef top sirloin steaks
- 2 garlic cloves, minced
- ¾ cup of cream
- ¼ cup of butter
- Salt and black pepper, to taste

Method:
1. Start by putting all the Ingredients: into your Crockpot.
2. Cover it and cook for 4 hours on High settings.
3. Once done, uncover the pot and mix well.
4. Garnish as desired.
5. Serve warm.

Nutritional Information per Serving:
- Calories 287
- Saturated Fat 4.8 g

- Cholesterol 283 mg
- Sodium 1212 mg
- Total Carbs 2.4 g
- Fiber 1.8 g
- Sugar 0.8 g
- Protein 17.4 g

Crock Pot Beef Fajitas

Prep Time: 10 minutes; Cooking Time: 9 hours; Servings: 2
Ingredients:
- 1 lb. beef, sliced
- 1 bell pepper, sliced
- 1 onion, sliced
- 1 tablespoon of butter
- 1 tablespoon of fajita seasoning

Method:
1. Start by putting all the Ingredients: into your Crockpot.
2. Cover it and cook for 9 hours on Low settings.
3. Once done, uncover the pot and mix well.
4. Garnish as desired.
5. Serve warm.

Nutritional Information per Serving:
- Calories 232
- Total Fat 16.4 g
- Saturated Fat 10.1 g
- Cholesterol 200 mg
- Sodium 272 mg
- Fiber 0.2 g
- Sugar 0 g
- Protein 15 g

Steak with cheese and herb butter

Prep Time: 10 minutes; Cooking Time: 10 hours; Servings: 8
Ingredients:
- 8 beef steaks
- 3 oz. cheddar cheese or gruyere cheese, cut into rods
- salt and pepper
- 2 tablespoons of butter
- ½ cup of beef stock
- 2 leeks, rinsed, trimmed and sliced
- 1 lb. mushrooms, cut into wedges
- 2 tablespoons of olive oil
- 5 oz. herb butter

Method:
1. Start by putting all the Ingredients: into your Crockpot except the cheese
2. Cover it and cook for 10 hours on Low settings.
3. Once done, uncover the pot and mix well.
4. Garnish with crumbled cheese.
5. Serve warm.

Nutritional Information per Serving:
- Calories 425
- Total Fat 12.7 g
- Saturated Fat 6.1 g
- Cholesterol 4 mg
- Sodium 227 mg
- Fiber 1.4 g
- Sugar 0.9 g
- Protein 21.2 g

Ground beef and green beans

Prep Time: 10 minutes; Cooking Time: 4 hours; Servings: 3
Ingredients:
- 2/3 lb. ground beef
- 9 oz. fresh green beans
- 3½ oz. butter
- salt and pepper

- ½ cup of beef stock
- 1/3 cup of mayonnaise or crème Fraiche

Method:
1. Start by putting all the Ingredients: into your Crockpot except mayonnaise.
2. Cover it and cook for 4 hours on Low settings.
3. Once done, uncover the pot and mix well.
4. Garnish with mayonnaise.
5. Serve warm.

Nutritional Information per Serving:
- Calories 361
- Total Fat 16.3 g
- Saturated Fat 4.9 g
- Cholesterol 114 mg
- Sodium 515 mg
- Fiber 0.1 g
- Sugar 8.2 g
- Protein 33.3 g

Chateaubriand with Hassel back

Prep Time: 10 minutes; Cooking Time: 10 hours; Servings: 4

Ingredients:
- 1 1/3 lbs. beef, tenderloin, diced
- 2 tablespoons of butter
- 1 tablespoon of olive oil
- 3 4 sprigs fresh rosemary
- salt and pepper
- Red wine butter
- 1 shallot, peeled and diced
- ¾ cup of red wine
- 5 oz. butter
- 1 tablespoon of finely fresh parsley, chopped
- 1 teaspoon of red wine vinegar
- salt and pepper
- 12 oz. celery root, rinsed, peeled and sliced
- 1 oz. butter
- salt and pepper

Method:
1. Start by putting all the Ingredients: into your Crockpot.
2. Cover it and cook for 10 hours on Low settings.
3. Once done, uncover the pot and mix well.
4. Garnish as desired.
5. Serve warm.

Nutritional Information per Serving:
- Calories 388
- Total Fat 6 g
- Saturated Fat 1 g
- Cholesterol 72 mg
- Sodium 472 mg
- Fiber 1.6 g
- Sugar 2.3 g
- Protein 22.5 g

Ground beef and broccoli

Prep Time: 10 minutes; Cooking Time: 2 hours; Servings: 4

Ingredients:
- 2/3 lb. ground beef
- 3 oz. butter
- ½ cup of beef stock
- 9 oz. broccoli, trimmed and diced
- Salt and black pepper-to taste
- ½ cup of mayonnaise or crème Fraiche

Method:
1. Start by putting all the Ingredients: into your Crockpot.

2. Cover it and cook for 2 hours on Low settings.
3. Once done, uncover the pot and mix well.
4. Garnish as desired.
5. Serve warm.

Nutritional Information per Serving:
- Calories 272
- Total Fat 18 g
- Saturated Fat 5 g
- Cholesterol 6.1 mg
- Sodium 3 mg
- Fiber 3 g
- Sugar 4 g
- Protein 19.4 g

Ribeye Steak and broccoli

Prep Time: 10 minutes; Cooking Time: 9 hours; Servings: 2
Ingredients:
- 4 oz. butter
- ¾ lb. ribeye steaks
- 9 oz. broccoli, trimmed and diced
- 1 yellow onion, peeled and diced
- 1 tablespoon of tamari soy
- 1 tablespoon of pumpkin seeds
- salt and pepper

Method:
1. Start by putting all the Ingredients: into your Crockpot.
2. Cover it and cook for 9 hours on Low settings.
3. Once done, uncover the pot and mix well.
4. Garnish as desired.
5. Serve warm.

Nutritional Information per Serving:
- Calories 421
- Total Fat 12.2 g
- Saturated Fat 2.4 g
- Cholesterol 110 mg
- Sodium 276 mg
- Fiber 0.9 g
- Sugar 1.4 g
- Protein 18.8 g

Blue cheese casserole

Prep Time: 10 minutes; Cooking Time: 10 hours; Servings: 4
Ingredients:
- 2 oz. butter
- 1 lb. ground beef
- 1 yellow onion, diced
- 7 oz. fresh green beans, trimmed and diced
- 5 oz. blue cheese
- 1 cup of heavy whipping cream
- 4 oz. shredded cheddar cheese
- salt and pepper
- Serving
- 5 oz. leafy greens
- 4 tablespoons of olive oil

Method:
1. Start by putting all the Ingredients: into your Crockpot except blue cheese.
2. Mix well and spread evenly then drizzle the cheese on top.
3. Cover it and cook for 10 hours on Low settings.
4. Once done, uncover the pot and mix well.
5. Garnish as desired.
6. Serve warm.

Nutritional Information per Serving:
- Calories 301
- Total Fat 12.2 g

- Saturated Fat 2.4 g
- Cholesterol 110 mg
- Sodium 276 mg
- Fiber 0.9 g
- Sugar 1.4 g
- Protein 28.8 g

Southwest Jalapeno Beef

Prep Time: 10 minutes; Cooking Time: 6 hours; Servings: 4

Ingredients:

- 1 lb. ground beef
- 1 red onion, diced
- ½ green pepper, diced
- 2 oz. olive oil
- 10 oz. diced tomatoes
- 1 cup of carrots, diced
- 3 diced jalapeños
- 3 cup of cauliflower rice
- 3 cup of chicken stock
- 3 tablespoons of chili powder
- 1 tablespoon of salt
- 1 tablespoon of pepper
- 2 oz. diced cilantro

Method:

1. Start by putting all the Ingredients: into your Crockpot.
2. Cover it and cook for 6 hours on Low settings.
3. Once done, uncover the pot and mix well.
4. Garnish as desired.
5. Serve warm.

Nutritional Information per Serving:

- Calories 391
- Total Fat 21.8 g
- Saturated Fat 12.6 g
- Cholesterol 16 mg
- Sodium 162 mg
- Fiber 9.2 g
- Sugar 4.5 g
- Protein 11.6 g

Debdoozie's Beef Chili

Prep Time: 10 minutes; Cooking Time: 4 hours; Servings: 6

Ingredients:

- 2 lbs. ground beef
- ½ onion, diced
- 1 teaspoon of black pepper
- ½ teaspoon of garlic salt
- 2 ½ cups of sugar-free tomato sauce
- 1 (8 oz.) jar salsa
- 4 tablespoons of chili seasoning mix
- ½ cup of green bell pepper, diced

Method:

1. Start by putting all the Ingredients: into your Crockpot.
2. Cover it and cook for 4 hours on Low settings.
3. Once done, uncover the pot and mix well.
4. Garnish as desired.
5. Serve warm.

Nutritional Information per Serving:

- Calories 416
- Total Fat 24.5 g
- Saturated Fat 10 g
- Cholesterol 32 mg
- Sodium 123 mg
- Fiber 3.6 g
- Sugar 5.5 g
- Protein 14.3 g

Garlic Sirloin

Prep Time: 10 minutes; Cooking Time: 12 hours; Servings: 12
Ingredients:

- 6 lbs. beef top sirloin steaks
- 4 teaspoons of garlic powder
- 8 cloves garlic, minced
- 1 cup of butter
- Salt and pepper, to taste
- ½ cup of beef stock

Method:

1. Start by putting all the Ingredients: into your Crockpot.
2. Cover it and cook for 12 hours on Low settings.
3. Once done, uncover the pot and mix well.
4. Garnish as desired.
5. Serve warm.

Nutritional Information per Serving:

- Calories 335
- Total Fat 10.7 g
- Saturated Fat 2.7 g
- Cholesterol 168 mg
- Sodium 121 mg
- Fiber 3.5 g
- Sugar 2.3 g
- Protein 19.7 g

Red Beef Steak

Prep Time: 10 minutes; Cooking Time: 9 hours; Servings: 8
Ingredients:

- 4 lbs. beef round steak
- 2 tablespoons of vegetable oil
- 4 teaspoons of Worcestershire sauce
- 6 garlic cloves
- 1 teaspoon of salt
- 1 teaspoon of black pepper
- 1 cup of ketchup
- 1 cup of diced onions

Method:

1. Start by putting all the Ingredients: into your Crockpot.
2. Cover it and cook for 9 hours on Low settings.
3. Once done, uncover the pot and mix well.
4. Garnish as desired.
5. Serve warm.

Nutritional Information per Serving:

- Calories 402
- Total Fat 13.7 g
- Saturated Fat 4.7 g
- Cholesterol 194 mg
- Sodium 607 mg
- Fiber 1.4 g
- Sugar 3.3 g
- Protein 10.2 g

Pepper Beef

Prep Time: 10 minutes; Cooking Time: 9 hours; Servings: 6
Ingredients:

- 2 large yellow bell pepper, seeded and sliced
- 2 lbs. grass-fed boneless beef, trimmed
- 4 cups of tomatoes, diced
- 6 garlic cloves, minced
- 2 large red bell pepper, seeded and sliced
- 2 cups of water
- 2 tablespoons of olive oil

- Salt and black pepper, to taste
- 2 teaspoons of rosemary, dried, crushed
- 2 large green bell pepper, seeded and sliced
- 3 cups of sugar-free tomato sauce

Method:
1. Start by putting all the Ingredients: into your Crockpot.
2. Cover it and cook for 9 hours on Low settings.
3. Once done, uncover the pot and mix well.
4. Garnish as desired.
5. Serve warm.

Nutritional Information per Serving:
- Calories 295
- Total Fat 23.5 g
- Saturated Fat 1.7 g
- Cholesterol 381 mg
- Sodium 245 mg
- Fiber 0.3 g
- Sugar 1.8. g
- Protein 18.2 g

Prime Rib Luncheon

Prep Time: 10 minutes; Cooking Time: 12 hours; Servings: 10
Ingredients:
- ½ (5 lb.) prime rib roast
- 1 tablespoon of olive oil
- Black pepper, to taste
- Salt, to taste
- 5 cloves garlic, minced
- 1 teaspoon of thyme, dried

Method:
1. Start by putting all the Ingredients: into your Crockpot.
2. Cover it and cook for 12 hours on Low settings.
3. Once done, uncover the pot and mix well.
4. Garnish as desired.
5. Serve warm.

Nutritional Information per Serving:
- Calories 259
- Total Fat 9 g
- Saturated Fat 13 g
- Cholesterol 52 mg
- Sugar 1 g
- Fiber 1 g
- Sodium 992 mg
- Protein 20 g

Chapter 5: Lamb

Smoked Lamb Chili

Prep Time: 10 minutes; Cooking Time: 8 hours; Servings: 4
Ingredients:

- 2 lbs. grass-fed ground lamb
- 8 bacon strips, diced
- 1 small onion, diced
- 3 tablespoons of chili powder
- 2 tablespoons of smoked paprika
- 4 teaspoons of cumin, ground
- 2 red bell pepper, seeded and diced
- Black pepper, to taste
- 4 garlic cloves, minced

Method:

1. Start by putting all the Ingredients: into your Crockpot.
2. Cover its lid and cook for 8 hours on Medium settings.
3. Once done, remove its lid and mix well.
4. Garnish as desired.
5. Serve warm.

Nutritional Information per Serving:

- Calories 511
- Total Fat 18.5 g
- Saturated Fat 11.5 g
- Cholesterol 51 mg
- Sodium 346 mg
- Sugar 0.5 g
- Fiber 0.4 g
- Protein 11.5 g

Lamb Chops Curry

Prep Time: 10 minutes; Cooking Time: 6 hours; Servings: 2
Ingredients:

- 1 lb. lamb loin chops
- 1 garlic clove, crushed
- ½ cup of bone broth
- 3/4 teaspoon of rosemary, dried, crushed
- 1 tablespoon of xanthan gum
- 1 ½ tablespoons of butter
- ½ small onion, sliced
- 3/4 cup of Sugar-free diced tomatoes
- 1 cup of carrots, peeled and sliced
- Salt and black pepper
- ½ tablespoon of cold water

Method:

1. Start by putting all the Ingredients: into your Crockpot.
2. Cover its lid and cook for 6 hours on Low settings.
3. Once done, remove its lid and mix well.
4. Garnish as desired.
5. Serve warm.

Nutritional Information per Serving

- Calories 184
- Total Fat 12.7 g
- Saturated Fat 7.3 g
- Cholesterol 35 mg
- Sodium 222 mg
- Sugar 2.7 g
- Fiber 1.6 g
- Protein 12.2 g

Dinner Lamb Shanks

Prep Time: 10 minutes; Cooking Time: 8 hours; Servings: 3
Ingredients:

- 1 ½ lb. grass-fed lamb shanks, trimmed
- 1 tablespoon of olive oil
- 3/4 cup of bone broth
- ½ teaspoon of rosemary, dried, crushed
- 1 tablespoon of melted butter
- 3 whole garlic cloves, peeled
- Salt and black pepper, to taste
- 3/4 tablespoon of *Sugar*-free tomato paste
- 1 ¼ tablespoon of fresh lemon juice

Method:
1. Start by putting all the Ingredients: into your Crockpot.
2. Cover its lid and cook for 8 hours on Low settings.
3. Once done, remove its lid and mix well.
4. Garnish as desired.
5. Serve warm.

Nutritional Information per Serving:
- Calories 188
- Total Fat 12.5 g
- Saturated Fat 4.4 g
- Cholesterol 53 mg
- Sodium 1098 mg
- Sugar 0.3 g
- Fiber 2 g
- Protein 14.6 g

Coconut Lamb Stew

Prep Time: 10 minutes; Cooking Time: 10 hours; Servings: 2
Ingredients:
- 1 lb. grass-fed lamb shoulder, cut into bite-sized pieces
- 1 tablespoon of curry powder, divided
- ¼ cup of unsweetened coconut milk
- 2 tablespoons of coconut cream
- 1 tablespoon of coconut oil
- 1 medium yellow onion, diced
- ½ cup of chicken broth
- 1 tablespoon of fresh lemon juice
- Salt and black pepper, to taste
- 2 tablespoons of fresh basil, diced

Method:
1. Start by putting all the Ingredients: into your Crockpot except basil.
2. Cover its lid and cook for 10 hours on Low settings.
3. Once done, remove its lid and mix well.
4. Garnish with basil
5. Serve warm.

Nutritional Information per Serving:
- Calories 141
- Total Fat 11.3 g
- Saturated Fat 3.8 g
- Cholesterol 181 mg
- Sodium 334 mg
- Sugar 0.5 g
- Fiber 0 g
- Protein 8.9 g

Herbed Lamb Stew

Prep Time: 10 minutes; Cooking Time: 9 hours; Servings: 2
Ingredients:
- 1 lb. grass-fed lamb shoulder, trimmed and cubed into 2-inch size
- 3/4 tablespoon of olive oil
- 1 celery stalk, diced
- 1 cup of tomatoes, diced

- 1 ½ tablespoon of fresh lemon juice
- ½ teaspoon of salt
- ½ teaspoon of black pepper
- ½ large green bell pepper, cut into 8 slices
- ½ large red bell pepper, cut into 8 slices
- ½ cup of bone broth
- ½ small onion, diced
- ½ tablespoon of garlic, minced
- ½ teaspoon of oregano, dried, crushed
- ½ teaspoon of dried basil, crushed

Method:
1. Start by putting all the Ingredients: into your Crockpot.
2. Cover its lid and cook for 9 hours on Low settings.
3. Once done, remove its lid and mix well.
4. Garnish as desired.
5. Serve warm.

Nutritional Information per Serving:
- Calories 260
- Total Fat 22.9 g
- Saturated Fat 7.3 g
- Cholesterol 0 mg
- Sodium 9 mg
- Sugar 1.8 g
- Fiber 1.4 g
- Protein 5.6 g

Vegetable Lamb Stew

Prep Time: 10 minutes; Cooking Time: 10.5 hours; Servings: 2
Ingredients:
- 1 lb. cubed lamb stew meat
- 1 tablespoon of fresh ginger, grated
- ½ teaspoon of lime juice
- ¼ teaspoon of black pepper
- 3/4 cup of diced tomatoes
- ½ teaspoon of turmeric powder
- 1 ½ medium carrots, sliced
- 2 garlic cloves, minced
- ½ cup of coconut milk
- ¼ teaspoon of salt
- 1 tablespoon of olive oil
- ½ medium onion, diced
- ½ medium zucchini, diced

Method:
1. Start by putting all the Ingredients: into your Crockpot except zucchini.
2. Cover its lid and cook for 10 hours on Low settings.
3. Once done, remove its lid and mix well.
4. Stir in zucchini and continue cooking for 30 minutes on high heat.
5. Garnish as desired.
6. Serve warm.

Nutritional Information per Serving
- Calories 108
- Total Fat 9 g
- Saturated Fat 4.3 g
- Cholesterol 180 mg
- Sodium 146 mg
- Sugar 0.5 g
- Fiber 0.1 g
- Protein 6 g

Lamb Leg with Thyme

Prep Time: 10 minutes; Cooking Time: 10 hours; Servings: 4
Ingredients:
- 2 lbs. leg of lamb
- 1 teaspoon of fine salt

- 2 ½ tablespoons of olive oil
- 6 sprigs thyme
- 1 ½ cup of bone broth
- 6 garlic cloves, minced
- 1 ½ teaspoon of black pepper
- 1 ½ small onion
- 3/4 cup of vegetable stock

Method:
1. Start by putting all the Ingredients: into your Crockpot.
2. Cover its lid and cook for 10 hours on Low settings.
3. Once done, remove its lid and mix well.
4. Garnish as desired.
5. Serve warm.

Nutritional Information per Serving
- Calories 112
- Total Fat 4.9 g
- Saturated Fat 1.9 g
- Cholesterol 10 mg
- Sodium 355 mg
- Sugar 0.8 g
- Fiber 0.4 g
- Protein 3 g

Full Meal Turmeric Lamb

Prep Time: 10 minutes; Cooking Time: 6 hours; Servings: 2
Ingredients:
- ½ lb. ground lamb meat
- ½ cup of onion diced
- ½ tablespoon of garlic
- ½ tablespoon of minced ginger
- ¼ teaspoon of turmeric
- ¼ teaspoon of ground coriander
- ½ teaspoon of salt
- ¼ teaspoon of cumin
- ¼ teaspoon of cayenne pepper

Method:
1. Start by putting all the Ingredients: into your Crockpot.
2. Cover its lid and cook for 6 hours on Low settings.
3. Once done, remove its lid and mix well.
4. Garnish as desired.
5. Serve warm.

Nutritional Information per Serving:
- Calories 132
- Total Fat 10.9 g
- Saturated Fat 2.7 g
- Cholesterol 164 mg
- Sodium 65 mg
- Sugar 0.5 g
- Fiber 2.3 g
- Protein 6.3 g

Lamb Cauliflower Curry

Prep Time: 10 minutes; Cooking Time: 10 hours; Servings: 4
Ingredients:
- 2 lbs. lamb roasted Wegmans
- 1 cup of onion soup
- ¼ cup of carrots
- 1 cup of cauliflower
- 1 cup of beef broth

Method:
1. Start by putting all the Ingredients: into your Crockpot.
2. Cover its lid and cook for 10 hours on Low settings.
3. Once done, remove its lid and mix well.
4. Garnish as desired.

5. Serve warm.

Nutritional Information per Serving:
- Calories 118
- Total Fat 9.7 g
- Saturated Fat 4.3 g
- Cholesterol 228 mg
- Sodium 160 mg
- Fiber 0 g
- Sugar 0.5 g
- Protein 7.4 g

Irish Chop stew

Prep Time: 10 minutes; Cooking Time: 10 hours; Servings: 8

Ingredients:
- 8 lamb shoulder chops, cubed
- 8 large onions, sliced into thin rounds
- 4 cups of water
- 4 tablespoons of olive oil
- 9 large carrots, chunked
- 4 sprigs thyme
- 2 teaspoons of salt
- 2 teaspoons of black pepper

Method:
1. Start by putting all the Ingredients: into your Crockpot.
2. Cover its lid and cook for 10 hours on Low settings.
3. Once done, remove its lid and mix well.
4. Garnish as desired.
5. Serve warm.

Nutritional Information per Serving:
- Calories 280
- Total Fat 23 g
- Saturated Fat 13.8 g
- Cholesterol 82 mg
- Sodium 28 mg
- Fiber 2.5 g
- Sugar 0.5 g
- Protein 3.9 g

Picante Glazed Chops

Prep Time: 10 minutes; Cooking Time: 6 hours; Servings: 6

Ingredients:
- 6 lamb chops, bone-in
- 1 ¼ cup of Picante sauce
- 1 cup of cherry tomatoes
- 3 tablespoons of olive oil
- 3 tablespoons of almond flour
- 3 tablespoons of brown swerve, packed

Method:
1. Start by putting all the Ingredients: into your Crockpot.
2. Cover its lid and cook for 6 hours on Low settings.
3. Once done, remove its lid and mix well.
4. Garnish as desired.
5. Serve warm.

Nutritional Information per Serving:
- Calories 206
- Total Fat 20.8 g
- Saturated Fat 14.2 g
- Cholesterol 315 mg
- Sodium 35 mg
- Fiber 0.1 g
- Sugar 1.5 g
- Protein 4.2 g

Pomegranate Lamb

Prep Time: 10 minutes; Cooking Time: 10 hours 15 minutes; Servings: 4

Ingredients:

- 1 leg of lamb, boneless (tied)
- 1 cup of pomegranate juice
- 1 cup of white wine
- 1 cup of chicken stock
- ½ cup of pomegranate seeds
- 4 mint leaves
- 4 cloves garlic, peeled and minced
- 1 teaspoon of black pepper, ground
- 1 teaspoon of salt
- 3 tablespoons of olive oil

Method:

1. Start by throwing all the Ingredients: except the pomegranate seeds, butter, and flour into your Crockpot.
2. Cover its lid and cook for 10 hours on Low settings.
3. Once done, remove its lid and mix well.
4. Slice the slow-cooked lamb then transfer to a plate
5. Mix flour with butter in a small bowl then pour into the crockpot.
6. Continue cooking the remaining sauce for 15 minutes on high heat.
7. Pour this sauce around the slices lamb.
8. Garnish with pomegranate seeds.
9. Serve warm.

Nutritional Information per Serving:

- Calories 225
- Total Fat 20.4 g
- Saturated Fat 8.7 g
- Cholesterol 30 mg
- Sodium 135 mg
- Fiber 4.3 g
- Sugar 2.2 g
- Protein 5.2 g

Persian Lamb Curry

Prep Time: 10 minutes; Cooking Time: 10 hours;Servings: 6

Ingredients:

- 1 tablespoon of turmeric
- 2 teaspoons of black pepper
- 1 teaspoon of salt
- 1 teaspoon of crushed red pepper flakes
- 3 tablespoons of extra virgin olive oil
- 2 medium onions, minced
- 3 lbs. lamb meat, cut into chunks
- 3 tablespoons of tomato paste
- ¼ cup of cilantro, diced

Method:

1. Start by putting all the Ingredients: into your Crockpot except cilantro.
2. Cover its lid and cook for 10 hours on Low settings.
3. Once done, remove its lid and mix well.
4. Garnish with cilantro.
5. Serve warm.

Nutritional Information per Serving:

- Calories 376
- Total Fat 12.1 g
- Saturated Fat 14.2 g
- Cholesterol 195 mg
- Sodium 73 mg
- Fiber 3.1 g
- Sugar 2.1 g
- Protein 25.7 g

Indian Lamb Stew

Prep Time: 10 minutes; Cooking Time: 10 hours 15 minutes; Servings: 8
Ingredients:

- 2 tablespoons of sweet paprika
- 1 ½ teaspoons of cayenne pepper
- 1 cup of Greek yogurt
- ¼ cup of vegetable oil
- 4 lbs. boneless lamb shoulder
- 1 ½ teaspoons of ground ginger
- 1 ½ teaspoon of ground coriander
- ½ teaspoon of ground turmeric
- ¼ teaspoon of cloves, ground
- 2 small cinnamon sticks
- 8 cardamom pods
- 1 medium tomato, diced
- Black pepper
- 1 tablespoon of xanthan gum
- 2 tablespoons of water

Method:

1. Start by throwing all the Ingredients: except the butter and flour into your Crockpot.
2. Cover its lid and cook for 10 hours on Low settings.
3. Once done, remove its lid and mix well.
4. Mix corn starch and water in a small bowl then pour into the crockpot.
5. Continue cooking the remaining sauce for 15 minutes on high heat until it thickens.
6. Garnish as desired.
7. Serve warm.

Nutritional Information per Serving:

- Calories 265
- Total Fat 26.1 g
- Saturated Fat 7.8 g
- Cholesterol 143 mg
- Sodium 65 mg
- Fiber 3.2 g
- Sugar 1.3 g
- Protein 6.1 g

Lamb Tomato Stew

Prep Time: 10 minutes; Cooking Time: 10 hours; Servings: 2
Ingredients:

- 4 tablespoons of olive oil
- 1 (½ -1 ¾) lb. lamb stew meat
- 2 onions, diced
- 8 garlic cloves, diced
- 2 teaspoons of salt
- 2 teaspoons of pepper
- 2 teaspoons of cumin
- 2 teaspoons of coriander
- 2 teaspoons of turmeric,
- 2 teaspoons of cinnamon
- 1 teaspoon of chili flakes
- 4 tablespoons of tomato paste
- ½ cup of apple cider vinegar
- 4 tablespoons of swerve
- 2 ½ cups of chicken broth

Method:

1. Start by throwing all the Ingredients: except the cilantro into your Crockpot.
2. Cover its lid and cook for 10 hours on Low settings.
3. Once done, remove its lid and mix well.
4. Garnish as desired.
5. Serve warm.

Nutritional Information per Serving:

- Calories 347
- Total Fat 11.6 g

- Saturated Fat 2.3 g
- Cholesterol 421 mg
- Sodium 54 mg

- Fiber 0.6 g
- Sugar 1.1 g
- Protein 2.4 g

Tangy Lamb Meat Balls

Prep Time: 10 minutes; Cooking Time: 9 hours; Servings: 6
Ingredients:

- 3/4 lb. ground lamb meat
- Salt and black pepper, to taste
- 2 small tomatoes, diced roughly
- ½ small yellow onion, diced roughly
- ½ cup of sugar-free tomato sauce

- ¼ teaspoon of red pepper flakes, crushed
- 2 garlic cloves, peeled
- 5 mini bell peppers, seeded and halved
- ½ tablespoon of olive oil
- 1 teaspoon of adobo seasoning

Method:
1. Mix lamb meat, adobo seasoning, black pepper, and salt in a suitable bowl.
2. Now use this lamb mixture to make small meatballs of 1-inch diameter.
3. Start putting all the Ingredients:, including the meatballs into your Crockpot.
4. Cover its lid and cook for 9 hours on Low settings.
5. Once done, remove its lid and mix well.
6. Garnish as desired.
7. Serve warm.

Nutritional Information per Serving:
- Calories 345
- Total Fat 27.2 g
- Saturated Fat 15.2 g
- Cholesterol 53 mg

- Sodium 65 mg
- Fiber 1.2 g
- Sugar 0.9 g
- Protein 6.4 g

Bacon Lamb Chili

Prep Time: 10 minutes; Cooking Time: 10 hours; Servings: 6
Ingredients:

- 2 lbs. grass-fed ground lamb
- 8 bacon strips, diced
- 1 small onion, diced
- 3 tablespoons of chili powder
- 2 tablespoons of smoked paprika

- 4 teaspoons of cumin, ground
- 2 red bell pepper, seeded and diced
- Black pepper, to taste
- 4 garlic cloves, minced

Method:
1. Start by putting all the Ingredients: into your Crockpot.
2. Cover its lid and cook for 2 hours on High settings.
3. Once done, remove its lid and mix well.
4. Garnish as desired.
5. Serve warm.

Nutritional Information per Serving:
- Calories 294
- Total Fat 19.3 g
- Saturated Fat 9.4 g
- Cholesterol 132 mg

- Sodium 76 mg
- Fiber 1.4 g
- Sugar 0.9 g
- Protein 5.1 g

Sauce Glazed Lamb Chops

Prep Time: 10 minutes; Cooking Time: 10 hours 20 minutes; Servings: 2
Ingredients:

- 1 lb. lamb loin chops
- 1 garlic clove, crushed
- 1/2 cup of bone broth
- 3/4 teaspoon of rosemary, dried, crushed
- 1 tablespoon of xanthan gum
- 1 1/2 tablespoons of butter
- 1/2 small onion, sliced
- 3/4 cup of *Sugar*-free diced tomatoes
- 1 cup of carrots, peeled and sliced
- Salt and black pepper
- 1/2 tablespoon of cold water

Method:
1. Start by putting all the Ingredients: into your Crockpot except xanthan gum and water.
2. Cover its lid and cook for 10 hours on Low settings.
3. Once done, remove its lid and mix well.
4. Mix the xanthan gum with water and pour it into the crockpot.
5. Continue cooking for another 20 minutes on high heat until the sauce thickens.
6. Garnish as desired.
7. Serve warm.

Nutritional Information per Serving:

- Calories 343
- Total Fat 21.4 g
- Saturated Fat 12.1 g
- Cholesterol 165 mg
- Sodium 45 mg
- Fiber 2.2 g
- Sugar 0.9 g
- Protein 3.4 g

Lamb Pepper Stew

Prep Time: 10 minutes; Cooking Time: 12 hours; Servings: 12
Ingredients:

- 6 lbs. lamb shoulder
- 4 garlic cloves sliced thin
- 2 teaspoons of salt
- 2 teaspoons of garlic powder
- 2 teaspoons of oregano
- 2 tablespoons of cumin
- 4 teaspoons of ground coriander
- 4 teaspoons of chili powder
- 1/2 teaspoon of black pepper
- 1/2 teaspoon of onion powder
- 1 tablespoon of olive oil
- 4 tablespoons of apple cider vinegar
- 2 cups of peppers sliced
- 1 onion sliced
- 1 7 oz. can of chipotle peppers
- 1 14.5 oz. can tomato, diced
- 1 4 oz. can of green chilis

Method:
1. Start by putting all the Ingredients: into your Crockpot.
2. Cover its lid and cook for 12 hours on medium setting.
3. Once done, remove its lid and mix well.
4. Garnish as desired.
5. Serve warm.

Nutritional Information per Serving:

- Calories 449
- Total Fat 28.7 g
- Saturated Fat 14.9 g
- Cholesterol 163 mg

- Sodium 844 mg
- Sugar 2.6 g
- Fiber 1.9 g
- Protein 39.3 g

Herbed Lamb Loin Chops

Prep Time: 10 minutes; Cooking Time: 8 hours; Servings: 1
Ingredients:
- 3 tablespoons of Mustard
- 2 tablespoons of Butter melted
- 1 tablespoon of swerve
- ¼ cup of dill, diced
- 3 green onions, diced
- 1 tablespoon of Lemon peel, grated
- Salt and black pepper- to taste
- 1 lamb loin chop

Method:
1. Start by putting all the Ingredients: into your Crockpot.
2. Cover its lid and cook for 8 hours on Low setting.
3. Once done, remove its lid and mix well.
4. Garnish as desired.
5. Serve warm.

Nutritional Information per Serving:
- Calories 298
- Total Fat 14.4 g
- Saturated Fat 2.4 g
- Cholesterol 73 mg
- Sodium 76 mg
- Fiber 0.3 g
- Sugar 0.6 g
- Protein 31.4 g

Lamb Chops with Balsamic Green

Prep Time: 10 minutes; Cooking Time: 10.5 hours; Servings: 4
Ingredients:
- 4 lamb chops, bone-in
- 2 tablespoons of swerves
- ½ cup of beef stock
- 1 tablespoon of balsamic vinegar
- 4 tablespoons of butter melted
- 4 oz. baby spinach

Method:
1. Start by putting all the Ingredients: into your Crockpot except spinach.
2. Cover its lid and cook for 10 hours on Low setting.
3. Once done, remove its lid and mix well.
4. Stir in spinach and cook for 30 minutes on high heat.
5. Garnish as desired.
6. Serve warm.

Nutritional Information per Serving:
- Calories 364
- Total Fat 13.2 g
- Saturated Fat 3.4 g
- Cholesterol 141 mg
- Sodium 274 mg
- Sugar 2.8g
- Fiber 5.7 g
- Protein 47.7 g

Tarragon Lamb Chops

Prep Time: 10 minutes; Cooking Time: 10 hours; Servings: 4
Ingredients:
- 4 lamb loin chops, boneless
- 2 tablespoons of tarragon, diced
- Salt and black pepper- to taste
- 1 lb. Asparagus, trimmed and halved
- 2 tablespoon of Olive oil

- 1 bunch green onions, diced
- ½ cup of vegetable broth
- 1 tablespoon of Mustard

Method:
1. Start by putting all the Ingredients: into your Crockpot and mix them well.
2. Cover its lid and cook for 10 hours on Low setting.
3. Once done, remove its lid and mix well.
4. Garnish as desired.
5. Serve warm.

Nutritional Information per Serving:
- Calories 355
- Total Fat 15 g
- Saturated Fat 1.4 g
- Cholesterol 128 mg
- Sodium 1271 mg
- Sugar 2.5 g
- Fiber 2.7 g
- Protein 44.2 g

Spicy Lamb Leg

Prep Time: 10 minutes; Cooking Time: 10 hours; Servings: 2
Ingredients:
- 1 lb. lamb leg, boneless, sliced
- 2 tablespoon of chili powder
- ½ cup of tomato passata
- 2 tablespoons of mustard
- 2 tablespoon of olive oil
- 2 tablespoons of balsamic vinegar
- Salt and black pepper- to taste

Method:
1. Start by putting all the Ingredients: into your Crockpot.
2. Cover its lid and cook for 10 hours on Low setting.
3. Once done, remove its lid and mix well.
4. Serve warm.

Nutritional Information per Serving:
- Calories 487
- Total Fat 37.4 g
- Saturated Fat 8.8 g
- Cholesterol 71 mg
- Sodium 501 mg
- Sugar 1.2 g
- Fiber 9.2 g
- Protein 28.1 g

Chard Mixed Lamb Shoulder

Prep Time: 10 minutes; Cooking Time: 10 hours; Servings: 4
Ingredients:
- 2 lbs. lamb shoulder
- 2 lemons, sliced
- 4 teaspoon of olive oil
- Salt and black pepper- to taste
- 2 garlic cloves, minced
- 2 bunches swiss chard, diced
- ½ cup of beef stock

Method:
1. Start by putting all the Ingredients: into your Crockpot.
2. Cover its lid and cook for 10 hours on Low setting.
3. Once done, remove its lid and mix well.
4. Garnish as desired.
5. Serve warm.

Nutritional Information per Serving:
- Calories 434
- Total Fat 36.4 g

- Saturated Fat 17.1 g
- Cholesterol 257 mg
- Sodium 1038 mg
- Sugar 0.9 g
- Fiber 0.2 g
- Protein 24.2 g

Sesame Topped Baby Ribs

Prep Time: 10 minutes; Cooking Time: 6 hours; Servings: 4
Ingredients:
- 2 lbs. Lamb leg, bone-in
- Salt and black pepper- to taste
- 1 cup of tomato passata
- 1 tablespoon of balsamic vinegar
- 2 garlic cloves, minced
- 1 teaspoon of sesame seeds

Method:
1. Start by putting all the Ingredients: into your Crockpot.
2. Cover its lid and cook for 6 hours on High setting.
3. Once done, remove its lid and mix well.
4. Garnish as desired.
5. Serve warm.

Nutritional Information per Serving:
- Calories 335
- Total Fat 21.6 g
- Saturated Fat 12.8 g
- Cholesterol 10 mg
- Sodium 851 mg
- Sugar 3.3 g
- Fiber 2.8 g
- Protein 23.8 g

Mustard Rubbed Lamb Chops

Prep Time: 10 minutes; Cooking Time: 6 hours; Servings: 4
Ingredients:
- 4 lamb chops, bone-in
- 1 tablespoon of olive oil
- ½ cup of vegetable broth
- ¼ cup of apricot preserves
- 3 tablespoons of mustard
- Salt and black pepper- to taste

Method:
1. Start by putting all the Ingredients: into your Crockpot.
2. Cover its lid and cook for 6 hours on High setting.
3. Once done, remove its lid and mix well.
4. Garnish as desired.
5. Serve warm.

Nutritional Information per Serving:
- Calories 324
- Total Fat 20.7 g
- Saturated Fat 6.7 g
- Cholesterol 45 mg
- Sodium 241 mg
- Sugar 1.4 g
- Fiber 0.5 g
- Protein 35.3 g

Tangy Lamb Chops

Prep Time: 10 minutes; Cooking Time: 4 hours; Servings: 4
Ingredients:
- 4 lamb loin chops, boneless
- 2 tablespoon of olive oil
- 1 teaspoon of chili powder
- Salt and black pepper- to taste
- ½ cup of beef stock

Salsa

- 1 tomato, cubed
- 1 teaspoon of Balsamic vinegar

Method:
1. Start by putting all the Ingredients: for lamb chops into your Crockpot.
2. Cover its lid and cook for 8 hours on a low setting.
3. Once done, remove its lid and mix well.
4. Mix the tomato with vinegar in a small bowl.
5. Garnish the lamb chops with tomato salsa.
6. Serve warm.

Nutritional Information per Serving:
- Calories 287
- Total Fat 29.5 g
- Saturated Fat 3 g
- Cholesterol 0 mg
- Sodium 388 mg
- Sugar 1.4g
- Fiber 4.3 g
- Protein 14.7 g

Sweet Lamb Chops

Prep Time: 10 minutes; Cooking Time: 10 hours; Servings: 4
Ingredients:
- ¼ cup of tomato passata
- 1 teaspoon of ginger, grated
- 1 tablespoon of mustard
- 1 garlic clove, minced
- 1 teaspoon of garlic, minced
- 1 tablespoon of brown swerve
- 1 tablespoon of olive oil
- 1 and ½ lbs. lamb chops

Method:
1. Start by putting all the Ingredients: into your Crockpot.
2. Cover it and cook for 10 hours on High settings.
3. Once done, uncover the pot and mix well.
4. Garnish as desired.
5. Serve warm.

Nutritional Information per Serving:
- Calories 371
- Total Fat 17.2 g
- Saturated Fat 9.4 g
- Cholesterol 141 mg
- Sodium 153 mg
- Fiber 0.9 g
- Sugar 1.4 g
- Protein 32 g

Traditional Lamb Goulash

Prep Time: 10 minutes; Cooking Time: 10 hours; Servings: 3
Ingredients:
- 1 and ½ lbs. lamb, cubed
- 1 red bell pepper, diced
- 1 yellow onion, diced
- 2 garlic cloves, minced
- 2 teaspoons of sweet paprika
- 3 oz. mushrooms halved
- 2 bay leaves
- a drizzle of olive oil
- ½ cup of beef stock
- ½ cup of coconut cream

Method:
1. Start by putting all the Ingredients: into your Crockpot.
2. Cover it and cook for 10 hours on Low settings.
3. Once done, uncover the pot and mix well.
4. Remove and discard the bay leaves.
5. Garnish as desired.

6. Serve warm.

Nutritional Information per Serving:
- Calories 291
- Total Fat 14.2 g
- Saturated Fat 4.4 g
- Cholesterol 180 mg
- Sodium 154 mg
- Fiber 3.1 g
- Sugar 3.6 g
- Protein 20.8 g

Lamb Onion Medley

Prep Time: 10 minutes; Cooking Time: 4 hours; Servings: 2

Ingredients:
- 1 tablespoon of olive oil
- 1 yellow onion, diced
- 1 lb. lamb meat, sliced
- 2 springs onions, diced
- 1 cup of tomato passata
- Salt and black pepper- to taste

Method:
1. Start by putting all the Ingredients: into your Crockpot except the spring onions.
2. Cover it and cook for 4 hours on medium settings.
3. Once done, uncover the pot and mix well.
4. Garnish with spring onions.
5. Serve warm.

Nutritional Information per Serving:
- Calories 419
- Total Fat 13.2 g
- Saturated Fat 21.4 g
- Cholesterol 140 mg
- Sodium 161 mg
- Fiber 2.9 g
- Sugar 3.4 g
- Protein 36.2 g

Saucy Lamb Chops

Prep Time: 10 minutes; Cooking Time: 10 hours; Servings: 2

Ingredients:
- 2 lamb chops
- 1 teaspoon of black peppercorns
- ¼ cup of sugar-free tomato sauce
- Salt and black pepper- to taste
- 1 tablespoon of olive oil

Method:
1. Start by putting all the Ingredients: into your Crockpot.
2. Cover it and cook for 10 hours on Low settings.
3. Once done, uncover the pot and mix well.
4. Garnish as desired.
5. Serve warm.

Nutritional Information per Serving:
- Calories 351
- Total Fat 12.2 g
- Saturated Fat 2.4 g
- Cholesterol 110 mg
- Sodium 276 mg
- Fiber 0.9 g
- Sugar 1.4 g
- Protein 15.8 g

Savoury Lamb Chili

Prep Time: 10 minutes; Cooking Time: 4 hours; Servings: 6

Ingredients:
- 1 tablespoon of olive oil
- 1 green bell pepper, diced

- 1 ½ lb. lamb ground
- 6 garlic cloves, minced
- 28 oz. canned tomatoes, diced
- 14 oz. pumpkin puree
- 1 cup of chicken stock
- 2 tablespoon of chili powder
- 1 ½ teaspoon of cumin, ground
- 1 teaspoon of cinnamon powder
- Salt and black pepper- to taste

Method:
1. Start by putting all the Ingredients: into your Crockpot.
2. Cover it and cook for 5 hours on Low settings.
3. Once done, uncover the pot and mix well.
4. Garnish as desired.
5. Serve warm.

Nutritional Information per Serving:
- Calories 238
- Total Fat 13.8 g
- Saturated Fat 1.7 g
- Cholesterol 221 mg
- Sodium 120 mg
- Fiber 2.4 g
- Sugar 11.2 g
- Protein 34.4g

Passata lamb Stew

Prep Time: 10 minutes; Cooking Time: 1o hours; Serving: 4
Ingredients:
- 28 oz. lamb meat, cubed
- 1 tablespoon of olive oil
- 1 tablespoon of parsley, chopped
- Salt and black pepper- to taste
- 8 oz. tomato passata
- 1 yellow onion, diced
- 1 cup of green olives pitted and sliced

Method:
1. Start by putting all the Ingredients: into your Crockpot.
2. Cover it and cook for 10 hours on Low settings.
3. Once done, uncover the pot and mix well.
4. Garnish as desired.
5. Serve warm.

Nutritional Information per Serving:
- Calories 359
- Total Fat 34 g
- Saturated Fat 10.3 g
- Cholesterol 112 mg
- Sugar 2 g
- Fiber 1.3 g
- Sodium 92 mg
- Protein 27.5 g

Lamb Meat Casserole

Prep Time: 10 minutes; Cooking Time: 8 hours; Servings: 6
Ingredients:
- ½ cabbage head, shredded
- 1 yellow onion, diced
- 3 garlic cloves, minced
- 1 ½ lb. Lamb meat, ground
- 1 ½ cups of tomatoes, crushed
- 2 cups of cauliflower rice
- A drizzle of olive oil
- Salt and black pepper- to taste
- ½ teaspoon of Red pepper, crushed
- ½ cup of parsley, chopped

Method:
1. Start by putting all the Ingredients: into your Crockpot and mix well.
2. Cover it and cook for 8 hours on Low settings.

3. Once done, uncover the pot and mix well.
4. Garnish as desired.
5. Serve warm.

Nutritional Information per Serving:
- Calories 204
- Total Fat 10.6 g
- Saturated Fat 13.1 g
- Cholesterol 131 mg
- Sodium 141 mg
- Fiber 0.2 g
- Sugar 14.3 g
- Protein 12.6 g

Vegetable Lamb Stew

Prep Time: 10 minutes; Cooking Time: 10 hours; Servings: 2

Ingredients:
- ½ lb. lamb meat, cubed
- ½ yellow onion, diced
- 3 oz. tomato paste
- 1 garlic clove, minced
- ½ tablespoon of thyme, diced
- 1 carrot, diced
- 1.5 celery stalks, diced
- 1 tablespoon of parsley, chopped
- 1 tablespoon of white vinegar
- salt and black pepper to taste

Method:
1. Start by putting all the Ingredients: into your Crockpot.
2. Cover it and cook for 10 hours on Low settings.
3. Once done, uncover the pot and mix well.
4. Garnish as desired.
5. Serve warm.

Nutritional Information per Serving:
- Calories 311
- Total Fat 25.5 g
- Saturated Fat 12.4 g
- Cholesterol 69 mg
- Sodium 58 mg
- Fiber 0.7 g
- Sugar 7.3 g
- Protein 17.5 g

Spicy Mexican Stew

Prep Time: 10 minutes; Cooking Time: 9 hours; Servings: 4

Ingredients:
- 2 lbs. lamb meat, cubed
- 6 tomatoes, diced
- 2 red onion, diced
- 10 oz. canned green chilies, diced
- 4 teaspoon of chili powder
- 2 teaspoon of cumin powder
- 2 teaspoons of oregano, dried
- 4 cups of vegetable broth
- salt and black pepper to taste

Method:
1. Start by putting all the Ingredients: into your Crockpot.
2. Cover it and cook for 9 hours on Low settings.
3. Once done, uncover the pot and mix well.
4. Garnish as desired.
5. Serve warm.

Nutritional Information per Serving:
- Calories 338
- Total Fat 34 g
- Saturated Fat 8.5 g
- Cholesterol 69 mg
- Sodium 217 mg
- Fiber 1.2 g

- Sugar 12 g
- Protein 30.3 g

Lamb Meatball Curry

Prep Time: 10 minutes; Cooking Time: 9 hours; Servings: 4

Ingredients:
- 2/3 lbs. lamb meat, ground
- ½ egg
- 1 tablespoon of parsley, chopped
- 1 garlic clove, minced
- Salt and black pepper- to taste
- ¼ cup of vegetable broth
- ½ cup of tomato passata
- ¼ teaspoon of nutmeg, ground
- ¼ teaspoon of sweet paprika
- 1 tablespoon of olive oil
- 1 carrot, diced

Method:
1. Thoroughly mix the meat with egg, parsley, salt, pepper, garlic, nutmeg, and paprika in a suitable bowl.
2. Mix well and make small meatballs out of this mixture.
3. Now start by putting all the Ingredients:, including the meatballs into your Crockpot.
4. Cover it and cook for 9 hours on Low settings.
5. Once done, uncover the pot and mix well.
6. Garnish as desired.
7. Serve warm.

Nutritional Information per Serving:
- Calories 328
- Total Fat 13.8 g
- Saturated Fat 5.1 g
- Cholesterol 200 mg
- Sodium 172 mg
- Fiber 1 g
- Sugar 3.3 g
- Protein 31.8 g

Barbecue Lamb Leg

Prep Time: 10 minutes; Cooking Time: 10 hours; Servings: 6

Ingredients:
- 3 lbs. lamb leg, boneless
- 1 1/2 teaspoons of kosher salt
- 1/2 teaspoon of black pepper
- 2 tablespoons of olive oil
- 1/3 cup of beef stock
- 1/4 cup of red wine
- 1/2 cup of water
- 1/2 teaspoon of liquid smoke
- 1 cup of barbecue sauce
- 1 teaspoon of Worcestershire sauce
- 1/2 teaspoon of onion powder
- 1/2 teaspoon of chili powder
- 1/2 teaspoon of garlic powder

Method:
1. Start by putting all the Ingredients: into your Crockpot.
2. Cover it and cook for 10 hours on Low settings.
3. Once done, uncover the pot and mix well.
4. Slice the leg and transfer it to a plate.
5. Pour the remaining sauce around.
6. Garnish as desired.
7. Serve warm.

Nutritional Information per Serving:
- Calories 314
- Total Fat 18.2 g

- Saturated Fat 2.4 g
- Cholesterol 110 mg
- Sodium 231 mg
- Fiber 0.9 g
- Sugar 1.4 g
- Protein 26.3 g

Lamb Mushroom Curry

Prep Time: 10 minutes; Cooking Time: 9 hours; Servings: 4
Ingredients:

- 2 lbs. lamb meat, diced
- 1 (1-ounce) packet onion soup mix
- 1 (10 3/4-ounce) can golden mushroom soup
- 1/2 cup of dry red wine
- 1 (4-ounce) can mushrooms

Method:

1. Start by putting all the Ingredients: into your Crockpot.
2. Cover it and cook for 9 hours on Low settings.
3. Once done, uncover the pot and mix well.
4. Garnish as desired.
5. Serve warm.

Nutritional Information per Serving:

- Calories 233
- Total Fat 20.2 g
- Saturated Fat 4.4 g
- Cholesterol 120 mg
- Sodium 76 mg
- Fiber 0.9 g
- Sugar 1.4 g
- Protein 41.9 g

Chapter 6: Snack and Appetizers

Parmesan cream Green Beans

Prep Time: 10 minutes; Cooking Time: 2 hours; Servings: 2
Ingredients:

- 10 oz. green beans, trimmed and halved
- A pinch of salt and black pepper
- 1/3 cup of parmesan (grated)
- 2 oz. cream cheese
- 1/3 cup of coconut cream
- 1 tablespoon of dill, diced

Method:

1. Start by throwing all the Ingredients: into the Crockpot.
2. Cover its lid and cook for 2 hours on Low setting.
3. Once done, remove its lid of the crockpot carefully.
4. Mix well and garnish as desired.
5. Serve warm.

Nutritional Information per Serving:

- Calories 292
- Total Fat 26.2 g
- Saturated Fat 16.3 g
- Cholesterol 100 mg
- Sodium 86 mg
- Sugar 6.6 g
- Fiber 0.2 g
- Protein 5.2 g

Radish Spinach Medley

Prep Time: 10 minutes; Cooking Time: 2 hours; Servings: 2
Ingredients:

- 1 lb. spinach, torn
- 2 cups of radishes, sliced
- A pinch of salt and black pepper
- ¼ cup of vegetable broth
- 1 teaspoon of chili powder
- 1 tablespoon of parsley, chopped

Method:

1. Start by throwing all the Ingredients: into the Crockpot.
2. Cover its lid and cook for 2 hours on Low setting.
3. Once done, remove its lid of the crockpot carefully.
4. Mix well and garnish as desired.
5. Serve warm.

Nutritional Information per Serving:

- Calories 244
- Total Fat 24.8 g
- Saturated Fat 15.6 g
- Cholesterol 32 mg
- Sodium 204 mg
- Sugar 0.4 g
- Fiber 0.1 g
- Protein 24 g

Citrus rich Cabbage

Prep Time: 10 minutes; Cooking Time: 3 hours; Servings: 2
Ingredients:

- 1 lb. green cabbage, shredded
- ½ cup of chicken stock
- A pinch of salt and black pepper
- 1 tablespoon of lemon juice
- 1 tablespoon of chives, diced
- 1 tablespoon of lemon zest (grated)

Method:

1. Start by throwing all the Ingredients: into the Crockpot.

2. Cover its lid and cook for 3 hours on Low setting.
3. Once done, remove its lid of the crockpot carefully.
4. Mix well and garnish as desired.
5. Serve warm.

Nutritional Information per Serving:
- Calories 145
- Total Fat 13.1 g
- Saturated Fat 9.1 g
- Cholesterol 96 mg
- Sodium 35 mg
- Sugar 1.2 g
- Fiber 1.5 g
- Protein 3.5 g

Herb Mixed Radish

Prep Time: 10 minutes; Cooking Time: 3 hours; Servings: 4
Ingredients:
- 3 cups of red radishes, halved
- ½ cup of vegetable broth
- 2 tablespoons of basil, diced
- 1 tablespoon of oregano, diced
- 1 tablespoon of chives, diced
- 1 tablespoon of green onion, diced
- A pinch of salt and black pepper

Method:
1. Start by throwing all the Ingredients: into the Crockpot.
2. Cover its lid and cook for 3 hours on Low setting.
3. Once done, remove its lid of the crockpot carefully.
4. Mix well and garnish as desired.
5. Serve warm.

Nutritional Information per Serving:
- Calories 266
- Total Fat 26.9 g
- Saturated Fat 15.8 g
- Cholesterol 18 mg
- Sodium 218 mg
- Sugar 0.4 g
- Fiber 0.2 g
- Protein 4.5 g

Creamy Mustard Asparagus

Prep Time: 10 minutes; Cooking Time: 3 hours; Servings: 2
Ingredients:
- 1 lb. asparagus, trimmed and halved
- 2 teaspoons of mustard
- ¼ cup of coconut cream
- 2 garlic cloves, minced
- 1 tablespoon of chives, diced
- Salt and black pepper- to taste

Method:
1. Start by throwing all the Ingredients: into the Crockpot.
2. Cover its lid and cook for 3 hours on Low setting.
3. Once done, remove its lid of the crockpot carefully.
4. Mix well and garnish as desired.
5. Serve warm.

Nutritional Information per Serving:
- Calories 149
- Total Fat 14.5 g
- Saturated Fat 8.1 g
- Cholesterol 56 mg
- Sodium 56 mg
- Sugar 0.3 g
- Fiber 0.2 g
- Protein 2.6 g

Savory Pine Nuts Cabbage

Prep Time: 10 minutes; Cooking Time: 2 hours; Servings: 2
Ingredients:
- 1 savoy cabbage, shredded
- 2 tablespoons of avocado oil
- 1 tablespoon of balsamic vinegar
- ¼ cup of pine nuts, toasted
- ½ cup of vegetable broth
- Salt and black pepper- to taste

Method:
1. Start by throwing all the Ingredients: into the Crockpot.
2. Cover its lid and cook for 2 hours on Low setting.
3. Once done, remove its lid of the crockpot carefully.
4. Mix well and garnish as desired.
5. Serve warm.

Nutritional Information per Serving:
- Calories 145
- Total Fat 13.1 g
- Saturated Fat 9.1 g
- Cholesterol 96 mg
- Sodium 35 mg
- Sugar 1.2 g
- Fiber 1.5 g
- Protein 3.5 g

Nutmeg Fennel

Prep Time: 10 minutes; Cooking Time: 3 hours; Servings: 2
Ingredients:
- 2 fennel bulbs, sliced
- 2 tablespoon of olive oil
- 4 garlic cloves, diced
- 2 tablespoons of balsamic vinegar
- 2 and ½ cups of baby spinach
- ½ teaspoon of nutmeg, ground
- ¼ cup of vegetable broth

Method:
1. Start by throwing all the Ingredients: into the Crockpot.
2. Cover its lid and cook for 3 hours on Low setting.
3. Once done, remove its lid of the crockpot carefully.
4. Mix well and garnish as desired.
5. Serve warm.

Nutritional Information per Serving:
- Calories 244
- Total Fat 24.8 g
- Saturated Fat 15.6 g
- Cholesterol 32 mg
- Sodium 204 mg
- Sugar 0.4 g
- Fiber 0.1 g
- Protein 24 g

Herbed Cherry Tomatoes

Prep Time: 10 minutes; Cooking Time: 1 hour; Servings: 2
Ingredients:
- 4 garlic cloves, minced
- A pinch of salt and black pepper
- 2 lbs. Cherry tomatoes halved
- 2 tablespoon of olive oil
- 1 tablespoon of dill, diced
- ½ cups of chicken stock
- ¼ cup of basil, diced

Method:
1. Start by throwing all the Ingredients: into the Crockpot.

2. Cover its lid and cook for 1 hour on Low setting.
3. Once done, remove its lid of the crockpot carefully.
4. Mix well and garnish as desired.
5. Serve warm.

Nutritional Information per Serving:
- Calories 145
- Total Fat 13.1 g
- Saturated Fat 9.1 g
- Cholesterol 96 mg
- Sodium 35 mg
- Protein 3.5 g

Viennese Coffee

Prep Time: 10 minutes; Cooking Time: 2.5 hours; Servings: 2

Ingredients:
- 3 cups of strong brewed coffee
- 3 tablespoons of sugar-free chocolate syrup
- 1 teaspoon of stevia
- 1/3 cup of heavy whipping cream
- 1/4 cup of crème de cacao
- Whipped cream, optional

Method:
1. Start by throwing all the Ingredients: into the Crockpot.
2. Cover its lid and cook for 2.5 hours on Low setting.
3. Once done, remove its lid of the crockpot carefully.
4. Garnish with whipped cream.
5. Serve warm.

Nutritional Information per Serving:
- Calories 231
- Total Fat 32.9 g
- Saturated Fat 6.1 g
- Cholesterol 10 mg
- Sodium 18 mg
- Protein 4.4 g

Ginger Tea Drink

Prep Time: 10 minutes; Cooking Time: 2 hours; Servings: 4

Ingredients:
- 4 cups of boiling water
- 15 individual green tea bags
- 4 cups of white grape juice
- 1 to 2 tablespoons of honey
- 1 tablespoon of minced fresh ginger root
- Crystallized ginger, optional

Method:
1. Start by throwing all the Ingredients: into the Crockpot.
2. Cover its lid and cook for 2 hours on Low setting.
3. Once done, remove its lid of the crockpot carefully.
4. Strain the slow-cooked tea into the glasses.
5. Serve warm.

Nutritional Information per Serving:
- Calories 179
- Total Fat 15.7 g
- Saturated Fat 8 g
- Cholesterol 0 mg
- Sodium 43 mg
- Protein 5.6 g

Hot Spiced Wine

Prep Time: 10 minutes; Cooking Time: 3 hours; Servings: 2

Ingredients:

- 2 cinnamon sticks (3 inches)
- 3 whole cloves
- 3 medium pears, peeled and sliced
- 1/2 cup of stevia
- 2 cups of sugar-free apple juice
- 1 teaspoon of lemon juice
- 2 bottles (750 ml) dry red wine

Method:

1. Start by tying the whole spices in cheesecloth.
2. Now place the tied spices along with all the Ingredients: into the Crockpot.
3. Cover its lid and cook for 3 hours on Low setting.
4. Once done, remove its lid of the crockpot carefully.
5. Strain the slow-cooked tea into the serving glass.
6. Serve warm.

Nutritional Information per Serving:

- Calories 220
- Total Fat 20.1 g
- Saturated Fat 7.4 g
- Cholesterol 132 mg
- Sodium 157 mg
- Protein 6.1 g

Sweet Kahlua Coffee

Prep Time: 10 minutes; Cooking Time: 4 hours; Servings: 4

Ingredients:

- 2 quarts hot water
- 1/2 cup of Kahlua (coffee liqueur)
- 1/4 cup of crème de cacao
- 3 tablespoons of instant coffee granules
- 2 cups of heavy whipping cream, to garnish
- 1/4 cup of stevia
- 1 teaspoon of vanilla extract
- 2 tablespoons of sugar-free chocolate chips, to garnish

Method:

1. Start by throwing all the Ingredients: into the Crockpot.
2. Cover its lid and cook for 4 hours on Low setting.
3. Once done, remove its lid of the crockpot carefully.
4. Garnish with whipping cream and chocolate chips.
5. Serve warm.

Nutritional Information per Serving:

- Calories 213
- Total Fat 28.4 g
- Saturated Fat 12.1 g
- Cholesterol 27 mg
- Sodium 39 mg
- Protein 8.1 g

Crockpot Milk Tea

Prep Time: 10 minutes; Cooking Time: 8 hours; Servings: 12

Ingredients:

- 15 slices fresh ginger root (about 3 oz.)
- 3 cinnamon sticks (3 inches)
- 25 whole cloves
- 15 cardamom pods, lightly crushed
- 3 whole peppercorns
- 31/2 quarts water
- 8 black tea bags
- 1 cup of evaporated milk
- 2 tablespoons of stevia

Method:

1. Start by tying all the whole spices in a cheesecloth.

2. Now place the tied spices along with all other Ingredients: into the Crockpot.
3. Cover its lid and cook for 8 hours on Low setting.
4. Once done, remove its lid of the crockpot carefully.
5. Strain the slow-cooked tea into the serving glasses.
6. Serve warm.

Nutritional Information per Serving:
- Calories 214
- Total Fat 19 g
- Saturated Fat 5.8 g
- Cholesterol 15 mg
- Sodium 123 mg
- Protein 6.5 g

Spiced Lemon Drink

Prep Time: 10 minutes; Cooking Time: 3 hours; Servings: 4
Ingredients:
- 21/2 quarts water
- 2 cups of stevia
- 11/2 cups of lime juice
- 1/2 cup of plus 2 tablespoons of lemon juice
- 1/4 cup of cranberry juice
- 1 cinnamon stick (3 inches)
- 1/2 teaspoon of whole cloves

Method:
1. Start by tying all the whole spices in a cheesecloth.
2. Now place the tied spices along with all other Ingredients: into the Crockpot.
3. Cover its lid and cook for 3 hours on Low setting.
4. Once done, remove its lid of the crockpot carefully.
5. Strain the slow-cooked tea into the serving glasses.
6. Serve warm.

Nutritional Information per Serving:
- Calories 158
- Total Fat 35.2 g
- Saturated Fat 15.2 g
- Cholesterol 69 mg
- Sodium 178 mg
- Protein 5.5 g

Truffle Hot Chocolate

Prep Time: 10 minutes; Cooking Time: 2 hours; Servings: 4
Ingredients:
- 4 cups of 2% milk
- 6 oz. 70% cacao dark baking chocolate, diced
- 3 tablespoons of stevia
- 1 teaspoon of instant espresso powder
- 1 teaspoon of vanilla extract
- Dash salt
- For Irish Whipped Cream:
- 1/2 cup of heavy whipping cream
- 1 tablespoon of Irish cream liqueur

Method:
1. Start by throwing all the Ingredients: into the Crockpot except Irish whipped cream.
2. Cover its lid and cook for 2 hours on Low setting.
3. Once done, remove its lid of the crockpot carefully.
4. Now mix whipping cream with Irish cream liqueur.
5. Top the slow-cooked coffee with this cream mixture.
6. Serve warm.

Nutritional Information per Serving:
- Calories 282
- Total Fat 25.1 g
- Saturated Fat 8.8 g
- Cholesterol 100 mg
- Sodium 117 mg
- Protein 8 g

Mulled Merlot

Prep Time: 10 minutes; Cooking Time: 1 hour; Servings: 2
Ingredients:
- 4 cinnamon sticks (3 inches)
- 4 whole cloves
- 2 bottles (750 milliliters each) merlot
- 1/2 cup of stevia
- 1 cup of brandy
- 1 lemon, sliced

Method:
1. Start by tying all the whole spices in a cheesecloth.
2. Now place the tied spices along with all other Ingredients: into the Crockpot.
3. Cover its lid and cook for 1 hour on High setting.
4. Once done, remove its lid of the crockpot carefully.
5. Strain the slow-cooked tea into the serving glasses.
6. Serve warm.

Nutritional Information per Serving:
- Calories 216
- Total Fat 10.9 g
- Saturated Fat 8.1 g
- Cholesterol 0 mg
- Sodium 8 mg
- Protein 6.4 g

Spiced Punch

Prep Time: 10 minutes; Cooking Time: 3 hours; Servings: 4
Ingredients:
- 31/2 cups of sugar-free apple juice
- 3 cups of apricot nectar
- 1/4 cup of water
- 3 tablespoons of lemon juice
- 1/2 teaspoon of ground cardamom
- 1/2 teaspoon of ground nutmeg
- 2 cinnamon sticks (3 inches)
- 1 teaspoon of diced fresh ginger root
- 1 teaspoon of grated orange peel
- 8 whole cloves

Method:
1. Start by throwing all the Ingredients: into the Crockpot.
2. Cover its lid and cook for 3 hours on Low setting.
3. Once done, remove its lid of the crockpot carefully.
4. Strain the slow-cooked tea into the serving glasses.
5. Serve warm.

Nutritional Information per Serving:
- Calories 331
- Total Fat 38.5 g
- Saturated Fat 19.2 g
- Cholesterol 141 mg
- Sodium 283 mg
- Protein 2.1 g

Chapter 7: Cranberry Cider

Creamy Coconut Spinach

Prep Time: 10 minutes; Cooking Time: 2 hours; Servings: 2

Ingredients:
- 1 and ½ lbs. Baby spinach
- ¼ cup of coconut cream
- 1 tablespoon of chili powder
- A pinch of salt and black pepper
- 1 tablespoon of cilantro, diced

Method:
1. Start by throwing all the Ingredients: into the Crockpot.
2. Cover its lid and cook for 2 hours on Low setting.
3. Once done, remove its lid of the crockpot carefully.
4. Mix well and garnish as desired.
5. Serve warm.

Nutritional Information per Serving:
- Calories 255
- Total Fat 23.4 g
- Saturated Fat 11.7 g
- Cholesterol 135 mg
- Sodium 112 mg
- Sugar 12.5 g
- Fiber 1 g
- Protein 27.9 g

White Mushrooms and Chard Mix

Prep Time: 10 minutes; Cooking Time: 3 hours; Servings: 2

Ingredients:
- 2 tablespoon of olive oil
- 1 lb. white mushrooms, sliced
- 1 red chard bunch (roughly diced)
- ¼ cup of chicken stock
- 1 teaspoon of garlic powder
- A pinch of salt and black pepper
- 3 tablespoons of parsley, chopped

Method:
1. Start by throwing all the Ingredients: into the Crockpot.
2. Cover its lid and cook for 3 hours on Low setting.
3. Once done, remove its lid of the crockpot carefully.
4. Mix well and garnish as desired.
5. Serve warm.

Nutritional Information per Serving:
- Calories 251
- Total Fat 24.5 g
- Saturated Fat 14.7 g
- Cholesterol 165 mg
- Sodium 142 mg
- Sugar 0.5 g
- Fiber 1 g
- Protein 15.9 g

Creamy Coconut Cauliflower

Prep Time: 10 minutes; Cooking Time: 3 hours; Servings: 2

Ingredients:
- 1 lb. cauliflower florets
- 1 cup of red onion, diced
- ¼ cup of chicken stock
- A pinch of salt and black pepper
- 2 tablespoons of balsamic vinegar
- 1 cup of coconut cream

Method:
1. Start by throwing all the Ingredients: into the Crockpot.

2. Cover its lid and cook for 3 hours on Low setting.
3. Once done, remove its lid of the crockpot carefully.
4. Mix well and garnish as desired.
5. Serve warm.

Nutritional Information per Serving:
- Calories 173
- Total Fat 16.2 g
- Saturated Fat 9.8 g
- Cholesterol 100 mg
- Sodium 42 mg
- Sugar 0.2 g
- Fiber1 g
- Protein 3.3 g

Herbed Green Beans

Prep Time: 10 minutes; Cooking Time: 2 hours; Servings: 2
Ingredients:
- 2 tablespoons of avocado oil
- ½ teaspoon of chili powder
- 1 lb. green beans, trimmed and halved
- 1 and ½ cups of chicken stock
- 1 tablespoon of rosemary, diced
- 1 tablespoon of basil, diced
- 1 tablespoon of dill, diced
- A pinch of salt and black pepper
- ½ cup of almonds, diced

Method:
1. Start by throwing all the Ingredients: into the Crockpot.
2. Cover its lid and cook for 2 hours on Low setting.
3. Once done, remove its lid of the crockpot carefully.
4. Mix well and garnish as desired.
5. Serve warm.

Nutritional Information per Serving:
- Calories 149
- Total Fat 14.5 g
- Saturated Fat 8.1 g
- Cholesterol 56 mg
- Sodium 56 mg
- Sugar 0.3 g
- Fiber 0.2 g
- Protein 2.6 g

Spicy Rosemary Cauliflower

Prep Time: 10 minutes; Cooking Time: 3 hours; Servings: 2
Ingredients:
- 1 lb. cauliflower florets
- 1 cup of chicken stock
- 2 garlic cloves, minced
- A pinch of salt and black pepper
- 1 tablespoon of rosemary, diced
- 1 teaspoon of hot chili sauce

Method:
1. Start by throwing all the Ingredients: into the Crockpot.
2. Cover its lid and cook for 3 hours on Low setting.
3. Once done, remove its lid of the crockpot carefully.
4. Mix well and garnish as desired.
5. Serve warm.

Nutritional Information per Serving:
- Calories 266
- Total Fat 26.9 g
- Saturated Fat 15.8 g
- Cholesterol 18 mg
- Sodium 218 mg
- Sugar 0.4 g
- Fiber 0.2 g
- Protein 4.5 g

Citrus Glazed Artichokes

Prep Time: 10 minutes; Cooking Time: 3 hours; Servings: 4
Ingredients:
- 4 artichokes, trimmed
- 1 tablespoon of olive oil
- 1 tablespoon of lemon juice
- 1 tablespoon of chives, diced
- 1 tablespoon of sweet paprika
- 1 tablespoon of parsley, chopped
- 2 cups of water

Method:
1. Start by throwing all the Ingredients: into the Crockpot.
2. Cover its lid and cook for 3 hours on Low setting.
3. Once done, remove its lid of the crockpot carefully.
4. Mix well and garnish as desired.
5. Serve warm.

Nutritional Information per Serving:
- Calories 158
- Total Fat 14.2 g
- Saturated Fat 6.2 g
- Cholesterol 35 mg
- Sodium 69 mg
- Sugar 0.5 g
- Fiber 2.7 g
- Protein 3.8 g

Celery and Broccoli Medley

Prep Time: 10 minutes; Cooking Time: 3 hours; Servings: 2
Ingredients:
- 2 garlic cloves, minced
- 1 tablespoon of olive oil
- 1 and ½ cups of broccoli florets
- 1 celery stalk, diced
- ½ cups of vegetable broth
- A pinch of salt and black pepper
- 2 tablespoon of lime juice

Method:
1. Start by throwing all the Ingredients: into the Crockpot.
2. Cover its lid and cook for 3 hours on Low setting.
3. Once done, remove its lid of the crockpot carefully.
4. Mix well and garnish as desired.
5. Serve warm.

Nutritional Information per Serving:
- Calories 131
- Total Fat 10.4 g
- Saturated Fat 9.5 g
- Cholesterol 10 mg
- Sodium 106 mg
- Sugar 0.5 g
- Fiber 3.4 g
- Protein 2.3 g

Paprika Zucchini

Prep Time: 10 minutes; Cooking Time: 5 hours; Servings: 3
Ingredients:
- ½ cup of vegetable broth
- 3 zucchinis, sliced
- A pinch of salt and black pepper
- 1 tablespoon of dill, diced
- ½ teaspoon of nutmeg (grated)
- 2 tablespoons of sweet paprika

Method:
1. Start by throwing all the Ingredients: into the Crockpot.

2. Cover its lid and cook for 5 hours on Low setting.
3. Once done, remove its lid of the crockpot carefully.
4. Mix well and garnish as desired.
5. Serve warm.

Nutritional Information per Serving:
- Calories 204
- Total Fat 15.7 g
- Saturated Fat 9.7 g
- Cholesterol 49 mg
- Sodium 141 mg
- Total Carbs 46 g
- Sugar 3.4 g
- Fiber 1.5 g

Dill Mixed Fennel Bulbs

Prep Time: 10 minutes; Cooking Time: 3 hours; Servings: 2
Ingredients:
- 2 fennel bulbs, sliced
- ¼ cup of chicken stock
- A pinch of salt and black pepper
- 1 tablespoon of dill, diced
- 1 tablespoon of parsley, chopped

Method:
1. Start by throwing all the Ingredients: into the Crockpot.
2. Cover its lid and cook for 3 hours on Low setting.
3. Once done, remove its lid of the crockpot carefully.
4. Mix well and garnish as desired.
5. Serve warm.

Nutritional Information per Serving:
- Calories 131
- Total Fat 10.4 g
- Saturated Fat 9.5 g
- Cholesterol 10 mg
- Sodium 106 mg
- Sugar 0.5 g
- Fiber 3.4 g
- Protein 2.3 g

Mushrooms Balsamic Mix

Prep Time: 10 minutes; Cooking Time: 3 hours; Servings: 2
Ingredients:
- 1 lb. white mushrooms, sliced
- 2 spring onions, diced
- 1 garlic clove, minced
- 2 endives, trimmed and halved
- 1 tablespoon of balsamic vinegar
- 1 tablespoon of chives, diced
- 1 cup of chicken stock

Method:
1. Start by throwing all the Ingredients: into the Crockpot.
2. Cover its lid and cook for 3 hours on Low setting.
3. Once done, remove its lid of the crockpot carefully.
4. Mix well and garnish as desired.
5. Serve warm.

Nutritional Information per Serving:
- Calories 204
- Total Fat 15.7 g
- Saturated Fat 9.7 g
- Cholesterol 49 mg
- Sodium 141 mg
- Sugar 3.4 g
- Fiber 1.5 g
- Protein 6.3 g

Nutty Green Beans with Avocado

Prep Time: 10 minutes; Cooking Time: 2 hours; Servings: 4

Ingredients:

- 2 cups of green beans, halved
- ½ cup of chicken stock
- ½ cup of walnuts, diced
- 1 avocado (peeled, pitted and cubed)
- ¼ teaspoon of sweet paprika
- A pinch of salt and black pepper
- 2 teaspoons of balsamic vinegar

Method:

1. Start by throwing all the Ingredients: into the Crockpot.
2. Cover its lid and cook for 2 hours on Low setting.
3. Once done, remove its lid of the crockpot carefully.
4. Mix well and garnish as desired.
5. Serve warm.

Nutritional Information per Serving:

- Calories 134
- Total Fat 21.4 g
- Saturated Fat 1.2 g
- Cholesterol 244 mg
- Sodium 10 mg
- Sugar 2.7 g
- Fiber 5.2 g
- Protein 2.3 g

Thyme Mixed Brussels Sprouts

Prep Time: 10 minutes; Cooking Time: 3 hours; Servings: 4

Ingredients:

- ½ cups of beef stock
- 2 and ½ lbs. brussels sprouts halved
- 2 tablespoon of olive oil
- 2 shallots, diced
- A pinch of salt and black pepper
- 1 tablespoon of thyme, diced

Method:

1. Start by throwing all the Ingredients: into the Crockpot.
2. Cover its lid and cook for 3 hours on Low setting.
3. Once done, remove its lid of the crockpot carefully.
4. Mix well and garnish as desired.
5. Serve warm.

Nutritional Information per Serving:

- Calories 104
- Total Fat 3.7 g
- Saturated Fat 0.7 g
- Cholesterol 33 mg
- Sodium 141 mg
- Sugar 1.4 g
- Fiber 0.7 g
- Protein 5.4 g

Mashed Broccoli

Prep Time: 10 minutes; Cooking Time: 3 hours; Servings: 2

Ingredients:

- ½ teaspoon of turmeric powder
- 1 broccoli, florets separated
- A pinch of salt and black pepper
- 1 tablespoon of butter, melted
- ½ cup of chicken stock
- 1 tablespoon of chives, diced

Method:

1. Start by throwing all the Ingredients: into the Crockpot.
2. Cover its lid and cook for 3 hours on Low setting.
3. Once done, remove its lid of the crockpot carefully.
4. Puree this mixture using an immersion blender.
5. Mix well and garnish as desired.
6. Serve warm.

Nutritional Information per Serving:
- Calories 124
- Total Fat 13.4 g
- Saturated Fat 7 g
- Cholesterol 20 mg
- Sodium 136 mg
- Total Carbs 6.4 g
- Sugar 2.1 g
- Fiber 4.8 g

Rich Creamy Endives

Prep Time: 10 minutes; Cooking Time: 3 hours; Servings: 4

Ingredients:
- ¼ cup of coconut cream
- 4 endives, trimmed and halved
- ½ cup of chicken stock
- 1 tablespoon of dill, diced
- 1 tablespoon of smoked paprika

Method:
1. Start by throwing all the Ingredients: into the Crockpot.
2. Cover its lid and cook for 3 hours on Low setting.
3. Once done, remove its lid of the crockpot carefully.
4. Mix well and garnish as desired.
5. Serve warm.

Nutritional Information per Serving:
- Calories 191
- Total Fat 8.4 g
- Saturated Fat 0.7 g
- Cholesterol 743 mg
- Sugar 0.1 g
- Fiber 1.4 g
- Sodium 226 mg
- Protein 6.3 g

Spiced Greens

Prep Time: 10 minutes; Cooking Time: 3 hours; Servings: 3

Ingredients:
- 1 and ½ lbs. baby spinach
- ½ lb. kale, torn
- 1 teaspoon of nutmeg, ground
- 1 tablespoon of butter, melted
- A pinch of salt and black pepper
- 1 cup of vegetable broth
- 1 tablespoon of chives, diced

Method:
1. Start by throwing all the Ingredients: into the Crockpot.
2. Cover its lid and cook for 3 hours on Low setting.
3. Once done, remove its lid of the crockpot carefully.
4. Mix well and garnish as desired.
5. Serve warm.

Nutritional Information per Serving:
- Calories 142
- Total Fat 8.4 g
- Saturated Fat 67 g
- Cholesterol 743 mg
- Sodium 346 mg
- Sugar 1 g

- Fiber 0.8 g
- Protein 4.1 g

Creamy Coconut Fennel

Prep Time: 10 minutes; Cooking Time: 3 hours; Servings: 2
Ingredients:
- 2 tablespoons of avocado oil
- 2 spring onions, diced
- 2 shallots, minced
- 1 garlic clove, minced
- 1 and ½ cups of coconut cream
- 2 big fennel bulbs, sliced
- ¼ teaspoon of nutmeg, ground
- A pinch of salt and black pepper

Method:
1. Start by throwing all the Ingredients: into the Crockpot.
2. Cover its lid and cook for 3 hours on Low setting.
3. Once done, remove its lid of the crockpot carefully.
4. Mix well and garnish as desired.
5. Serve warm.

Nutritional Information per Serving:
- Calories 279
- Total Fat 4.8 g
- Saturated Fat 1 g
- Cholesterol 45 mg
- Sodium 24 mg
- Sugar 2.3 g
- Fiber 4.5 g
- Protein 5 g

Saffron Bell Peppers

Prep Time: 10 minutes; Cooking Time: 3 hours; Servings: 3
Ingredients:
- 2 yellow bell peppers, julienned
- 2 red bell peppers, sliced
- 3 garlic cloves, minced
- 1 shallot, diced
- A pinch of salt and black pepper
- 1 teaspoon of saffron powder
- ¼ cup of chicken stock
- 1 tablespoon of cilantro, diced

Method:
1. Start by throwing all the Ingredients: into the Crockpot.
2. Cover its lid and cook for 3 hours on Low setting.
3. Once done, remove its lid of the crockpot carefully.
4. Mix well and garnish as desired.
5. Serve warm.

Nutritional Information per Serving:
- Calories 199
- Total Fat 17.4 g
- Saturated Fat 11.3 g
- Cholesterol 47 mg
- Sodium 192 mg
- Sugar 1.5 g
- Fiber 4.3 g
- Protein 6.4 g

Broccoli Yogurt Dip

Prep Time: 10 minutes; Cooking Time: 6 hours; Servings: 12
Ingredients:
- 2 tablespoons of avocado oil
- 8 garlic cloves, minced
- 2 cups of vegetable broth
- 6 cups of broccoli florets
- 1 cup of Greek yogurt
- 1 tablespoon of dill, diced
- A pinch of salt and black pepper
- ½ cup of coconut cream

Method:

1. Start by throwing all the Ingredients: into the Crockpot.
2. Cover its lid and cook for 6 hours on Low setting.
3. Once done, remove its lid of the crockpot carefully.
4. Blend this dip mixture using an immersion blender.
5. Mix well and garnish as desired.
6. Serve warm.

Nutritional Information per Serving:

- Calories 135
- Total Fat 9.9 g
- Saturated Fat 3.2 g
- Cholesterol 34 mg
- Sodium 10 mg
- Sugar 3.4 g
- Fiber 1.5 g
- Protein 8.6 g

Cheesy Mushroom Spread

Prep Time: 10 minutes; Cooking Time: 6 hours; Servings: 8

Ingredients:

- 1 shallot diced
- 2 tablespoon of olive oil
- 1 tablespoon of rosemary, diced
- A pinch of salt and black pepper
- 3 garlic cloves, minced
- 1 cup of chicken stock
- 2 lbs. white mushrooms, sliced
- ½ cup of parmesan (grated)
- ½ cup of coconut cream
- 1 tablespoon of parsley, chopped

Method:

1. Start by throwing all the Ingredients: into the Crockpot.
2. Cover its lid and cook for 6 hours on Low setting.
3. Once done, remove its lid of the crockpot carefully.
4. Blend this dip mixture using an immersion blender.
5. Mix well and garnish as desired.
6. Serve warm.

Nutritional Information per Serving:

- Calories 294
- Total Fat 16.4 g
- Saturated Fat 57 g
- Cholesterol 120 mg
- Sodium 343 mg
- Sugar 0.1 g
- Fiber 0.3 g
- Protein 35 g

Tomato Zucchini Dip

Prep Time: 10 minutes; Cooking Time: 3 hours; Servings: 12

Ingredients:

- 2 cups of tomatoes, cubed
- 2 cups of zucchinis, cubed
- 1 tablespoon of hot paprika
- 2 red chilies, diced
- ¼ cup of vegetable broth
- 1 tablespoon of basil, diced
- A pinch of salt and black pepper
- 2 scallions, diced
- 1 tablespoon of olive oil

Method:

1. Start by throwing all the Ingredients: into the Crockpot except basil.
2. Cover its lid and cook for 3 hours on Low setting.
3. Once done, remove its lid of the crockpot carefully.
4. Blend this dip mixture using an immersion blender.

5. Mix well and garnish with basil.
6. Serve warm.

Nutritional Information per Serving:
- Calories 304
- Total Fat 20 g
- Saturated Fat 3 g
- Cholesterol 12 mg
- Sodium 645 mg
- Sugar 2 g
- Fiber 5 g
- Protein 22 g

Spinach Leeks Dip

Prep Time: 10 minutes; Cooking Time: 6 hours; Servings: 6

Ingredients:
- 1 shallot, diced
- 2 tablespoons of avocado oil
- 2 leeks, diced
- 2 garlic cloves, minced
- 4 cups of spinach, torn
- ¼ cup of vegetable broth
- ¼ cup of lime juice
- 1 bunch basil, diced
- A pinch of salt and black pepper

Method:
1. Start by throwing all the Ingredients: into the Crockpot.
2. Cover its lid and cook for 6 hours on Low setting.
3. Once done, remove its lid of the crockpot carefully.
4. Blend this dip mixture using an immersion blender.
5. Mix well and garnish as desired.
6. Serve warm.

Nutritional Information per Serving:
- Calories 136
- Total Fat 18.3 g
- Saturated Fat 2.6 g
- Cholesterol 75 mg
- Sodium 104 mg
- Sugar 6.2 g
- Fiber 2.9 g
- Protein 5.9 g

Capers Zucchini Dip

Prep Time: 10 minutes; Cooking Time: 5 hours; Servings: 10

Ingredients:
- 1 shallot, diced
- 1 and ½ lbs. zucchinis, diced
- 1 tablespoon of olive oil
- 2 garlic cloves, minced
- A pinch of salt and black pepper
- 1 tablespoon of capers, drained and diced
- ¼ cup of vegetable broth
- 1 bunch basil, diced

Method:
1. Start by throwing all the Ingredients: into the Crockpot.
2. Cover its lid and cook for 5 hours on Low setting.
3. Once done, remove its lid of the crockpot carefully.
4. Blend this dip mixture using an immersion blender.
5. Mix well and garnish as desired.
6. Serve warm.

Nutritional Information per Serving:
- Calories 194
- Total Fat 21.7 g
- Saturated Fat 9.4 g
- Cholesterol 105 mg

- Sodium 384 mg
- Sugar 1.6 g
- Fiber 1.3 g
- Protein 3.2 g

Zucchini Eggplant Spread

Prep Time: 10 minutes; Cooking Time: 5 hours; Servings: 12

Ingredients:
- 2 and ½ teaspoon of lemon zest, grated
- 3 tablespoon of lemon juice
- 2 zucchinis, diced
- 2 eggplants, diced
- 1 tablespoon of olive oil
- ½ cup of vegetable broth
- 2 tablespoons of dill, diced

Method:
1. Start by throwing all the Ingredients: into the Crockpot.
2. Cover its lid and cook for 5 hours on Low setting.
3. Once done, remove its lid of the crockpot carefully.
4. Blend this dip mixture using an immersion blender.
5. Mix well and garnish as desired.
6. Serve warm.

Nutritional Information per Serving:
- Calories 132
- Total Fat 7.1 g
- Saturated Fat 1 g
- Cholesterol 101 mg
- Sodium 94 mg
- Sugar 1.9 g
- Fiber 0.6 g
- Protein 13.5 g

Chapter 8: Pork

Pork Chops with Spice Rub

Prep Time: 10 minutes; Cooking Time: 6 hours; Servings: 2

Ingredients:
- 1 tablespoon of rosemary dried
- 1 tablespoon of thyme dried
- 1 tablespoon of curry powder dried
- 1 tablespoon of chives diced, fresh
- 1 tablespoon of fennel seeds
- 1 tablespoon of cumin, ground
- 1 teaspoon of salt
- 4 tablespoons of olive oil
- 2 lbs. pork chops

Method:
1. Start by putting all the Ingredients: into your Crockpot.
2. Cover its lid and cook for 6 hours on Low setting.
3. Once done, remove its lid and mix well.
4. Garnish as desired.
5. Serve warm.

Nutritional Information per Serving:
- Calories 394
- Total Fat 21.7 g
- Saturated Fat 9.4 g
- Cholesterol 105 mg
- Sodium 384 mg
- Sugar 1.6 g
- Fiber 1.3 g
- Protein 43.2 g

Pork Butt Carnitas

Prep Time: 10 minutes; Cooking Time: 8 hours; Servings: 8

Ingredients:
- ½ tablespoon of salt
- ½ tablespoon of black pepper
- 1 tablespoon of chili powder
- 1 tablespoon of bacon grease
- 1 small onion
- 1 tablespoon of cumin
- 1 tablespoon of thyme, dried
- 4 lb. pork butt
- 2 tablespoons of garlic, minced
- ½ cup of water

Method:
1. Start by putting all the Ingredients: into your Crockpot.
2. Cover its lid and cook for 8 hours on High setting.
3. Once done, remove its lid and mix well.
4. Garnish as desired.
5. Serve warm.

Nutritional Information per Serving:
- Calories 329
- Total Fat 34 g
- Saturated Fat 10.3 g
- Cholesterol 112 mg
- Sugar 2 g
- Fiber 1.3 g
- Sodium 92 mg
- Protein 27.5 g

Pork Steaks

Prep Time: 10 minutes; Cooking Time: 6 hours; Servings: 4

Ingredients:
- 4 pork steaks
- 2 tablespoons of pork rub
- 1 teaspoon of Celtic salt
- 1 teaspoon of fresh cracked pepper

- ¼ cup of beef stock

Method:
1. Start by putting all the Ingredients: into your Crockpot.
2. Cover its lid and cook for 6 hours on High setting.
3. Once done, remove its lid and mix well.
4. Garnish as desired.
5. Serve warm.

Nutritional Information per Serving:
- Calories 259
- Total Fat 9 g
- Saturated Fat 13 g
- Cholesterol 52 mg
- Sugar 1 g
- Fiber 1 g
- Sodium 992 mg
- Protein 20 g

Pork Roast

Prep Time: 10 minutes; Cooking Time: 4 hours; Servings: 5

Ingredients:
- 2.5-lb. pork loin roast
- 1.5 cups of BBQ sauce
- 5 slices thick-cut bacon

Method:
1. Start by putting all the Ingredients: into your Crockpot.
2. Cover its lid and cook for 4 hours on Low setting.
3. Once done, remove its lid and mix well.
4. Garnish as desired.
5. Serve warm.

Nutritional Information per Serving:
- Calories 254
- Total Fat 15 g
- Saturated Fat 7 g
- Cholesterol 79 mg
- Sugar 3 g
- Fiber 1 g
- Sodium 812 mg
- Protein 21 g

Ranch Pork Chops

Prep Time: 10 minutes; Cooking Time: 8 hours; Servings: 4

Ingredients:
- 2 lbs. of Pork Loin, thawed
- 2 cans Cream of Chicken Soup
- 2 cups of Water
- 1 Packet Ranch Dressing Mix
- 1 8oz Container of Sliced Mushrooms

Method:
1. Start by putting all the Ingredients: into your Crockpot.
2. Cover its lid and cook for 8 hours on Low setting.
3. Once done, remove its lid and mix well.
4. Garnish as desired.
5. Serve warm.

Nutritional Information per Serving:
- Calories 231
- Total Fat 17.8 g
- Saturated Fat 10.3 g
- Cholesterol 112 mg
- Sugar 0.2 g
- Fiber 0 g
- Sodium 92 mg
- Protein 16.4 g

Pork Roast with Cheese

Prep Time: 10 minutes; Cooking Time: 6 hours 5 minutes; Servings: 2
Ingredients:

- 1 large pork roast   bone-in
- 1 1/2 cups of chicken stock
- 1 cup of diced onion
- 1/2 cup of diced mushrooms
- 3 4 celery stalks, diced

For the Gravy

- 1 cup of heavy cream
- 4 oz. cream cheese, cubed
- 1/2 stick butter

- 1/4 cup of parsley, dried
- 1/2 stick butter
- 2 teaspoons of salt
- 1 teaspoon of garlic powder
- 1 teaspoon of black pepper

- 1/2 1 teaspoon of Glucomannan powder
- 1 1/2 2 cups of cooking liquid from the roast

Method:
1. Start by putting all the Ingredients: except those for the gravy into your Crockpot.
2. Cover its lid and cook for 6 hours on high setting.
3. Once done, remove its lid and mix well.
4. Mix all the gravy Ingredients: in a saucepan and stir cook for 5 minutes.
5. Pour this gravy over the slow-cooked pork.
6. Garnish as desired.
7. Serve warm.

Nutritional Information per Serving:

- Calories 359
- Total Fat 34 g
- Saturated Fat 10.3 g
- Cholesterol 112 mg

- Sugar 2 g
- Fiber 1.3 g
- Sodium 92 mg
- Protein 27.5 g

Chipotle Pork

Prep Time: 10 minutes; Cooking Time: 8 hours; Servings: 12
Ingredients:

- 6 lbs. pork shoulder
- 4 garlic cloves sliced thin
- 2 teaspoons of salt
- 2 teaspoons of garlic powder
- 2 teaspoons of oregano
- 2 tablespoons of cumin
- 4 teaspoons of ground coriander
- 4 teaspoons of chili powder
- 1/2 teaspoon of black pepper

- 1/2 teaspoon of onion powder
- 1 tablespoon of olive oil
- 4 tablespoons of apple cider vinegar
- 2 cups of peppers sliced
- 1 onion sliced
- 1 7 oz. can of chipotle peppers
- 1 14.5 oz. can tomato, diced
- 1 4 oz. can of green chilis

Method:
1. Start by putting all the Ingredients: into your Crockpot.
2. Cover its lid and cook for 8 hours on medium setting.
3. Once done, remove its lid and mix well.
4. Shred the slow-cooked pork and return it to the pork.
5. Garnish as desired.
6. Serve warm.

Nutritional Information per Serving:
- Calories 449
- Total Fat 28.7 g
- Saturated Fat 14.9 g
- Cholesterol 163 mg
- Sodium 844 mg
- Sugar 2.6 g
- Fiber 1.9 g
- Protein 39.3 g

Dill Rubbed Pork Loin

Prep Time: 10 minutes; Cooking Time: 8 hours; Servings: 2

Ingredients:
- 3 tablespoons of Mustard
- 2 tablespoons of Butter melted
- 1 tablespoon of Swerve
- ¼ cup of dill, diced
- 3 green onions, diced
- 1 tablespoon of Lemon peel, grated
- Salt and black pepper to taste
- 1 pork loin, boneless

Method:
1. Start by putting all the Ingredients: into your Crockpot.
2. Cover its lid and cook for 8 hours on Low setting.
3. Once done, remove its lid and mix well.
4. Garnish as desired.
5. Serve warm.

Nutritional Information per Serving:
- Calories 202
- Total Fat 9.5g
- Saturated Fat 2 g
- Cholesterol 62 mg
- Sodium 526 mg
- Sugar 5.8 g
- Fiber 2.6 g
- Protein 22 g

Balsamic Pork Chops with Spinach

Prep Time: 10 minutes; Cooking Time: 8.5 hours; Servings: 4

Ingredients:
- 4 pork chops, bone-in
- 2 tablespoons of swerves
- ½ cup of beef stock
- 1 tablespoon of balsamic vinegar
- 4 tablespoons of butter melted
- 4 oz. baby spinach

Method:
1. Start by putting all the Ingredients: into your Crockpot except spinach.
2. Cover its lid and cook for 8 hours on Low setting.
3. Once done, remove its lid and mix well.
4. Stir in spinach and cook for 30 minutes on high heat.
5. Garnish as desired.
6. Serve warm.

Nutritional Information per Serving:
- Calories 364
- Total Fat 13.2 g
- Saturated Fat 3.4 g
- Cholesterol 141 mg
- Sodium 274 mg
- Sugar 2.8g
- Fiber 5.7 g
- Protein 47.7 g

Lemongrass Pork Meatballs

Prep Time: 10 minutes; Cooking Time: 8 hours; Servings: 2

Ingredients:

- ¼ cup of mint, diced
- 3 garlic cloves, minced
- 1 shallot, diced
- 1 lemongrass stalk, diced
- 1 lb. pork, ground
- 1 teaspoon of tomato passata
- ½ teaspoon of chili pepper
- 1 tablespoon of cilantro, diced
- 2 tablespoon of olive oil
- 1/2 cup of beef stock

Method:
1. Thoroughly mix garlic, mint, lemongrass, pork, shallots, chili, cilantro, and tomato passata in a bowl.
2. Make small meatballs out of this mixture and keep them aside.
3. Now start by putting all the Ingredients:, including the meatballs into your Crockpot.
4. Cover its lid and cook for 8 hours on Low setting.
5. Once done, remove its lid and mix well.
6. Garnish as desired.
7. Serve warm.

Nutritional Information per Serving:
- Calories 455
- Total Fat 34.4 g
- Saturated Fat 3.4 g
- Cholesterol 64 mg
- Sodium 58 mg
- Sugar 1.7 g
- Fiber 5.2 g
- Protein 29.6 g

Pork Chops Asparagus Sautee

Prep Time: 10 minutes; Cooking Time: 8 hours; Servings: 4
Ingredients:
- 4 pork loin chops, boneless
- 2 tablespoons of tarragon, diced
- Salt and black pepper- to taste
- 1 lb. asparagus, trimmed and halved
- 2 tablespoon of olive oil
- 1 bunch green onions, diced
- ½ cup of vegetable broth
- 1 tablespoon of mustard

Method:
1. Start by putting all the Ingredients: into your Crockpot and mix them well.
2. Cover its lid and cook for 8 hours on Low setting.
3. Once done, remove its lid and mix well.
4. Garnish as desired.
5. Serve warm.

Nutritional Information per Serving:
- Calories 355
- Total Fat 15 g
- Saturated Fat 1.4 g
- Cholesterol 128 mg
- Sodium 1271 mg
- Sugar 2.5 g
- Fiber 2.7 g
- Protein 44.2 g

Passata Mixed Pulled Pork

Prep Time: 10 minutes; Cooking Time: 10 hours; Servings: 2
Ingredients:
- 1 lb. pork tenderloin, sliced
- 2 tablespoon of chili powder
- ½ cup of tomato passata
- 2 tablespoons of mustard
- 2 tablespoon of olive oil
- 2 tablespoons of balsamic vinegar

- Salt and black pepper- to taste

Method:
1. Start by putting all the Ingredients: into your Crockpot.
2. Cover its lid and cook for 10 hours on Low setting.
3. Once done, remove its lid and mix well.
4. Shred the slow-cooked pork and return the pot.
5. Mix well and garnish as desired.
6. Serve warm.

Nutritional Information per Serving:
- Calories 487
- Total Fat 37.4 g
- Saturated Fat 8.8 g
- Cholesterol 71 mg
- Sodium 501 mg
- Sugar 1.2 g
- Fiber 9.2 g
- Protein 28.1 g

Pork Tenderloin with Swiss Chard

Prep Time: 10 minutes; Cooking Time: 10 hours; Servings: 4
Ingredients:
- 2 lbs. pork tenderloin
- 2 lemons, sliced
- 4 teaspoon of olive oil
- Salt and black pepper- to taste
- 2 garlic cloves, minced
- 2 bunches swiss chard, diced
- ½ cup of beef stock

Method:
1. Start by putting all the Ingredients: into your Crockpot.
2. Cover its lid and cook for 10 hours on Low setting.
3. Once done, remove its lid and mix well.
4. Garnish as desired.
5. Serve warm.

Nutritional Information per Serving:
- Calories 434
- Total Fat 36.4 g
- Saturated Fat 17.1 g
- Cholesterol 257 mg
- Sodium 1038 mg
- Sugar 0.9 g
- Fiber 0.2 g
- Protein 24.2 g

Sesame Topped Baby Ribs

Prep Time: 10 minutes; Cooking Time: 4 hours; Servings: 4
Ingredients:
- 2 lbs. baby back ribs
- Salt and black pepper- to taste
- 1 cup of tomato passata
- 1 tablespoon of balsamic vinegar
- 2 garlic cloves, minced
- 1 teaspoon of sesame seeds

Method:
1. Start by putting all the Ingredients: into your Crockpot.
2. Cover its lid and cook for 4 hours on High setting.
3. Once done, remove its lid and mix well.
4. Garnish as desired.
5. Serve warm.

Nutritional Information per Serving:
- Calories 335
- Total Fat 21.6 g

- Saturated Fat 12.8 g
- Cholesterol 10 mg
- Sodium 851 mg
- Sugar 3.3 g
- Fiber 2.8 g
- Protein 23.8 g

Saucy Apricot Glazed Pork Chops

Prep Time: 10 minutes; Cooking Time: 4 hours; Servings: 4
Ingredients:
- 4 pork chops, bone-in
- 1 tablespoon of olive oil
- ½ cup of vegetable broth
- ¼ cup of apricot jam
- 3 tablespoons of mustard
- Salt and black pepper- to taste

Method:
6. Start by putting all the Ingredients: into your Crockpot.
7. Cover its lid and cook for 4 hours on High setting.
8. Once done, remove its lid and mix well.
9. Garnish as desired.
10. Serve warm.

Nutritional Information per Serving:
- Calories 324
- Total Fat 20.7 g
- Saturated Fat 6.7 g
- Cholesterol 45 mg
- Sodium 241 mg
- Sugar 1.4 g
- Fiber 0.5 g
- Protein 35.3 g

Pork Chops with Salsa

Prep Time: 10 minutes; Cooking Time: 4 hours; Servings: 4
Ingredients:
- 4 pork loin chops, boneless
- 2 tablespoon of Olive oil
- 1 teaspoon of Chili powder
- Salt and black pepper- to taste
- ½ cup of beef stock

Salsa
- 1 tomato, cubed
- 1 teaspoon of Balsamic vinegar

Method:
1. Start by putting all the Ingredients: for pork chops into your Crockpot.
2. Cover its lid and cook for 4 hours on High setting.
3. Once done, remove its lid and mix well.
4. Mix the tomato with vinegar in a small bowl.
5. Garnish the pork chops with tomato salsa.
6. Serve warm.

Nutritional Information per Serving:
- Calories 287
- Total Fat 29.5 g
- Saturated Fat 3 g
- Cholesterol 0 mg
- Sodium 388 mg
- Sugar 1.4g
- Fiber 4.3 g
- Protein 14.7 g

Pork Roast with Cabbage Stir Fry

Prep Time: 10 minutes; Cooking Time: 4 hours 5minutes; Servings: 2
Ingredients:
- 2 tablespoon of Olive oil
- 1 Pork tenderloin

- ¼ cup of Tomato passata

Cabbage Stir fry
- 1 Red cabbage head, shredded
- 4 Green onions diced
- ¼ cup of beef stock
- 2 tablespoons of Balsamic vinegar
- 1 Jalapeno diced

Method:
1. Start by putting all the Ingredients: into your Crockpot.
2. Cover its lid and cook for 4 hours on High setting.
3. Once done, remove its lid and mix well.
4. Now prepare the cabbage stir fry by sautéing all its Ingredients: for 5 minutes.
5. Garnish the pork with cabbage stir fry.
6. Serve warm.

Nutritional Information per Serving:
- Calories 338
- Total Fat 9.5 g
- Saturated Fat 2.7 g
- Cholesterol 103 mg
- Sodium 403 mg
- Sugar 0 g
- Fiber 0 g
- Protein 34.2 g

Pork Roast with Cinnamon

Prep Time: 10 minutes; Cooking Time: 4 hours; Servings: 2
Ingredients:
- 1 pork loin, boneless
- 1 ½ teaspoon of red pepper, crushed
- 2 tablespoon of olive oil
- 2 yellow onions, cut into wedges
- 2 tablespoons of butter, melted
- ¼ cup of apple vinegar
- 2 teaspoons of cinnamon powder
- 3-star anise
- 5 garlic slices, diced
- 1 tablespoon of parsley, chopped

Method:
1. Start by putting all the Ingredients: into your Crockpot.
2. Cover its lid and cook for 4 hours on High setting.
3. Once done, remove its lid and mix well.
4. Garnish as desired.
5. Serve warm.

Nutritional Information per Serving:
- Calories 369
- Total Fat 24.9 g
- Saturated Fat 8.5 g
- Cholesterol 112 mg
- Sodium 537 mg
- Sugar 1.4 g
- Fiber 3.4 g
- Protein 31.5 g

Pork Chops with Poblano Stir Fry

Prep Time: 10 minutes; Cooking Time: 4 hours; Servings: 4
Ingredients:
- 5 teaspoon of olive oil
- 4 pork loin chops, bone-in
- Salt and black pepper- to taste
- 1 cup of red onion, diced
- 4 garlic cloves, minced
- 1 poblano chili, diced
- 1 red bell pepper, diced
- 1 yellow bell pepper, diced
- 3 tablespoons of parsley, chopped
- 2 tablespoons of capers
- 3 tablespoons of red vinegar
- ¼ teaspoon of red pepper, crushed

- ¼ cup of beef stock

Method:
1. Start by putting all the Ingredients: into your Crockpot.
2. Cover its lid and cook for 4 hours on High setting.
3. Once done, remove its lid and mix well.
4. Garnish as desired.
5. Serve warm.

Nutritional Information per Serving:
- Calories 376
- Total Fat 21.9 g
- Saturated Fat 7.8 g
- Cholesterol 110 mg
- Sodium 345 mg
- Sugar 4.6 g
- Fiber 5.7 g
- Protein 33.2 g

Pork Tenderloin with Juicy Shallots

Prep Time: 10 minutes; Cooking Time: 8 hours; Servings: 2
Ingredients:
- 3 tablespoon of olive oil
- 2 garlic cloves, minced
- 1 tablespoon of thyme, diced
- 1 and ½ lbs. pork tenderloin
- 3 shallots, cut into medium wedges
- 4 tablespoons of butter, melted
- 1 ½ cups of chicken stock
- ¾ cup of pear juice, unsweetened

Method:
1. Start by putting all the Ingredients: into your Crockpot.
2. Cover its lid and cook for 8 hours on Low setting.
3. Once done, remove its lid and mix well.
4. Garnish as desired.
5. Serve warm.

Nutritional Information per Serving:
- Calories 349
- Total Fat 31.9 g
- Saturated Fat 15 g
- Cholesterol 46 mg
- Sodium 237 mg
- Sugar 1.4 g
- Fiber 3.4 g
- Protein 11 g

Rosemary Rainbow Pork Sautee

Prep Time: 10 minutes; Cooking Time: 9 hours; Servings: 2
Ingredients:
- 1 lb. pork tenderloin, trimmed and cut into medallions
- Salt and black pepper- to taste
- 1 and ½ teaspoon of rosemary, diced
- 1 tablespoon of olive oil
- 3 garlic cloves, minced
- 1 red bell pepper, cut into strips
- 1 yellow bell pepper, cut into strips
- 2 teaspoons of balsamic vinegar
- ¼ cup of vegetable stock

Method:
1. Start by putting all the Ingredients: into your Crockpot.
2. Cover its lid and cook for 9 hours on Low setting.
3. Once done, remove its lid and mix well.
4. Garnish as desired.
5. Serve warm.

Nutritional Information per Serving:

- Calories 238
- Total Fat 23.2 g
- Saturated Fat 13 g
- Cholesterol 61 mg
- Sodium 115 mg
- Sugar 0 g
- Fiber 0.9 g
- Protein 22.3 g

Pork with Green Onion Sauce

Prep Time: 10 minutes; Cooking Time: 8 hours; Servings: 2
Ingredients:

- 1 lb. pork tenderloin, cut into strips
- 1/3 cup of chicken stock
- 2 tablespoon of coconut aminos
- 1 teaspoon of garlic sauce
- Salt and black pepper- to taste
- cooking spray
- 1 and ½ teaspoon of olive oil
- ¼ cup of water
- 2 teaspoons of ginger, grated
- ¼ cup of green onions, diced

Method:

1. Start by putting all the Ingredients: into your Crockpot.
2. Cover its lid and cook for 8 hours on Low setting.
3. Once done, remove its lid and mix well.
4. Garnish as desired.
5. Serve warm.

Nutritional Information per Serving:

- Calories 474
- Total Fat 40.8 g
- Saturated Fat 25.5 g
- Cholesterol 105 mg
- Sodium 345 mg
- Sugar 1.8 g
- Fiber 0.8 g
- Protein 24.5 g

Jalapeno Pork Tenderloin Soup

Prep Time: 10 minutes; Cooking Time: 8 hours; Servings: 2
Ingredients:

- 1 cup of yellow onion, diced
- cooking spray
- 2/3 cup of green bell pepper, diced
- 1 tablespoon of garlic, minced
- 1 jalapeno pepper, diced
- 1 lb. pork tenderloin, cubed
- 2 cups of chicken stock
- 2 teaspoon of chili powder
- 1 teaspoon of cumin, ground
- Salt and black pepper -to taste
- 14 oz. canned tomatoes, diced
- 2 tablespoons of Cilantro, diced

Method:

1. Start by putting all the Ingredients: into your Crockpot.
2. Cover its lid and cook for 8 hours on Low setting.
3. Once done, remove its lid and mix well.
4. Garnish as desired.
5. Serve warm.

Nutritional Information per Serving:

- Calories 392
- Total Fat 40.4 g
- Saturated Fat 6 g
- Cholesterol 20 mg
- Sodium 423 mg
- Sugar 3 g
- Fiber 4.2 g
- Protein 21 g

Pork Mushroom Stew

Prep Time: 10 minutes; Cooking Time: 8 hours; Servings: 3
Ingredients:
- 1 tablespoon of olive oil
- ½ garlic clove, minced
- 1 lb. pork loin, cubed
- Salt and black pepper to taste
- 1 tablespoon of oregano, dried
- ¼ teaspoon of nutmeg, ground
- 1 lb. mushrooms, sliced
- 1 tablespoon of white vinegar
- 2/3 cups of vegetable broth
- 1/8 cup of coconut milk

Method:
1. Start by putting all the Ingredients: into your Crockpot.
2. Cover its lid and cook for 8 hours on Low setting.
3. Once done, remove its lid and mix well.
4. Garnish as desired.
5. Serve warm.

Nutritional Information per Serving:
- Calories 213
- Total Fat 23.4 g
- Saturated Fat 6.1 g
- Cholesterol 102 mg
- Sodium 86 mg
- Sugar 2.1 g
- Fiber 1.5 g
- Protein 33.2 g

Mushroom Chops Stew

Prep Time: 10 minutes; Cooking Time: 4 hours; Servings: 2
Ingredients:
- 1.5 bacon strips, diced
- 1.5 garlic cloves, minced
- ½ tablespoon of olive oil
- ½ small yellow onion, diced
- 4 oz. mushrooms, sliced
- 2 pork chops, bone-in
- ½ cup of vegetable broth
- ½ thyme spring, diced
- 5 oz. coconut cream
- ½ tablespoon of parsley, chopped

Method:
1. Start by putting all the Ingredients: into your Crockpot.
2. Cover its lid and cook for 4 hours on High setting.
3. Once done, remove its lid and mix well.
4. Garnish as desired.
5. Serve warm.

Nutritional Information per Serving:
- Calories 234
- Total Fat 12 g
- Saturated Fat 6.4 g
- Cholesterol 231 mg
- Sodium 153 mg
- Fiber 3.5 g
- Sugar 3.4 g
- Protein 22.2 g

Pork Tomatillo Salsa

Prep Time: 10 minutes; Cooking Time: 10 hours; Servings: 8
Ingredients:
- 4 lbs. Pork sirloin roast, cubed
- Salt and black pepper to taste
- 4 teaspoon of Garlic powder
- 2 tablespoon of Olive oil
- 36 oz. Green chili tomatillo salsa

Method:
1. Start by putting all the Ingredients: into your Crockpot.
2. Cover its lid and cook for 10 hours on medium setting.
3. Once done, remove its lid and mix well.
4. Garnish as desired.
5. Serve warm.

Nutritional Information per Serving:
- Calories 274
- Total Fat 13 g
- Saturated Fat 7.4 g
- Cholesterol 132 mg
- Sodium 115 mg
- Fiber 0.9 g
- Sugar 1.4 g
- Protein 25.1 g

Bouillon Pork Chops

Prep Time: 10 minutes; Cooking Time: 4 hours; Servings: 4
Ingredients:
- 4 boneless pork chops
- Salt and black pepper, to taste
- 1 cup of water
- 2 teaspoons of extra virgin olive oil
- 2 teaspoons of chicken bouillon powder
- 10 oz canned cream of mushroom soup
- 1 cup of sour cream
- ½ small bunch fresh parsley, chopped

Method:
1. Start by putting all the Ingredients: into your Crockpot.
2. Cover its lid and cook for 4 hours on High setting.
3. Once done, remove its lid and mix well.
4. Garnish as desired.
5. Serve warm.

Nutritional Information per Serving:
- Calories 287
- Total Fat 10.3 g
- Saturated Fat 2.1 g
- Cholesterol 132 mg
- Sodium 342 mg
- Fiber 3.9 g
- Sugar 1.4 g
- Protein 23 g

Cider Rich Pork Loin

Prep Time: 10 minutes; Cooking Time: 6 hours; Servings: 4
Ingredients:
- 2 tablespoons of extra virgin olive oil
- 2 lbs pork loin
- 1 tablespoon of minced dried onion
- Salt and black pepper to taste
- 1 yellow onion, diced
- 2 cups of apple cider
- ¼ cup of vegetable stock

Method:
1. Start by putting all the Ingredients: into your Crockpot.
2. Cover its lid and cook for 6 hours on medium setting.
3. Once done, remove its lid and mix well.
4. Garnish as desired.
5. Serve warm.

Nutritional Information per Serving:
- Calories 265
- Total Fat 22.2 g
- Saturated Fat 12.4 g
- Cholesterol 151 mg
- Sodium 211 mg
- Fiber 0.9 g
- Sugar 1.4 g
- Protein 24.2 g

Char Siu Glazed Pork

Prep Time: 10 minutes; Cooking Time: 4 hours; Servings: 4
Ingredients:
- 4 cups of chicken broth
- 4 tablespoons of Char Siu sauce
- 2 tablespoons of soy sauce
- 2 tablespoons of dry sherry
- 2 lbs pork belly
- 1 teaspoon of peanut oil
- 2 tablespoons of sugar-free ketchup
- 2 teaspoons of sesame oil
- ¼ cup of vegetable stock

Method:
1. Start by putting all the Ingredients: into your Crockpot.
2. Cover its lid and cook for 4 hours on High setting.
3. Once done, remove its lid and mix well.
4. Garnish as desired.
5. Serve warm.

Nutritional Information per Serving:
- Calories 257
- Total Fat 7.5 g
- Saturated Fat 1.1 g
- Cholesterol 20 mg
- Sodium 97 mg
- Fiber 0 g
- Sugar 0 g
- Protein 20.1g

Jalapeno Pork Gumbo

Prep Time: 10 minutes; Cooking Time: 8 hours; Servings: 4
Ingredients:
- ¼ tablespoon of olive oil
- ¼ lb. grass-fed ground beef
- ¼ lb. ground pork
- 1 medium tomatillo, diced
- ⅛ small yellow onion, diced
- ½ jalapeño pepper, diced
- ½ garlic clove, minced
- ¼ (6 oz.) can sugar-free tomato paste
- ¼ tablespoon of chili powder
- ¼ tablespoon of cumin, ground
- Salt and black pepper to taste
- 1 tablespoon of water

Method:
1. Start by putting all the Ingredients: into your Crockpot.
2. Cover its lid and cook for 8 hours on Low setting.
3. Once done, remove its lid and mix well.
4. Garnish as desired.
5. Serve warm.

Nutritional Information per Serving:
- Calories 127
- Total Fat 23.5 g
- Saturated Fat 10.5 g
- Cholesterol 162 mg
- Sodium 142 mg
- Fiber 0.4 g
- Sugar 0.5 g
- Protein 21.5 g

Pork Carne Asada

Prep Time: 10 minutes; Cooking Time: 8 hours; Servings: 4
Ingredients:

- 2 lbs pork belly meat, sliced
- ¾ tablespoon of chili powder
- Salt to taste
- 1½ tablespoons of olive oil
- ½ cup of beef bone broth
- ½ large onion, sliced
- ¾ tablespoon of cumin
- 1 tablespoon of lemon juice
- 1½ oz tomato paste

Method:

1. Start by putting all the Ingredients: into your Crockpot.
2. Cover its lid and cook for 8 hours on Low setting.
3. Once done, remove its lid and mix well.
4. Garnish as desired.
5. Serve warm.

Nutritional Information per Serving:

- Calories 272
- Total Fat 11.1 g
- Saturated Fat 5.8 g
- Cholesterol 610 mg
- Sodium 749 mg
- Fiber 0.2 g
- Sugar 0.2 g
- Protein 23.5 g

Pork Thai Curry

Prep Time: 10 minutes; Cooking Time: 8 hours; Servings: 2
Ingredients:

- ½ lb pork loin, boneless, diced
- ½ cup of coconut milk, canned
- 1 tablespoon of Thai curry paste
- ¼ cup of water

Method:

1. Start by putting all the Ingredients: into your Crockpot.
2. Cover its lid and cook for 8 hours on Low setting.
3. Once done, remove its lid and mix well.
4. Garnish as desired.
5. Serve warm.

Nutritional Information per Serving:

- Calories 248
- Total Fat 2.4 g
- Saturated Fat 0.1 g
- Cholesterol 320 mg
- Sodium 350 mg
- Fiber 0.7 g
- Sugar 0.7 g
- Protein 13.7 g

Wine Dipped Pork Ribs

Prep Time: 10 minutes; Cooking Time: 8.5 hours; Servings: 4
Ingredients:

- 2 lbs pork ribs
- ¾ teaspoon of erythritol
- ½ teaspoon of garlic powder
- ½ teaspoon of allspice
- ½ teaspoon of salt
- ¼ teaspoon of black pepper
- ½ teaspoon of onion powder
- ¼ teaspoon of coriander powder
- ¼ cup of tomato ketchup
- ¾ tablespoon of red wine vinegar
- ½ teaspoon of ground mustard
- ¼ teaspoon of liquid smoke

Method:
1. Start by putting all the Ingredients: into your Crockpot.
2. Cover its lid and cook for 8 hours on Low setting.
3. Once done, remove its lid and mix well.
4. Transfer the ribs to the serving plate.
5. Cook the remaining sauce in the crockpot for 30 minutes on high heat.
6. Pour this sauce over the ribs on the plate.
7. Garnish as desired.
8. Serve warm.

Nutritional Information per Serving:
- Calories 244
- Total Fat 17.4 g
- Saturated Fat 14.8 g
- Cholesterol 44 mg
- Sodium 164 mg
- Fiber 2.4 g
- Sugar 0.1 g
- Protein 31.2 g

Pork Brisket Bo Kho

Prep Time: 10 minutes; Cooking Time: 4 hours; Servings: 2
Ingredients:
- 1¼ lbs pork brisket
- 1 tablespoon of oil
- ½ small onion, diced
- 1 tablespoon of fresh ginger, grated
- 1 tablespoon of red boat fish sauce
- ½ large stalk lemongrass, cut into 3-inch lengths
- ½ bay leaf
- ½ cup of diced tomatoes
- ½ lb carrots, peeled and diced
- 1 teaspoon of Madras curry powder
- 1 tablespoon of sugar free applesauce
- 1 whole star anises
- ½ cup of bone broth
- Salt to taste

Method:
1. Start by putting all the Ingredients: into your Crockpot.
2. Cover its lid and cook for 4 hours on High setting.
3. Once done, remove its lid and mix well.
4. Garnish as desired.
5. Serve warm.

Nutritional Information per Serving:
- Calories 303
- Total Fat 11.9 g
- Saturated Fat 1.7 g
- Cholesterol 78 mg
- Sodium 79 mg
- Protein 20 g

Parmesan Pork Schnitzel

Prep Time: 10 minutes; Cooking Time: 8 hours; Servings: 4
Ingredients:
- 2 lbs boneless pork chops, sliced
- ½ cup of water
- ¼ cup of parmesan cheese, grated
- ½ teaspoon of garlic powder
- 1 teaspoon of salt
- 1 teaspoon of black pepper

Method:
1. Start by putting all the Ingredients: into your Crockpot except the cheese.
2. Cover its lid and cook for 8 hours on Low setting.
3. Once done, remove its lid and mix well.

4. Garnish with cheese on top.
5. Serve warm.

Nutritional Information per Serving:
- Calories 248
- Total Fat 15.7 g
- Saturated Fat 2.7 g
- Cholesterol 75 mg
- Sodium 94 mg
- Protein 12.9 g

Earthy Pork Briskets

Prep Time: 10 minutes; Cooking Time: 12 hours; Servings: 8
Ingredients:
- 4 lbs pork brisket, flat cut
- ½ teaspoon of celery salt
- ½ teaspoon of garlic salt
- ½ teaspoon of Lowry's seasoned salt
- 2 tablespoons of Worcestershire sauce
- 2 cups of barbecue sauce
- 4 tablespoons of liquid smoke
- 1 cup of water

Method:
1. Start by putting all the Ingredients: into your Crockpot.
2. Cover its lid and cook for 12 hours on Low setting.
3. Once done, remove its lid and mix well.
4. Garnish as desired.
5. Serve warm.

Nutritional Information per Serving:
- Calories 442
- Total Fat 13.1 g
- Saturated Fat 11.3 g
- Cholesterol 132 mg
- Sodium 156 mg
- Protein 26.1 g

Pork Filled Avocado

Prep Time: 10 minutes; Cooking Time: 4 hours; Servings: 6
Ingredients:
- ½ pork tenderloin
- ½ tablespoon of cumin, ground
- 1 teaspoon of salt
- ½ tablespoon of chili powder
- ½ tablespoon of garlic powder
- ½ tablespoon of butter
- 6 avocados, cut in half, pits removed and scooped

Method:
1. Start by putting all the Ingredients: into your Crockpot except the avocados
2. Cover its lid and cook for 4 hours on High setting.
3. Once done, remove its lid and mix well.
4. Shred the slow-cooked pork and return to the crockpot.
5. Mix well and divide this mixture into the avocados.
6. Garnish as desired.
7. Serve warm.

Nutritional Information per Serving:
- Calories 397
- Total Fat 17.1 g
- Saturated Fat 13.4 g
- Cholesterol 56 mg
- Sodium 146 mg
- Potassium 322mg
- Protein 41.2 g

Chapter 9: Fish and Seafood

Fish Curry

Prep Time: 10 minutes; Cooking Time: 2 hours; Servings: 2

Ingredients:

- 1 lb. salmon fillets, cut into bite-sized pieces
- 1 curry leaves
- ½ tablespoon of olive oil
- ½ teaspoon of red chili powder
- ½ small yellow onion, diced
- 1 garlic clove, minced
- 1 tablespoon of curry powder
- 1 teaspoon of cumin, ground
- 1 teaspoon of ground coriander
- ½ teaspoon of ground turmeric
- 1 cup of unsweetened coconut milk
- 1 cups of tomato, diced
- ½ Serrano pepper, seeded and diced
- ½ tablespoon of fresh lemon juice

Method:

1. Start by throwing all the Ingredients: into your Crockpot.
2. Cover its lid and cook for 2 hours on High setting.
3. Once done, remove its lid and give it a stir.
4. Serve warm.

Nutritional Information per Serving:

- Calories 216
- Total Fat 21.7 g
- Saturated Fat 6.1 g
- Cholesterol 16 mg
- Sodium 111 mg
- Protein 28.9 g

Elegant Dinner Mussels

Prep Time: 10 minutes; Cooking Time: 2 hours; Servings: 4

Ingredients:

- 2 lbs. mussels, cleaned and de-bearded
- 2 tablespoons of butter
- 1 medium yellow onion, diced
- 1 garlic clove, minced
- ½ teaspoon of rosemary, dried, crushed
- 1 cup of homemade chicken broth
- 2 tablespoons of fresh lemon juice
- ½ cup of sour cream
- Salt and black pepper, to taste

Method:

1. Start by throwing all the Ingredients: into your Crockpot except cream.
2. Cover its lid and cook for 2 hours on High setting.
3. Once done, remove its lid and give it a stir.
4. Stir in cream and mix it all gently
5. Serve warm.

Nutritional Information per Serving:

- Calories 245
- Total Fat 16g
- Saturated Fat 10 g
- Cholesterol 16 mg
- Sodium 111 mg
- Protein 32 g

Lobster Dinner

Prep Time: 10 minutes; Cooking Time: 1 hour; Servings: 4

Ingredients:

- 2 lbs. lobster tails, cut in half

- 2 tablespoons of unsalted butter, melted
- Pinch of salt
- 2 oz. white wine
- 4 oz. water

Method:
1. Start by throwing all the Ingredients: into your Crockpot.
2. Cover its lid and cook for 1 hour on Low setting.
3. Once done, remove its lid and give it a stir.
4. Serve warm.

Nutritional Information per Serving:
- Calories 324
- Total Fat 20.7 g
- Saturated Fat 6.7 g
- Cholesterol 45 mg
- Sodium 241 mg
- Protein 15.3 g

Curried Shrimp

Prep Time: 10 minutes; Cooking Time: 2.5 hours; Servings: 4
Ingredients:
- 1 tablespoon of olive oil
- 1 medium onion, diced
- ½ teaspoon of cumin, ground
- 1½ teaspoons of red chili powder
- 1 teaspoon of ground turmeric
- Pinch of salt
- 2 medium tomatoes, diced
- ¼ cup of water
- 1¾ lbs. medium shrimp, peeled and deveined
- 1 tablespoon of fresh lemon juice
- ¼ cup of fresh cilantro, diced

Method:
1. Start by throwing all the Ingredients: into your Crockpot except shrimp.
2. Cover its lid and cook for 2 hours on Low setting.
3. Once done, remove its lid and give it a stir.
4. Add shrimp and continue cooking for 30 minutes on low heat.
5. Serve warm.

Nutritional Information per Serving:
- Calories 287
- Total Fat 29.5 g
- Saturated Fat 3 g
- Cholesterol 743 mg
- Sodium 388 mg
- Protein 4.2 g

Lemon Salmon

Prep Time: 10 minutes; Cooking Time: 2 hours; Servings: 4
Ingredients:
- 2 lbs. skin-on salmon fillets
- Salt, to taste
- Fresh black pepper to taste
- 1 lemon, sliced
- ¼ cup of onion
- ¼ cup of fennel
- 1 to 1 1/2 cups of water

Method:
1. Start by throwing all the Ingredients: into your Crockpot.
2. Cover its lid and cook for 2 hours on Low setting.
3. Once done, remove its lid and give it a stir.
4. Serve warm.

Nutritional Information per Serving:
- Calories 238
- Total Fat 9.5 g

- Saturated Fat 2.7 g
- Cholesterol 103 mg
- Sodium 403 mg
- Protein 34.2 g

Seafood Stew

Prep Time: 10 minutes; Cooking Time: 2.5 hours; Servings: 6
Ingredients:
- 1 can (28 oz.) Crushed tomatoes
- 1 tablespoon of tomato paste
- 4 cups of vegetable broth
- 3 garlic cloves, minced
- 1/2 cup of diced white onion
- 1 teaspoon of thyme, dried
- 1 teaspoon of dried basil
- 1 teaspoon of oregano, dried
- 1/2 teaspoon of celery salt
- 1/4 teaspoon of crushed red pepper flakes
- 1/8 teaspoon of cayenne pepper
- Salt and pepper to taste
- 1 lb. large shrimp
- 1 lb. scallops
- A handful of fresh parsley, chopped

Method:
1. Start by throwing all the Ingredients: into your Crockpot except seafood.
2. Cover its lid and cook for 2 hours on Low setting.
3. Once done, remove its lid and give it a stir.
4. Stir in seafood and continue cooking for 30 minutes on low heat.
5. Serve warm.

Nutritional Information per Serving:
- Calories 335
- Total Fat 5.4 g
- Saturated Fat 3.3 g
- Cholesterol 16 mg
- Sodium 708 mg
- Protein 18.5 g

Rich Salmon Soup

Prep Time: 10 minutes; Cooking Time: 4 hours; Servings: 3
Ingredients:
- 1 lb. salmon fillets
- 1 tablespoon of coconut oil
- 1 cups of carrot, peeled and diced
- ½ cup of celery stalk, diced
- ½ cup of yellow onion, diced
- 1 cup of cauliflower, diced
- 2 cups of homemade chicken broth
- Salt and black pepper, to taste
- ¼ cup of fresh parsley, chopped

Method:
1. Start by throwing all the Ingredients: into your Crockpot.
2. Cover its lid and cook for 4 hours on Low setting.
3. Once done, remove its lid and give it a stir.
4. Serve warm.

Nutritional Information per Serving:
- Calories 376
- Total Fat 21.9 g
- Saturated Fat 7.8 g
- Cholesterol 110 mg
- Sodium 345 mg
- Protein 33.2 g

Citrus Glazed Salmon

Prep Time: 10 minutes; Cooking Time: 2 hours; Servings: 2
Ingredients:
- 2 (4-ounce) salmon fillets
- ½ teaspoon of fresh ginger, minced

- 1 teaspoon of fresh orange zest, grated finely
- ½ cup of white wine
- ½ tablespoon of olive oil
- 1 tablespoon of fresh lemon juice
- Black pepper, to taste

Method:
1. Start by throwing all the Ingredients: into your Crockpot.
2. Cover its lid and cook for 2 hours on Low setting.
3. Once done, remove its lid and give it a stir.
4. Serve warm.

Nutritional Information per Serving:
- Calories 269
- Total Fat 11.9 g
- Saturated Fat 5.5 g
- Cholesterol 36 mg
- Sodium 437 mg
- Protein 15 g

Cod & Peas with Sour Cream

Prep Time: 10 minutes; Cooking Time: 1 hour; Servings: 2
Ingredients:
- 2 (4-ounce) cod fillets
- 1 tablespoon of fresh parsley
- 1 garlic clove, diced
- ½ lb. frozen peas
- ½ teaspoon of paprika
- 1 cup of sour cream
- ½ cup of white wine

Method:
1. Start by throwing all the Ingredients: into your Crockpot except sour cream.
2. Cover its lid and cook for 1 hour on High setting.
3. Once done, remove its lid and give it a stir.
4. Stir in sour cream and mix it gently
5. Serve warm.

Nutritional Information per Serving:
- Calories 349
- Total Fat 31.9 g
- Saturated Fat 15 g
- Cholesterol 46 mg
- Sodium 237 mg
- Protein 11 g

Nutritious Salmon Dinner

Prep Time: 10 minutes; Cooking Time: 3 hours; Servings: 2
Ingredients:
- 1 lb. salmon fillet, cut into 3 pieces
- 1 garlic clove, minced
- 1 teaspoon of powdered stevia
- 1 tablespoon of red chili powder
- 1 teaspoon of cumin, ground
- Salt and Black pepper
- ½ cup of red wine
- ½ cup of broth

Method:
1. Start by throwing all the Ingredients: into your Crockpot.
2. Cover its lid and cook for 3 hours on Low setting.
3. Once done, remove its lid and give it a stir.
4. Serve warm.

Nutritional Information per Serving:
- Calories 238
- Total Fat 23.2 g
- Saturated Fat 13 g
- Cholesterol 61 mg
- Sodium 115 mg
- Protein 22.3 g

Shrimp & Pepper Stew

Prep Time: 10 minutes; Cooking Time: 2 hours; Servings: 4

Ingredients:

- 2 tablespoons of sriracha sauce
- 14 oz. canned diced tomatoes
- ¼ cup of yellow onion, peeled and diced
- 2 tablespoon of lime juice
- ¼ cup of olive oil
- 1½ lbs. shrimp, peeled and deveined
- ¼ cup of red pepper, roasted and diced
- 1 garlic clove, peeled and diced
- 1 cup of coconut milk
- ¼ cup of fresh cilantro, diced
- Salt and black pepper ground, to taste

Method:

1. Start by throwing all the Ingredients: into your Crockpot except shrimp.
2. Cover its lid and cook for 2 hours on Low setting.
3. Once done, remove its lid and give it a stir.
4. Stir in shrimp and continue cooking for 1 hour on low heat.
5. Serve warm.

Nutritional Information per Serving:

- Calories 392
- Total Fat 40.4 g
- Saturated Fat 6 g
- Cholesterol 20 mg
- Sodium 423 mg
- Protein 21 g

Shrimp Mushroom Alfredo

Prep Time: 10 minutes; Cooking Time: 4 hours; Servings: 4

Ingredients:

- ¼ cup of butter
- 2 tablespoon of olive oil
- 1 onion, peeled and diced
- 8 oz. mushrooms, diced
- 1 asparagus bunch, cut into pieces
- 1 lb. shrimp, peeled and deveined
- Salt and black pepper ground, to taste
- 2 teaspoons of Italian seasoning
- 1 teaspoon of red pepper flakes
- 1 cup of heavy cream
- 1 cup of Parmesan cheese, shredded
- 2 garlic cloves, peeled and minced

Method:

1. Start by throwing all the Ingredients: into your Crockpot except shrimp.
2. Cover its lid and cook for 4 hours on High setting.
3. Once done, remove its lid and give it a stir.
4. Stir in shrimp and continue cooking for 1 hour on low heat.
5. Serve warm.

Nutritional Information per Serving:

- Calories 213
- Total Fat 23.4 g
- Saturated Fat 6.1 g
- Cholesterol 102 mg
- Sodium 86 mg
- Protein 33.2 g

Shrimp Tomato Medley

Prep Time: 10 minutes; Cooking Time: 1 hour; Servings: 8

Ingredients:
- ½ tablespoon of chili oil
- 4 scallions, diced
- 1½ tablespoon of coconut oil
- 1 small ginger root, diced
- 8 cups of chicken stock
- ¼ cup of coconut aminos
- ¼ teaspoon of fish sauce
- 1 lb. shrimp, peeled and deveined
- ½ lb. tomatoes
- Black pepper ground, to taste
- 1 tablespoon of sesame oil
- 1 (5 oz.) can bamboo shoots, sliced

Method:
1. Start by throwing all the Ingredients: into your Crockpot.
2. Cover its lid and cook for 1 hour on Low setting.
3. Once done, remove its lid and give it a stir.
4. Serve warm.

Nutritional Information per Serving:
- Calories 371
- Total Fat 3.7 g
- Saturated Fat 2.7 g
- Cholesterol 168 mg
- Sodium 121 mg
- Protein 26.5 g

Butter Glazed Mussels

Prep Time: 10 minutes; Cooking Time: 2 hours; Servings: 6
Ingredients:
- 1 tablespoon of butter
- A splash of lemon juice
- 2 lb. mussels, debearded and scrubbed
- 2 garlic cloves, peeled and minced

Method:
1. Start by throwing all the Ingredients: into your Crockpot.
2. Cover its lid and cook for 2 hours on High setting.
3. Once done, remove its lid and give it a stir.
4. Serve warm.

Nutritional Information per Serving:
- Calories 266
- Total Fat 26.4 g
- Saturated Fat 4 g
- Cholesterol 13 mg
- Sodium 455 mg
- Protein 20.6 g

Citrus Rich Octopus Salad

Prep Time: 10 minutes; Cooking Time: 2 hours; Servings: 2
Ingredients:
- 3 oz. olive oil
- Juice of 1 lemon
- 21 oz. octopus, rinsed
- 4 celery stalks, roughly diced
- Salt and black pepper ground, to taste
- 4 tablespoons of fresh parsley, roughly diced

Method:
1. Start by throwing all the Ingredients: into your Crockpot.
2. Cover its lid and cook for 2 hours on Low setting.
3. Once done, remove its lid and give it a stir.
4. Serve warm.

Nutritional Information per Serving:
- Calories 225
- Total Fat 17.7 g

- Saturated Fat 3.2 g
- Cholesterol 5 mg
- Sodium 386 mg
- Protein 7.4 g

Creamy Clam Chowder Luncheon

Prep Time: 10 minutes; Cooking Time: 2 hours; Servings: 4
Ingredients:
- 2 cups of chicken stock
- 1 teaspoon of ground thyme
- 14 oz. canned baby clams
- 1 cup of celery stalks, roughly diced
- 2 cups of heavy cream
- Salt and black pepper ground, to taste
- 1 cup of onion, peeled and roughly diced
- 12 bacon strips, roughly diced

Method:
1. Start by throwing all the Ingredients: into your Crockpot.
2. Cover its lid and cook for 2 hours on High setting.
3. Once done, remove its lid and give it a stir.
4. Serve warm.

Nutritional Information per Serving:
- Calories 449
- Total Fat 28.7 g
- Saturated Fat 14.9 g
- Cholesterol 163 mg
- Sodium 744 mg
- Protein 39.3 g

Flounder with Shrimp

Prep Time: 10 minutes; Cooking Time: 2 hours; Servings: 6
Ingredients:
- 1 teaspoon of oregano, dried
- A pinch of cinnamon ground
- ¼ teaspoon of ground nutmeg
- ½ teaspoon of allspice
- ¼ teaspoon of cloves, ground
- 2 cups of chicken stock
- 2 tablespoon of coconut flour
- 1 tablespoon of butter
- 8 oz. bacon, sliced
- 1 green bell pepper, seeded and diced
- 1 celery stalk, diced
- 1 tomato, cored and diced
- 2 shallots, peeled and roughly diced
- 8 oz. shrimp, peeled, deveined, and diced
- 4 garlic cloves, peeled and minced
- 1 tablespoon of coconut milk
- ½ cup of fresh parsley, diced
- 2 tablespoons of butter
- 4 flounder fillets

Method:
1. Start by throwing all the Ingredients: into your Crockpot except shrimp.
2. Cover its lid and cook for 2 hours on High setting.
3. Once done, remove its lid and give it a stir.
4. Stir in shrimp and continue cooking for 1 hour on low heat.
5. Serve warm.

Nutritional Information per Serving:
- Calories 202
- Total Fat 9.5g
- Saturated Fat 2 g
- Cholesterol 62 mg
- Sodium 526 mg
- Protein 22 g

Tangy Pepper Oysters

Prep Time: 10 minutes; Cooking Time: 1 hour; Servings: 6
Ingredients:

- ¼ cup of olive oil
- 1 Serrano chili pepper, diced
- 12 oysters, shucked
- Juice from 1 lime
- ½ teaspoon of fresh ginger, shredded
- Juice of 2 lemons
- ¼ teaspoon of garlic, minced
- Zest from 2 limes
- ¼ cup of scallions, diced
- 1 cup of tomato juice
- Salt, to taste
- ¼ cup of fresh cilantro, diced

Method:

1. Start by throwing all the Ingredients: into your Crockpot.
2. Cover its lid and cook for 1 hour on High setting.
3. Once done, remove its lid and give it a stir.
4. Serve warm.

Nutritional Information per Serving:

- Calories 449
- Total Fat 28.7 g
- Saturated Fat 14.9 g
- Cholesterol 163 mg
- Sodium 744 mg
- Protein 39.3 g

Mediterranean Cod Salad

Prep Time: 10 minutes; Cooking Time: 2 hours; Servings: 4
Ingredients:

- 1 escarole head, leaves separated
- 6 tablespoons of capers
- 2 lbs. salt cod
- ¾ cup of olive oil
- 1 cup of fresh parsley, roughly diced
- 2 cups of jarred pimiento peppers, diced
- 1 cup of olives (Kalamata), pitted and roughly diced
- Salt and black pepper ground, to taste
- ½ teaspoon of red chili flakes
- Juice from 2 lemons
- 4 garlic cloves, peeled and minced
- 2 celery stalks, roughly diced

Method:

1. Start by throwing all the Ingredients: into your Crockpot except escarole leaves.
2. Cover its lid and cook for 2 hours on High setting.
3. Once done, remove its lid and give it a stir.
4. Divide the seafood mixture into the escarole leaves.
5. Serve warm.

Nutritional Information per Serving:

- Calories 364
- Total Fat 13.2 g
- Saturated Fat 3.4 g
- Cholesterol 141 mg
- Sodium 274 mg
- Protein 47.7 g

Luscious Herbed Clams

Prep Time: 10 minutes; Cooking Time: 2 hours; Servings: 12
Ingredients:

- 1 tablespoon of oregano, dried
- ½ cup of butter

- 2 cups of white wine
- 1 teaspoon of red pepper flakes
- 1 teaspoon of fresh parsley, roughly diced
- 36 clams, scrubbed
- 5 garlic cloves, peeled and minced

Method:
1. Start by throwing all the Ingredients: into your Crockpot.
2. Cover its lid and cook for 2 hours on Low setting.
3. Once done, remove its lid and give it a stir.
4. Serve warm.

Nutritional Information per Serving:
- Calories 455
- Total Fat 34.4 g
- Saturated Fat 3.4 g
- Cholesterol 64 mg
- Sodium 58 mg
- Protein 29.6 g

Cider Soaked Pancetta Clams

Prep Time: 10 minutes; Cooking Time: 2 hours; Servings: 6
Ingredients:
- 3 oz. pancetta
- 2 lbs. clams, scrubbed
- 1 tablespoon of olive oil
- Juice from ½ lemon
- 1 bottle infused cider
- 3 tablespoons of butter
- Salt and black pepper ground, to taste
- 2 garlic cloves, peeled and diced
- 2 thyme sprigs, diced

Method:
1. Start by throwing all the Ingredients: into your Crockpot.
2. Cover its lid and cook for 2 hours on Low setting.
3. Once done, remove its lid and give it a stir.
4. Serve warm.

Nutritional Information per Serving:
- Calories 355
- Total Fat 15 g
- Saturated Fat 1.4 g
- Cholesterol 128 mg
- Sodium 1271 mg
- Protein 44.2 g

Scallops with Romanesco

Prep Time: 10 minutes; Cooking Time: 1 hour; Servings: 4
Ingredients:
- 1/2 Romanesco head, trimmed
- 3 tablespoon of olive oil
- 1 cup of chicken stock
- 1 tablespoon of butter
- 1 shallot, peeled and diced
- 3 garlic cloves, peeled and minced
- 1 lb. scallops
- 2 cups of spinach, chopped
- ¼ cup of walnuts, toasted and diced
- 1½ cups of pomegranate seeds
- Salt and black pepper ground, to taste

Method:
1. Start by throwing all the Ingredients: into your Crockpot.
2. Cover its lid and cook for 1 hour on Low setting.
3. Once done, remove its lid and give it a stir.
4. Serve warm.

Nutritional Information per Serving:
- Calories 307
- Total Fat 29 g
- Saturated Fat 14g
- Cholesterol 111 mg
- Sodium 122 mg
- Protein 6 g

Jalapeno Cheese Oysters

Prep Time: 10 minutes; Cooking Time: 2 hours; Servings: 9
Ingredients:
- 1 jalapeño pepper, diced
- 2 tomatoes, cored and diced
- 18 oysters, scrubbed
- 2 limes, cut into wedges
- ½ cup of fresh cilantro, diced
- Salt and black pepper ground, to taste
- ½ cup of Monterey Jack cheese, shredded
- ¼ cup of onion, diced
- ½ cup of vegetable stock
- Juice from 1 lime

Method:
1. Start by throwing all the Ingredients: into your Crockpot.
2. Cover its lid and cook for 2 hours on Low setting.
3. Once done, remove its lid and give it a stir.
4. Serve warm.

Nutritional Information per Serving:
- Calories 487
- Total Fat 37.4 g
- Saturated Fat 8.8 g
- Cholesterol 71 mg
- Sodium 501 mg
- Protein 28.1 g

Salmon with Mushroom

Prep Time: 10 minutes; Cooking Time: 3 hours; Servings: 4
Ingredients:
- ¼ cup of mayonnaise
- 2 salmon fillets
- 2 cups of spinach, chopped
- A drizzle of olive oil
- 6 mushrooms, diced
- ¼ cup of macadamia nuts, toasted and roughly diced
- 3 green onions, diced
- Salt and black pepper ground, to taste
- A pinch of nutmeg
- 5 oz. tiger shrimp, peeled, deveined, and diced

Method:
1. Start by throwing all the Ingredients: into your Crockpot except shrimp
2. Cover its lid and cook for 2 hours on High setting.
3. Once done, remove its lid and give it a stir.
4. Stir in shrimp and continue cooking for 1 hour on low heat.
5. Serve warm.

Nutritional Information per Serving:
- Calories 282
- Total Fat 4.6 g
- Saturated Fat 1.4 g
- Cholesterol 75 mg
- Sodium 560 mg
- Protein 22.2 g

Maple Glazed Salmon Fillet

Prep Time: 10 minutes; Cooking Time: 2 hours; Servings: 1
Ingredients:
- 1 tablespoon of coconut oil
- 1 salmon fillet
- 2 tablespoons of mustard
- 1 tablespoon of maple syrup (sugar-free)
- Salt and black pepper ground, to taste

Method:
1. Start by throwing all the Ingredients: into your Crockpot.
2. Cover its lid and cook for 2 hours on High setting.
3. Once done, remove its lid and give it a stir.
4. Serve warm.

Nutritional Information per Serving:
- Calories 434
- Total Fat 36.4 g
- Saturated Fat 17.1 g
- Cholesterol 257 mg
- Sodium 1038 mg
- Protein 24.2 g

Salmon with Juicy Shallots

Prep Time: 10 minutes; Cooking Time: 2 hours; Servings: 2
Ingredients:
- 1 tablespoon of lemon juice
- 1 shallot, peeled and diced
- 2 medium salmon fillets
- Salt and black pepper ground, to taste
- ¼ cup of and 1 tablespoon of olive oil
- 1 lemon, cut into thin wedges
- 2 tablespoons of fresh parsley, diced

Method:
1. Start by throwing all the Ingredients: into your Crockpot.
2. Cover its lid and cook for 2 hours on High setting.
3. Once done, remove its lid and give it a stir.
4. Serve warm.

Nutritional Information per Serving:
- Calories 207
- Total Fat 15 g
- Saturated Fat 5.2 g
- Cholesterol 64 mg
- Sodium 252 mg
- Protein 11.1 g

Warming Mussels Tomato Soup

Prep Time: 10 minutes; Cooking Time: 3 hours; Servings: 4
Ingredients:
- 2 lbs. mussels
- 1 tablespoon of olive oil
- 2 cups of chicken stock
- 1 onion, peeled and diced
- 1 teaspoon of red pepper flakes
- 1 (28 oz.) can diced tomatoes
- 3 garlic cloves, peeled and minced
- ½ cup of fresh parsley, diced
- 1 (28 oz.) can crushed tomatoes
- Salt and black pepper ground, to taste

Method:
1. Start by throwing all the Ingredients: into your Crockpot.

2. Cover its lid and cook for 3 hours on Low setting.
3. Once done, remove its lid and give it a stir.
4. Serve warm.

Nutritional Information per Serving:
- Calories 321
- Total Fat 9 g
- Saturated Fat 4.9 g
- Cholesterol 108 mg
- Sodium 184 mg
- Protein 24.3 g

Herbed Swordfish Delight

Prep Time: 10 minutes; Cooking Time: 2 hours; Servings: 4
Ingredients:
- ½ teaspoon of dried sage
- 4 swordfish steaks
- 1 tablespoon of fresh parsley, diced
- 3 tablespoon of olive oil
- 1 lemon, cut into wedges
- 3 garlic cloves, peeled and minced
- ½ teaspoon of dried marjoram
- ½ teaspoon of rosemary, dried
- ⅓ cup of chicken stock
- Salt and black pepper ground, to taste
- ¼ cup of lemon juice

Method:
1. Start by throwing all the Ingredients: into your Crockpot.
2. Cover its lid and cook for 2 hours on High setting.
3. Once done, remove its lid and give it a stir.
4. Serve warm.

Nutritional Information per Serving:
- Calories 311
- Total Fat 8.3 g
- Saturated Fat 4.9 g
- Cholesterol 69 mg
- Sodium 896 mg
- Protein 17.4 g

Seafood Jambalaya

Prep Time: 10 minutes; Cooking Time: 1 hour; Servings: 4-6
Ingredients:
- 4 oz. catfish, cubed
- 4 oz. shrimp, peeled and deveined
- 1 tablespoon of olive oil
- 2 bacon strips, diced
- 1 1/5 cups of vegetable broth
- ¾ cup of sliced celery stalk
- 1/4 teaspoon of minced garlic
- 1/2 cup of diced onion
- 1 cup of canned diced tomatoes
- 1 cup of uncooked cauliflower rice
- 1/2 tablespoon of Cajun seasoning
- 1/4 teaspoon of thyme, dried
- 1/4 teaspoon of cayenne pepper
- 1/2 teaspoon of oregano, dried
- Salt and black pepper, to taste

Method:
1. Start by throwing all the Ingredients: into your Crockpot.
2. Cover its lid and cook for 1 hour on High setting.
3. Once done, remove its lid and give it a stir.
4. Serve warm.

Nutritional Information per Serving:
- Calories 231
- Total Fat 17.6 g
- Saturated Fat 7.6 g
- Cholesterol 383 mg
- Sodium 244 mg
- Protein 15.7 g

Shrimp Creole

Prep Time: 10 minutes; Cooking Time: 1 hour; Servings: 4
Ingredients:

- 1 lb. shrimps, peeled and deveined
- 1 tablespoon of olive oil
- 1 (28 oz.) can crush whole tomatoes
- 1 cup of celery stalk, sliced
- ¾ cup of diced white onion
- 1/2 cup of green bell pepper, diced
- 1 (8oz.) can sugar-free tomato sauce
- 1/2 teaspoon of minced garlic
- ¼ teaspoon of black pepper
- 1 tablespoon of Worcestershire sauce
- 4 drops hot pepper sauce
- Salt, to taste

Method:

1. Start by throwing all the Ingredients: into your Crockpot.
2. Cover its lid and cook for 1 hour on High setting.
3. Once done, remove its lid and give it a stir.
4. Serve warm.

Nutritional Information per Serving:

- Calories 139
- Total Fat 10.1 g
- Saturated Fat 5 g
- Cholesterol 216 mg
- Sodium 238 mg
- Protein 10.1 g

Mouth-Watering Casserole

Prep Time: 10 minutes; Cooking Time: 4 hours; Servings: 4
Ingredients:

- 1/2 cup of milk
- 2 teaspoons of olive oil
- 12 oz. water-packed tuna
- 15 oz. cream of mushroom soup
- 8 oz. egg noodles, cooked and drained
- 8 oz. thawed frozen mixed vegetables
- 2 tablespoons of parsley, dried
- Salt and black pepper, to taste
- 1/4 cup of toasted almonds, sliced

Method:

1. Start by throwing all the Ingredients: into your Crockpot.
2. Cover its lid and cook for 4 hours on High setting.
3. Once done, remove its lid and give it a stir.
4. Serve warm.

Nutritional Information per Serving:

- Calories 489
- Total Fat 43.3 g
- Saturated Fat 15.2 g
- Cholesterol 128 mg
- Sodium 662 mg
- Protein 22.2 g

Salmon Casserole

Prep Time: 10 minutes; Cooking Time: 8 hours; Servings: 6
Ingredients:

- 1/2 tablespoon of olive oil
- 8 oz. cream of mushroom soup
- 1 cup of mushrooms, diced
- ¼ cup of water
- 3 tablespoons of almond flour
- 1 (16oz.) can salmon (drained and flaked)
- ½ cup of diced scallion

- ¼ teaspoon of ground nutmeg
- Salt and black pepper, to taste

Method:
1. Start by throwing all the Ingredients: into your Crockpot.
2. Cover its lid and cook for 8 hours on medium setting.
3. Once done, remove its lid and give it a stir.
4. Serve warm.

Nutritional Information per Serving:
- Calories 211
- Total Fat 18.5 g
- Saturated Fat 11.5 g
- Cholesterol 173 mg
- Sodium 280 mg
- Protein 11.5 g

Salmon Soup

Prep Time: 10 minutes; Cooking Time: 4 hours; Servings: 4
Ingredients:
- 1 lb. salmon fillets
- 1 tablespoon of coconut oil
- 1 cup of carrots, peeled and diced
- 1/2 cup of celery stalk, diced
- 1/2 cup of yellow onion, diced
- 1 cup of cauliflower, diced
- 2 cups of homemade chicken broth
- 1½ cups of half-and-half cream
- Salt and black pepper, to taste
- 2 tablespoons of fresh parsley, chopped

Method:
1. Start by throwing all the Ingredients: into your Crockpot except parsley.
2. Cover its lid and cook for 4 hours on Low setting.
3. Once done, remove its lid and give it a stir.
4. Garnish with parsley.
5. Serve warm.

Nutritional Information per Serving:
- Calories 238
- Total Fat 9.5 g
- Saturated Fat 2.7 g
- Cholesterol 103 mg
- Sodium 403 mg
- Protein 34.2 g

Salmon Curry

Prep Time: 10 minutes; Cooking Time: 4 hours; Servings: 6
Ingredients:
- 3lbs. salmon fillets, diced
- 2 tablespoons of olive oil
- 2 Serrano peppers, diced
- 1 teaspoon of ground turmeric
- 4 tablespoons of curry powder
- 4 teaspoons of cumin, ground
- 4 curry leaves
- 4 teaspoons of ground coriander
- 2 small yellow onion, diced
- 2 teaspoons of red chili powder
- 4 garlic cloves, minced
- 4 cups of unsweetened coconut milk
- 2 ½ cups of tomatoes, diced
- 2 tablespoons of fresh lemon juice
- Fresh cilantro leaves (Garnish)

Method:
1. Start by throwing all the Ingredients: into your Crockpot.
2. Cover its lid and cook for 4 hours on Low setting.
3. Once done, remove its lid and give it a stir.
4. Garnish with cilantro.

5. Serve warm.

Nutritional Information per Serving:
- Calories 335
- Total Fat 5.4 g
- Saturated Fat 3.3 g
- Cholesterol 16 mg
- Sodium 708 mg
- Protein 18.5 g

Cod Platter

Prep Time: 10 minutes; Cooking Time: 4 hours; Servings: 6

Ingredients:
- 1 ½ lb. cherry tomatoes halved
- 2 ½ tablespoons of fresh rosemary, diced
- 6 (4-oz.) cod fillets
- 3 garlic cloves, minced
- 2 tablespoon of olive oil
- Salt and black pepper, to taste

Method:
1. Start by throwing all the Ingredients: into your Crockpot.
2. Cover its lid and cook for 4 hours on Low setting.
3. Once done, remove its lid and give it a stir.
4. Serve warm.

Nutritional Information per Serving:
- Calories 335
- Total Fat 5.4 g
- Saturated Fat 3.3 g
- Cholesterol 16 mg
- Sodium 708 mg
- Protein 18.5 g

Dinner Mussels

Prep Time: 10 minutes; Cooking Time: 3 hours; Servings: 8

Ingredients:
- 2 tablespoons of olive oil
- 2 medium yellow onions, diced
- 1 teaspoon of rosemary, dried, crushed
- 2 garlic cloves, minced
- 2 cups of chicken broth
- 4 lbs. mussels, cleaned and de-bearded
- ¼ cup of fresh lemon juice
- Salt and black pepper, to taste

Method:
1. Start by throwing all the Ingredients: into your Crockpot.
2. Cover its lid and cook for 3 hours on Low setting.
3. Once done, remove its lid and give it a stir.
4. Serve warm.

Nutritional Information per Serving:
- Calories 238
- Total Fat 9.5 g
- Saturated Fat 2.7 g
- Cholesterol 103 mg
- Sodium 403 mg
- Protein 34.2 g

Butter-Dipped Lobsters

Prep Time: 10 minutes; Cooking Time: 1 hour; Servings: 8

Ingredients:
- 1 cup of water
- 4 lbs. lobster tails, cut in half
- 4 tablespoons of unsalted butter, melted
- Salt to taste

- Black pepper to taste

Method:
1. Start by throwing all the Ingredients: into your Crockpot.
2. Cover its lid and cook for 1 hour on Low setting.
3. Once done, remove its lid and give it a stir.
4. Serve warm.

Nutritional Information per Serving:
- Calories 324
- Total Fat 20.7 g
- Saturated Fat 6.7 g
- Cholesterol 45 mg
- Sodium 241 mg
- Protein 15.3 g

Creamy Lobster

Prep Time: 10 minutes; Cooking Time: 1 hour; Servings: 8
Ingredients:
- 1½ cups of water
- 4 lbs. fresh lobster tails
- 2 teaspoons of old bay seasoning
- 1 cup of mayonnaise
- 2 scallions, diced
- ¼ cup of unsalted butter, melted
- 4 tablespoons of fresh lemon juice

Method:
1. Start by throwing all the Ingredients: into your Crockpot except mayonnaise.
2. Cover its lid and cook for 1 hour on Low setting.
3. Once done, remove its lid and give it a stir.
4. Peel the slow-cooked lobster tail and transfer the meat to a bowl.
5. Mix the meat with mayonnaise in that bowl.
6. Garnish as desired.
7. Serve warm.

Nutritional Information per Serving:
- Calories 349
- Total Fat 31.9 g
- Saturated Fat 15 g
- Cholesterol 46 mg
- Sodium 237 mg
- Protein 11 g

Citrus Enriched Salmon

Prep Time: 10 minutes; Cooking Time: 2 hours; Servings: 6
Ingredients:
- 6 (4-oz.) salmon fillets
- 1 ½ teaspoon of fresh ginger, minced
- 1 ½ tablespoon of olive oil
- 1 ½ cup of white wine
- 4 tablespoons of fresh lemon juice
- 2 ½ teaspoons of fresh orange zest, grated finely
- Black pepper, to taste
- Fresh herbs (garnish)

Method:
1. Start by throwing all the Ingredients: into your Crockpot.
2. Cover its lid and cook for 2 hours on Low setting.
3. Once done, remove its lid and give it a stir.
4. Garnish with cilantro.
5. Serve warm.

Nutritional Information per Serving:
- Calories 487
- Total Fat 37.4 g

- Saturated Fat 8.8 g
- Cholesterol 71 mg
- Sodium 501 mg
- Protein 28.1 g

Wine Sauce Glazed Cod

Prep Time: 10 minutes; Cooking Time: 4 hours; Servings: 7
Ingredients:
- 7 (4 oz.) cod fillets
- 1 tablespoon of fresh parsley
- 1 garlic clove, diced
- 1/4 teaspoon of paprika
- 1/2 cup of white wine
- 1 cup of water

Method:
1. Start by throwing all the Ingredients: into your Crockpot.
2. Cover its lid and cook for 4 hours on Low setting.
3. Once done, remove its lid and give it a stir.
4. Serve warm.

Nutritional Information per Serving:
- Calories 434
- Total Fat 36.4 g
- Saturated Fat 17.1 g
- Cholesterol 257 mg
- Sodium 1038 mg
- Protein 24.2 g

Fish Curry Delight

Prep Time: 10 minutes; Cooking Time: 4 hours; Servings: 6
Ingredients:
- 3 lbs. cod fillets, cut into bite-sized pieces
- 2 tablespoons of olive oil
- 4 curry leaves
- 4 medium onions, diced
- 2 tablespoons of fresh ginger, grated finely
- 4 garlic cloves, minced
- 4 tablespoons of curry powder
- 4 teaspoons of cumin, ground
- 4 teaspoons of ground coriander
- 2 teaspoons of red chili powder
- 1 teaspoon of ground turmeric
- 4 cups of unsweetened coconut milk
- 2 ½ cups of tomatoes, diced
- 2 Serrano peppers, seeded and diced
- 2 tablespoons of fresh lemon juice

Method:
1. Start by throwing all the Ingredients: into your Crockpot.
2. Cover its lid and cook for 4 hours on Low setting.
3. Once done, remove its lid and give it a stir.
4. Garnish with cilantro.
5. Serve warm.

Nutritional Information per Serving:
- Calories 231
- Total Fat 17.6 g
- Saturated Fat 7.6 g
- Cholesterol 383 mg
- Sodium 244 mg
- Protein 15.7 g

Chapter 10: Vegetables

Spinach with Tomato Sauce

Prep Time: 10 minutes; Cooking Time: 3; Serving: 4

Ingredients:

- 2 tablespoons of olive oil
- 1 medium onion, diced
- 1 tablespoon of garlic, minced
- ½ teaspoon of red pepper flakes, crushed
- 8 cups of fresh spinach, chopped
- 1 cup of tomatoes, diced
- ½ cup of homemade tomato puree
- ½ cup of white wine
- ¾ cup of vegetable broth
- ½ cup of cream cheese

Method:

1. Start by throwing all the Ingredients: into your Crockpot except cream cheese.
2. Cover its lid and cook for 3 hours on Low setting.
3. Once done, remove its lid and give it a stir.
4. Stir in cream cheese and mix gently.
5. Garnish as desired.
6. Serve warm.

Nutritional Information per Serving:

- Calories 347
- Total Fat 11.6 g
- Saturated Fat 2.3 g
- Cholesterol 421 mg
- Sodium 54 mg
- Protein 2.4 g

Carrots with Mushroom Sauce

Prep Time: 10 minutes; Cooking Time: 4 hours; Serving: 4

Ingredients:

- 2 tablespoons of butter
- 2 garlic cloves, minced
- 1 tablespoon of fresh sage leaves, diced
- 1 lb. fresh mushrooms, sliced
- Salt and black pepper, to taste
- ¼ cup of heavy cream
- 1 scallion, diced
- 3 large carrots, spiralized with blade C
- 1 cup of whipping cream

Method:

1. Start by throwing all the Ingredients: into your Crockpot.
2. Cover its lid and cook for 4 hours on Low setting.
3. Once done, remove its lid and give it a stir.
4. Garnish as desired.
5. Serve warm.

Nutritional Information per Serving:

- Calories 376
- Total Fat 12.1 g
- Saturated Fat 14.2 g
- Cholesterol 195 mg
- Sodium 73 mg
- Protein 5.7 g

Tomato Soup

Prep Time: 10 minutes; Cooking Time: 2 hours; Serving: 4

Ingredients:

- ½ tablespoon of olive oil
- 1 small onion, diced

- 1 garlic clove, minced
- 1 ½ lb. tomatoes, diced
- 1 tablespoon of sugar-free tomato sauce
- 1 teaspoon of parsley, dried, crushed
- 1 teaspoon of dried basil, crushed
- Black pepper, to taste
- 2 cups of vegetable broth
- 2 tablespoons of Erythritol
- ½ tablespoon of balsamic vinegar
- ¼ cup of fresh basil, diced

Method:
1. Start by throwing all the Ingredients: into your Crockpot.
2. Cover its lid and cook for 2 hours on High setting.
3. Once done, remove its lid and give it a stir.
4. Garnish as desired.
5. Serve warm.

Nutritional Information per Serving:
- Calories 321
- Total Fat 5.2 g
- Saturated Fat 12.4 g
- Cholesterol 85 mg
- Sodium 48 mg
- Protein 5.7 g

Pesto Peppers

Prep Time: 10 minutes; Cooking Time: 4 hours; Serving: 4
Ingredients:
- 12 Baby bell peppers, cut into halves lengthwise
- 6 tablespoon of Jarred basil pesto
- 1 tablespoon of Lemon juice
- 1 tablespoon of Olive oil
- 1 lb. zucchini, sliced
- 1/4 teaspoon of Red pepper flakes, crushed
- Salt and black pepper- to taste
- Handful parsley, chopped
- ½ cup of vegetable stock

Method:
1. Start by throwing all the Ingredients: into your Crockpot.
2. Cover its lid and cook for 4 hours on Low setting.
3. Once done, remove its lid and give it a stir.
4. Garnish as desired.
5. Serve warm.

Nutritional Information per Serving:
- Calories 291
- Total Fat 34.1 g
- Saturated Fat 12.4 g
- Cholesterol 321 mg
- Sodium 54 mg
- Protein 9.2 g

Rich Cheesy Broccoli Soup

Prep Time: 10 minutes; Cooking Time: 5 hours; Serving: 6
Ingredients:
- 1 tablespoon of olive oil
- 2 tablespoons of butter
- 2 medium carrots, peeled and diced
- 1 small yellow onion, diced
- 2 tablespoons of almond flour
- 1 garlic clove, minced
- 3 cups of homemade vegetable broth
- 5 cups of broccoli florets
- 1 teaspoon of dill weed
- 1 teaspoon of smoked paprika
- Salt and black pepper, to taste

- 4 American cheese slices, cut into pieces
- 1 cup of Colby Jack cheese, shredded
- 1 cup of Pepper Jack cheese, shredded
- ½ cup of Parmesan cheese, shredded

Method:
1. Start by throwing all the Ingredients: into your Crockpot.
2. Cover its lid and cook for 5 hours on Low setting.
3. Once done, remove its lid and give it a stir.
4. Garnish as desired.
5. Serve warm.

Nutritional Information per Serving:
- Calories 352
- Total Fat 4.2 g
- Saturated Fat 22.4 g
- Cholesterol 93 mg
- Sodium 38 mg
- Protein 7.4 g

Nutty Brussels Sprout

Prep Time: 10 minutes; Cooking Time: 3 hours; Serving: 2
Ingredients:
- 1 lb. Brussels sprouts, trimmed and halved
- ¼ cup of butter, melted
- ½ cup of almonds, diced
- ½ cup of vegetable stock

Method:
1. Start by throwing all the Ingredients: into your Crockpot.
2. Cover its lid and cook for 3 hours on Low setting.
3. Once done, remove its lid and give it a stir.
4. Garnish as desired.
5. Serve warm.

Nutritional Information per Serving:
- Calories 233
- Total Fat 21.3 g
- Saturated Fat 10.1 g
- Cholesterol 321 mg
- Sodium 65 mg
- Protein 4.8 g

Broccoli Florets

Prep Time: 10 minutes; Cooking Time: 3 hours; Serving: 6
Ingredients:
- 2 lbs. broccoli florets
- 4 tablespoons of butter, melted
- 1 cup of whipping cream
- Salt and black pepper, to taste

Method:
1. Start by throwing all the Ingredients: into your Crockpot.
2. Cover its lid and cook for 3 hours on Low setting.
3. Once done, remove its lid and give it a stir.
4. Garnish as desired.
5. Serve warm.

Nutritional Information per Serving:
- Calories 281
- Total Fat 3.5 g
- Saturated Fat 3.1 g
- Cholesterol 344 mg
- Sodium 322 mg
- Protein 3.4 g

Veggies Dish

Prep Time: 10 minutes; Cooking Time: 5 hours; Serving: 4

Ingredients:

- 6-ounce fresh mushrooms, sliced
- ½ cup of onion, diced
- 2 zucchinis, cut into ½ inch slices
- 1 tablespoon of fresh basil, diced
- ½ tablespoon of olive oil
- ½ cup of cream
- ½ cup of cheddar cheese
- ½ cup of feta cheese
- 1 garlic clove, minced
- Salt and black pepper, to taste
- ½ (7 oz.) can sugar-free crushed tomatoes with juice

Method:

1. Start by throwing all the Ingredients: into your Crockpot.
2. Cover its lid and cook for 5 hours on Low setting.
3. Once done, remove its lid and give it a stir.
4. Garnish as desired.
5. Serve warm.

Nutritional Information per Serving:

- Calories 381
- Total Fat 18.1 g
- Saturated Fat 2.4 g
- Cholesterol 139 mg
- Sodium 78 mg
- Protein 5.4 g

Cheesy Cauliflower

Prep Time: 10 minutes; Cooking Time: 3 hours; Serving: 5

Ingredients:

- 1 head cauliflower
- 1 tablespoon of prepared mustard
- 1 teaspoon of mayonnaise
- ¼ cup of butter, cut into small pieces
- ½ cup of Parmesan cheese, grated

Method:

1. Start by throwing all the Ingredients: into your Crockpot.
2. Cover its lid and cook for 3 hours on High setting.
3. Once done, remove its lid and give it a stir.
4. Garnish as desired.
5. Serve warm.

Nutritional Information per Serving:

- Calories 231
- Total Fat 14.3 g
- Saturated Fat 3.9 g
- Cholesterol 349 mg
- Sodium 45 mg
- Protein 3.6 g

Tangy Fennel Bulbs

Prep Time: 10 minutes; Cooking Time: 5 hours; Serving: 4

Ingredients:

- 2 fennel bulbs, cut into quarters
- 1 red chili pepper, diced
- 3/4 cup of vegetable broth
- 1/4 cup of white wine
- 3 tablespoon of olive oil
- 1/2 lemon juice
- Salt and black pepper- to taste
- 1 garlic clove, minced
- 1/4 cup of parmesan, grated

Method:

1. Start by throwing all the Ingredients: into your Crockpot.
2. Cover its lid and cook for 5 hours on Low setting.
3. Once done, remove its lid and give it a stir.
4. Garnish as desired.
5. Serve warm.

Nutritional Information per Serving:
- Calories 412
- Total Fat 17.3 g
- Saturated Fat 10.4 g
- Cholesterol 329 mg
- Sodium 212 mg
- Protein 5.7 g

Parmesan Tomatoes

Prep Time: 10 minutes; Cooking Time: 4 hours; Serving: 6
Ingredients:
- 1 jalapeno pepper, diced
- 4 garlic cloves, minced
- 1/2 teaspoon of oregano, dried
- 1/4 cup of olive oil
- 1/2 cup of parmesan, grated
- 1/4 cup of basil, diced
- 2 lb. cherry tomatoes, halved
- Salt and black pepper- to taste

Method:
1. Start by throwing all the Ingredients: into your Crockpot.
2. Cover its lid and cook for 4 hours on Low setting.
3. Once done, remove its lid and give it a stir.
4. Garnish as desired.
5. Serve warm.

Nutritional Information per Serving:
- Calories 231
- Total Fat 14.3 g
- Saturated Fat 3.9 g
- Cholesterol 349 mg
- Sodium 45 mg
- Protein 3.6 g

Beet and Goat Cheese

Prep Time: 10 minutes; Cooking Time: 3 hours; Serving: 4
Ingredients:
- 8 small beets, trimmed, peeled and halved
- 2 tablespoon of olive oil
- 4-ounce goat cheese, crumbled
- 1 tablespoon of balsamic vinegar
- 1 red onion, sliced
- 2 tablespoons of swerves
- 1-pint mixed cherry tomatoes, halved
- 2-ounce pecans
- Salt and black pepper- to taste

Method:
1. Start by throwing all the Ingredients: into your Crockpot except cheese.
2. Cover its lid and cook for 3 hours on Low setting.
3. Once done, remove its lid and give it a stir.
4. Garnish with goat cheese.
5. Serve warm.

Nutritional Information per Serving:
- Calories 355
- Total Fat 26.2 g
- Saturated Fat 7.4 g
- Cholesterol 98 mg
- Sodium 75 mg
- Protein 5.4 g

Eggplant and Zucchini Medley

Prep Time: 10 minutes; Cooking Time: 5 hours; Serving: 4

Ingredients:

- 1 eggplant, roughly cubed
- 3 zucchinis, roughly cubed
- 2 tablespoon of lemon juice
- 1 teaspoon of oregano, dried
- 3 tablespoon of olive oil
- 1 teaspoon of thyme, dried
- Salt and black pepper- to taste
- ½ cup of vegetable stock

Method:

1. Start by throwing all the Ingredients: into your Crockpot.
2. Cover its lid and cook for 5 hours on Low setting.
3. Once done, remove its lid and give it a stir.
4. Garnish as desired.
5. Serve warm.

Nutritional Information per Serving:

- Calories 288
- Total Fat 25.5 g
- Saturated Fat 7.4 g
- Cholesterol 66 mg
- Sodium 73 mg
- Protein 3.4 g

Okra Mix

Prep Time: 10 minutes; Cooking Time: 4 hours; Serving: 4

Ingredients:

- 1 lb. okra, trimmed
- 28-ounce canned tomatoes, diced
- 6 scallions, diced
- 2 tablespoon of olive oil
- 1 teaspoon of swerve
- ½ cup of vegetable stock
- 3 green bell peppers, diced
- Salt and black pepper- to taste

Method:

1. Start by throwing all the Ingredients: into your Crockpot.
2. Cover its lid and cook for 4 hours on Low setting.
3. Once done, remove its lid and give it a stir.
4. Garnish as desired.
5. Serve warm.

Nutritional Information per Serving:

- Calories 371
- Total Fat 14.5 g
- Saturated Fat 3.4 g
- Cholesterol 361 mg
- Sodium 66 mg
- Protein 5.1 g

Quinoa Stuffed Bell Peppers

Prep Time: 10 minutes; Cooking Time: 3 hours; Serving: 4

Ingredients:

- ¼ cup of vegetable stock
- 4 bell peppers, top off and seeded
- 1/2 cup of tomato juice
- 1/4 cup of yellow onion, diced
- 1/4 cup of green peppers, diced
- 2 cups of sugar-free tomato sauce
- 2 tablespoons of jarred jalapenos, diced
- 1/2 teaspoon of red pepper, crushed
- 1 cup of quinoa, boiled
- 1 teaspoon of chili powder
- 1/2 teaspoon of garlic powder

- 1 cup of tomatoes, diced
- Salt and black pepper- to taste
- 2 teaspoons of onion powder
- 1 teaspoon of cumin, ground

Method:
1. Start by throwing all the Ingredients: except the peppers and the stock.
2. Divide this mixture into the deseeded peppers.
3. Pour the stock into the Crockpot and place the stuffed peppers in it.
4. Cover its lid and cook for 3 hours on Low setting.
5. Once done, remove its lid and give it a stir.
6. Garnish as desired.
7. Serve warm.

Nutritional Information per Serving:
- Calories 412
- Total Fat 16.5 g
- Saturated Fat 2.4 g
- Cholesterol 76 mg
- Sodium 49 mg
- Protein 2.4 g

Artichokes with Anchovy Sauce

Prep Time: 10 minutes; Cooking Time: 2 hours; Serving: 3
Ingredients:
- 2 artichokes, trimmed
- 1 tablespoon of lemon juice
- 2 garlic cloves, minced
- a drizzle olive oil
- 3 anchovy fillets
- 1/4 cup of extra virgin olive oil
- 1/4 cup of coconut oil
- 3 garlic cloves

Method:
1. Start by throwing all the Ingredients: into your Crockpot.
2. Cover its lid and cook for 2 hours on Low setting.
3. Once done, remove its lid and give it a stir.
4. Garnish as desired.
5. Serve warm.

Nutritional Information per Serving:
- Calories 422
- Total Fat 23.5 g
- Saturated Fat 12.4 g
- Cholesterol 159 mg
- Sodium 43 mg
- Protein 5.8 g

Creamy Parmesan Green Beans

Prep Time: 10 minutes; Cooking Time: 2 hours; Serving: 4
Ingredients:
- 2 lb. green beans
- 1/2 cup of heavy cream
- 1 cup of mozzarella, shredded
- 2/3 cup of parmesan, grated
- 2 teaspoon of lemon zest, grated
- Salt and black pepper- to taste
- A pinch red pepper flake

Method:
1. Start by throwing all the Ingredients: into your Crockpot.
2. Cover its lid and cook for 2 hours on Low setting.
3. Once done, remove its lid and give it a stir.
4. Garnish as desired.
5. Serve warm.

Nutritional Information per Serving:

- Calories 331
- Total Fat 16.2 g
- Saturated Fat 8.4 g
- Cholesterol 47 mg
- Sodium 63 mg
- Protein 3.4 g

Green Beans and Zucchini Medley

Prep Time: 10 minutes; Cooking Time: 4 hours; Serving: 2
Ingredients:
- 2 lb. green beans
- 6 bacon strips, cooked and diced
- 6 zucchinis, halved
- Salt and black pepper- to taste
- a drizzle olive oil
- ½ cup of vegetable stock

Method:
1. Start by throwing all the Ingredients: into your Crockpot.
2. Cover its lid and cook for 4 hours on Low setting.
3. Once done, remove its lid and give it a stir.
4. Garnish as desired.
5. Serve warm.

Nutritional Information per Serving:
- Calories 311
- Total Fat 0.5 g
- Saturated Fat 2.4 g
- Cholesterol 69 mg
- Sodium 58 mg
- Protein 1.4 g

Vegetable Mix

Prep Time: 10 minutes; Cooking Time: 3 hours; Serving: 3
Ingredients:
- 2 bell peppers, cut in large slices
- 2 large carrots, peeled and diced
- 3 small zucchinis, cut in thick slices
- 1/2 cup of peeled garlic cloves
- Salt to taste
- Black pepper to taste
- 2 tablespoons of olive oil

Method:
1. Start by throwing all the Ingredients: into your Crockpot.
2. Cover its lid and cook for 3 hours on Low setting.
3. Once done, remove its lid and give it a stir.
4. Garnish as desired.
5. Serve warm.

Nutritional Information per Serving:
- Calories 412
- Total Fat 16.5 g
- Saturated Fat 2.4 g
- Cholesterol 76 mg
- Sodium 49 mg
- Protein 2.4 g

Saucy Brussels Sprouts

Prep Time: 10 minutes; Cooking Time: 4 hours; Serving: 4
Ingredients:
- 1 lb. brussels sprouts, trimmed
- 2 tablespoons of dill, a diced
- 1 tablespoon of mustard
- 1/2 cup of bacon, cooked and diced
- 1 tablespoon of butter, melted
- Salt and black pepper- to taste
- ½ cup of vegetable stock

Method:
1. Start by throwing all the Ingredients: into your Crockpot.
2. Cover its lid and cook for 4 hours on Low setting.
3. Once done, remove its lid and give it a stir.
4. Garnish as desired.
5. Serve warm.

Nutritional Information per Serving:
- Calories 231
- Total Fat 14.3 g
- Saturated Fat 3.9 g
- Cholesterol 349 mg
- Sodium 45 mg
- Protein 3.6 g

Butter, Cheese Brussels Sprouts

Prep Time: 10 minutes; Cooking Time: 3 hours; Serving: 4
Ingredients:
- 1 lb. brussels sprouts, washed
- 3 tablespoons of parmesan, grated
- 1 lemon, juiced
- 2 tablespoons of butter, melted
- Salt and black pepper- to taste

Method:
1. Start by throwing all the Ingredients: into your Crockpot.
2. Cover its lid and cook for 3 hours on Low setting.
3. Once done, remove its lid and give it a stir.
4. Garnish as desired.
5. Serve warm.

Nutritional Information per Serving:
- Calories 229
- Total Fat 0.5 g
- Saturated Fat 2.4 g
- Cholesterol 69 mg
- Sodium 58 mg
- Protein 1.4 g

Mushroom Filled Poblano

Prep Time: 10 minutes; Cooking Time: 4 hours; Serving: 5
Ingredients:
- 10 poblano peppers, tops cut off and deseeded
- 2 teaspoons of garlic, minced
- 8-ounce mushrooms, diced
- 1/2 cup of cilantro, diced
- 1 white onion, diced
- 1 tablespoon of olive oil
- Salt and black pepper- to taste
- ¼ cup of vegetable stock

Method:
1. Start by throwing all the Ingredients: except the peppers and the stock.
2. Divide this mixture into the deseeded peppers.
3. Pour the stock into the Crockpot and place the stuffed peppers in it.
4. Cover its lid and cook for 4 hours on Low setting.
5. Once done, remove its lid and give it a stir.
6. Garnish as desired.
7. Serve warm.

Nutritional Information per Serving:
- Calories 287
- Total Fat 18.4 g
- Saturated Fat 2.8 g
- Cholesterol 59 mg

- Sodium 176 mg
- Protein 1.3 g

Mushroom Stuffed Tomatoes

Prep Time: 10 minutes; Cooking Time: 4 hours; Serving: 4
Ingredients:
- 4 tomatoes, tops cut off and pulp scooped and diced
- 1 yellow onion, diced
- 1/2 cup of mushrooms, diced
- 1 tablespoon of panko crumbs
- 1 tablespoon of butter, melted
- 1/4 teaspoon of caraway seeds
- 1 tablespoon of parsley, chopped
- 2 tablespoons of celery, diced
- 1 cup of cottage cheese
- Salt and black pepper- to taste
- ¼ cup of vegetable stock

Method:
1. Start by throwing all the Ingredients: except the tomatoes and the stock.
2. Divide this mixture into the cored tomatoes.
3. Pour the stock into the Crockpot and place the stuffed tomatoes in it.
4. Cover its lid and cook for 4 hours on Low setting.
5. Once done, remove its lid and give it a stir.
6. Garnish as desired.
7. Serve warm.

Nutritional Information per Serving:
- Calories 229
- Total Fat 0.5 g
- Saturated Fat 2.4 g
- Cholesterol 69 mg
- Sodium 58 mg
- Protein 1.4 g

Spinach Filled Portobello Cups

Prep Time: 10 minutes; Cooking Time: 3 hours; Serving: 4
Ingredients:
- 4 portobello mushrooms, stems removed and diced
- 10 basil leaves
- 1 tablespoon of parsley
- 1/4 cup of olive oil
- 8 cherry tomatoes, halved
- 1 cup of baby spinach
- 3 garlic cloves, diced
- 1 cup of almonds, roughly diced
- ½ cup of vegetable stock
- Salt and black pepper- to taste

Method:
1. Start by throwing all the Ingredients: except the mushrooms and the stock.
2. Divide this mixture into the mushroom caps.
3. Pour the stock into the Crockpot and place the stuffed mushrooms in it.
4. Cover its lid and cook for 3 hours on Low setting.
5. Once done, remove its lid and give it a stir.
6. Garnish as desired.
7. Serve warm.

Nutritional Information per Serving:
- Calories 231
- Total Fat 14.3 g
- Saturated Fat 3.9 g
- Cholesterol 349 mg
- Sodium 45 mg
- Protein 3.6 g

Ginger Broccoli Stew

Prep Time: 10 minutes; Cooking Time: 3 hours; Serving: 4

Ingredients:

- 28-ounce canned tomatoes, pureed
- A pinch red pepper, crushed
- 1 small ginger piece, diced
- 1 garlic clove, minced
- 1 broccoli head, florets separated
- 2 teaspoon of coriander seeds
- 1 tablespoon of olive oil
- 1 yellow onion, diced
- Salt and black pepper- to taste

Method:

1. Start by throwing all the Ingredients: into your Crockpot.
2. Cover its lid and cook for 3 hours on Low setting.
3. Once done, remove its lid and give it a stir.
4. Garnish as desired.
5. Serve warm.

Nutritional Information per Serving:

- Calories 412
- Total Fat 16.5 g
- Saturated Fat 2.4 g
- Cholesterol 76 mg
- Sodium 49 mg
- Protein 2.4 g

Seasoned eggplant

Prep Time: 10 minutes; Cooking Time: 2 hours; Serving: 4

Ingredients:

- 1 tablespoon of coriander seeds
- 1/2 teaspoon of turmeric powder
- 1/2 teaspoon of red chili powder
- 1 teaspoon of pomegranate powder
- 1 tablespoon of pickled mango, diced
- 1 tablespoon of cumin seeds
- 2 teaspoons of fenugreeks, dried
- 5 eggplants, peeled and cubed
- Salt and black pepper- to taste
- 2 tablespoon of olive oil

Method:

1. Start by throwing all the Ingredients: into your Crockpot.
2. Cover its lid and cook for 5 hours on Low setting.
3. Once done, remove its lid and give it a stir.
4. Garnish as desired.
5. Serve warm.

Nutritional Information per Serving:

- Calories 311
- Total Fat 0.5 g
- Saturated Fat 2.4 g
- Cholesterol 69 mg
- Sodium 58 mg
- Protein 1.4 g

Mayo Artichokes Hearts

Prep Time: 10 minutes; Cooking Time: 4 hours; Serving: 4

Ingredients:

- 14-ounce canned artichoke hearts
- 8-ounce cream cheese
- 16-ounce parmesan cheese, grated
- 10-ounce spinach
- 1/2 cup of chicken stock
- 1/2 cup of mayonnaise
- 8-ounce mozzarella, shredded
- 1/2 cup of sour cream

- 3 garlic cloves, minced
- 1 teaspoon of onion powder

Method:
1. Start by throwing all the Ingredients: into your Crockpot.
2. Cover its lid and cook for 4 hours on Low setting.
3. Once done, remove its lid and give it a stir.
4. Garnish as desired.
5. Serve warm.

Nutritional Information per Serving:
- Calories 412
- Total Fat 16.5 g
- Saturated Fat 2.4 g
- Cholesterol 76 mg
- Sodium 49 mg
- Protein 2.4 g

Balsamic Collard Greens

Prep Time: 10 minutes; Cooking Time: 2 hours; Serving: 2
Ingredients:
- 1 bunch collard greens, trimmed
- 2 tablespoon of olive oil
- 1 teaspoon of swerve
- 1 yellow onion, diced
- 3 garlic cloves, minced
- 2 tablespoon of tomato puree
- 1 tablespoon of balsamic vinegar
- Salt and black pepper- to taste

Method:
1. Start by throwing all the Ingredients: into your Crockpot.
2. Cover its lid and cook for 2 hours on Low setting.
3. Once done, remove its lid and give it a stir.
4. Garnish as desired.
5. Serve warm.

Nutritional Information per Serving:
- Calories 371
- Total Fat 14.5 g
- Saturated Fat 3.4 g
- Cholesterol 361 mg
- Sodium 66 mg
- Protein 5.1 g

Cauliflower with Eggplants

Prep Time: 10 minutes; Cooking Time: 5 hours; Serving: 4
Ingredients:
- 2 small eggplants, diced
- 1/2 cup of cauliflower, diced
- 1 teaspoon of oregano, diced
- 1/2 cup of parsley, chopped
- Salt and black pepper- to taste
- 10 tablespoons of olive oil
- 2 ½ lb. tomatoes, cut into halves and grated
- 1 green bell pepper, diced
- 1 yellow onion, diced
- 1 tablespoon of garlic, minced
- 3-ounce feta cheese, crumbled
- ½ cup of vegetable stock

Method:
1. Start by throwing all the Ingredients: into your Crockpot except cheese.
2. Cover its lid and cook for 5 hours on Low setting.
3. Once done, remove its lid and give it a stir.
4. Garnish with feta cheese.
5. Serve warm.

Nutritional Information per Serving:

- Calories 288
- Total Fat 25.5 g
- Saturated Fat 7.4 g
- Cholesterol 66 mg
- Sodium 73 mg
- Protein 3.4 g

Carrot & Cabbage Medley

Prep Time: 10 minutes; Cooking Time: 2 hours; Serving: 4

Ingredients:

- 1/4 cup of vegetable stock
- 1 carrot, grated
- 1/4 cup of apple cider vinegar
- 1/2 teaspoon of cayenne pepper
- 1 cabbage, cut into 8 wedges
- 1 tablespoon of sesame seed oil
- 1 teaspoon of red pepper flakes, crushed

Method:

1. Start by throwing all the Ingredients: into your Crockpot.
2. Cover its lid and cook for 2 hours on Low setting.
3. Once done, remove its lid and give it a stir.
4. Garnish as desired.
5. Serve warm.

Nutritional Information per Serving:

- Calories 355
- Total Fat 26.2 g
- Saturated Fat 7.4 g
- Cholesterol 98 mg
- Sodium 75 mg
- Protein 5.4 g

Tabasco Eggplant Hash

Prep Time: 10 minutes; Cooking Time: 4 hours; Serving: 4

Ingredients:

- 1 eggplant, roughly diced
- 1/2 lb. cherry tomatoes, halved
- 1/4 cup of mint, diced
- 1/4 cup of basil, diced
- 1/2 cup of olive oil
- 1 teaspoon of tabasco sauce
- Salt and black pepper- to taste
- ¼ cup of vegetable stock

Method:

1. Start by throwing all the Ingredients: into your Crockpot.
2. Cover its lid and cook for 4 hours on Low setting.
3. Once done, remove its lid and give it a stir.
4. Garnish as desired.
5. Serve warm.

Nutritional Information per Serving:

- Calories 311
- Total Fat 0.5 g
- Saturated Fat 2.4 g
- Cholesterol 69 mg
- Sodium 58 mg
- Protein 1.4 g

Cider Dipped Greens with Bacon

Prep Time: 10 minutes; Cooking Time: 2 hours; Serving: 2

Ingredients:

- 1 lb. kale
- 2 tablespoon of chicken stock
- 3 bacon strips, diced
- 1/4 cup of cherry tomatoes, halved
- 1 tablespoon of apple cider vinegar
- Salt and black pepper- to taste

Method:

1. Start by throwing all the Ingredients: into your Crockpot.
2. Cover its lid and cook for 2 hours on Low setting.
3. Once done, remove its lid and give it a stir.
4. Garnish as desired.
5. Serve warm.

Nutritional Information per Serving:
- Calories 421
- Total Fat 19.5 g
- Saturated Fat 2.4 g
- Cholesterol 69 mg
- Sodium 58 mg
- Protein 1.4 g

Crispy Zucchini Wedges

Prep Time: 10 minutes; Cooking Time: 2 hours; Serving: 2
Ingredients:
- 2 medium zucchinis, cut into wedges
- 1 yellow onion, diced
- 1 bay leaf
- 1 small carrot, roughly chopped
- 1 ½ tablespoon of almond flour
- 1/2 cup of chicken stock
- 2 tablespoons of Greek yogurt
- 2 tablespoons of butter, melted
- Salt and black pepper- to taste

Method:
1. Start by throwing all the Ingredients: into your Crockpot and mix well.
2. Cover its lid and cook for 5 hours on Low setting.
3. Once done, remove its lid and give it a stir.
4. Garnish as desired.
5. Serve warm.

Nutritional Information per Serving:
- Calories 355
- Total Fat 4.2 g
- Saturated Fat 21.4 g
- Cholesterol 53 mg
- Sodium 67 mg
- Protein 6.1 g

Mushroom Zoodles with Tomato Sauce

Prep Time: 10 minutes; Cooking Time: 2 hours; Serving: 4
Ingredients:
- 2 tablespoon of olive oil
- 3 zucchinis, cut with a spiralizer
- 1/4 cup of sun-dried tomatoes, diced
- 1 teaspoon of garlic, minced
- 1/2 cup of cherry tomatoes, halved
- 16-ounce mushrooms, sliced
- 2 cups of tomatoes sauce
- 2 cups of spinach, torn
- Salt and black pepper- to taste
- basil, diced a handful

Method:
1. Start by throwing all the Ingredients: into your Crockpot except zucchini noodles.
2. Cover its lid and cook for 2 hours on Low setting.
3. Meanwhile, place the noodles in a colander and drizzle salt on top.
4. Leave it until the mushroom sauce is ready.
5. Once the sauce is done, remove its lid and give it a stir.
6. Serve warm on top of strained zucchini.
7. Enjoy.

Nutritional Information per Serving:

- Calories 269
- Total Fat 4.6 g
- Saturated Fat 4.4 g
- Cholesterol 78 mg
- Sodium 75 mg
- Protein 7.1 g

Broccoli Mushroom Hash

Prep Time: 10 minutes; Cooking Time: 3 hours; Serving: 2

Ingredients:

- 10-ounce mushrooms, halved
- 1 broccoli head, florets separated
- 1 yellow onion, diced
- 1 tablespoon of olive oil
- 1 garlic clove, minced
- 1 teaspoon of basil, dried
- 1 tablespoon of balsamic vinegar
- 1 avocado, peeled and pitted
- A pinch red pepper flake
- salt and black pepper –to taste
- ¼ cup of vegetable stock

Method:

1. Start by throwing all the Ingredients: into your Crockpot except avocado.
2. Cover its lid and cook for 3 hours on Low setting.
3. Once done, remove its lid and give it a stir.
4. Garnish with avocado.
5. Serve warm.

Nutritional Information per Serving:

- Calories 431
- Total Fat 27.6 g
- Saturated Fat 2.4 g
- Cholesterol 44 mg
- Sodium 65 mg
- Protein 5.4 g

Wine Glazed Mushrooms

Prep Time: 10 minutes; Cooking Time: 2 hours; Serving: 2

Ingredients:

- 2 tablespoons of olive oil
- 6 garlic cloves, minced
- 2 lbs. fresh mushrooms, sliced
- 1/3 cup of balsamic vinegar
- 1/3 cup of white wine
- Salt to taste
- Black pepper to taste

Method:

1. Start by throwing all the Ingredients: into your Crockpot.
2. Cover its lid and cook for 3 hours on Low setting.
3. Once done, remove its lid and give it a stir.
4. Garnish as desired.
5. Serve warm.

Nutritional Information per Serving:

- Calories 344
- Total Fat 16.3 g
- Saturated Fat 3.4 g
- Cholesterol 54 mg
- Sodium 77 mg
- Protein 6.2 g

Vegetable Salad

Prep Time: 10 minutes; Cooking Time: 1 hour; Serving: 2

Ingredients:

- ½ bunch kale, chopped
- ½ carrot, peeled and shredded
- 1 cup of water
- ¼ teaspoon of salt

- ½ cup of cabbage, sliced
- ½ cup of green onions, diced
- ½ cup of red onions, sliced
- 1 tablespoon of brown swerve
- 2 tablespoons, balsamic vinegar
- 1 tablespoon of vegetable oil
- 1 tablespoon of ginger, grated
- 1 tablespoon of sunflower seeds
- 1 garlic clove, minced
- Black pepper, to taste

Method:
1. Start by adding throwing all the Ingredients: into your Crockpot.
2. Cover its lid and cook for 1 hour on Low setting.
3. Once done, remove its lid and give it a stir.
4. Garnish as desired.
5. Serve fresh.

Nutritional Information per Serving:
- Calories 254
- Total Fat 23.5 g
- Saturate Fat 2.4 g
- Cholesterol 69 mg
- Sodium 58 mg
- Protein 7.9 g

Nutritious Bean Bowl

Prep Time: 10 minutes; Cooking Time: 9 hours; Serving: 2
Ingredients:
- ½ tablespoon of olive oil
- ½ onion, diced
- ½ tablespoon of fresh ginger, minced
- ½ tablespoon of garlic, minced
- ½ teaspoons of curry powder
- ½ teaspoon of cumin, ground
- ½ teaspoon of ground coriander
- 1 medium tomato, diced
- ½ cup of edamame beans
- ½ cup of water
- Pinch of salt
- Black pepper, to taste
- 1 tablespoon of fresh parsley, chopped

Method:
1. Start by throwing all the Ingredients: into your Crockpot.
2. Cover its lid and cook for 3 hours on Low setting.
3. Once done, remove its lid and give it a stir.
4. Garnish as desired.
5. Serve warm.

Nutritional Information per Serving:
- Calories 265
- Total Fat 15.5 g
- Saturated Fat 12.4 g
- Cholesterol 154 mg
- Sodium 57 mg
- Protein 5.4 g

Crockpot Eggplant

Prep Time: 10 minutes; Cooking Time: 2 hours; Serving: 2
Ingredients:
- 1 cup of water
- 2 medium eggplants, peeled
- Salt and black pepper-to taste
- 1 tablespoon of olive oil
- Parsley to garnish
- Pomegranate seeds, to garnish

Method:
1. Start by throwing all the Ingredients: into your Crockpot.
2. Cover its lid and cook for 5 hours on Low setting.

3. Once done, remove its lid and give it a stir.
4. Garnish with parsley and pomegranate seed.
5. Serve warm.

Nutritional Information per Serving:
- Calories 359
- Total Fat 34 g
- Saturated Fat 10.3 g
- Cholesterol 112 mg
- Sodium 92 mg
- Protein 7.5 g

Mushrooms Squash

Prep Time: 10 minutes; Cooking Time: 2 hours; Serving: 4
Ingredients:
- 1 tablespoon of olive oil
- ½ cup of onion, diced
- 3 garlic cloves, minced
- 1 red bell pepper, diced
- 2 cups of zucchini squash, peeled and diced
- 1 ½ cups of cauliflower rice
- 3 ½ cup of vegetable broth
- ½ cup of dry white wine
- 8 oz. white mushrooms, sliced
- 1 teaspoon of salt
- 1 teaspoon of black pepper
- ¼ teaspoon of oregano
- 1 ½ a tablespoon of nutritional yeast

Method:
1. Start by throwing all the Ingredients: into your Crockpot.
2. Cover its lid and cook for 3 hours on Low setting.
3. Once done, remove its lid and give it a stir.
4. Garnish as desired.
5. Serve warm.

Nutritional Information per Serving:
- Calories 295
- Total Fat 33.1 g
- Saturated Fat 2.4 g
- Cholesterol 69 mg
- Sodium 58 mg
- Protein 1.4 g

Chapter 11: Side Dishes

Greens Mix

Prep Time: 10 minutes; Cooking Time: 8 hours; Servings: 6

Ingredients:

- 2 cups of spinach, chopped
- 2 cups of kale, chopped
- 1 lb. ham shanks, sliced
- 4 pickled jalapeno peppers, diced
- 1/2 teaspoon of baking soda
- 1 teaspoon of olive oil
- black pepper to taste
- garlic powder to taste

Method:

1. Start by throwing all the Ingredients: into the Crockpot.
2. Cover its lid and cook for 8 hours on Low setting.
3. Once done, remove its lid of the crockpot carefully.
4. Mix well and garnish as desired.
5. Serve warm.

Nutritional Information per Serving:

- Calories 77.8
- Total Fat 7.13 g
- Saturated Fat 4.5 g
- Cholesterol 15 mg
- Sodium 15 mg
- Potassium 33 mg
- Protein 2.3 g

Mayo Salad

Prep Time: 10 minutes; Cooking Time: 5 hours; Servings: 8

Ingredients:

- 1 cup of water
- 3 media eggplant, peeled and cubed
- 3 large eggs, boiled, peeled and cubed
- 1/8 cup of diced onion
- ½ cup of mayonnaise
- 1 tablespoon of finely fresh parsley, chopped
- ½ tablespoon of dill pickle juice
- ½ tablespoon of mustard
- Salt and black pepper-to taste

Method:

1. Start by putting eggplant and water into the Crockpot.
2. Cover its lid and cook for 5 hours on Low setting.
3. Once done, remove its lid of the crockpot carefully.
4. Toss the slow-cooked eggplant with the remaining Ingredients: in a salad bowl.
5. Mix well and garnish as desired.
6. Serve warm.

Nutritional Information per Serving:

- Calories 114
- Total Fat 9.6 g
- Saturated Fat 4.5 g
- Cholesterol 10 mg
- Sodium 155 mg
- Potassium 93 mg
- Protein 3.5 g

Seasoned Carrots

Prep Time: 10 minutes; Cooking Time: 4 hours; Servings: 8

Ingredients:

- ½ cup of avocado oil
- 3 lbs. carrots, sliced

- 1 teaspoon of onion powder
- 2 teaspoons of garlic powder
- 2 teaspoons of salt
- ½ teaspoon of paprika
- ½ teaspoon of black pepper
- 2 cups of chicken broth

Method:
1. Start by throwing all the Ingredients: into the Crockpot.
2. Cover its lid and cook for 4 hours on Low setting.
3. Once done, remove its lid of the crockpot carefully.
4. Mix well and garnish as desired.
5. Serve warm.

Nutritional Information per Serving:
- Calories 252
- Total Fat 17.3 g
- Saturated Fat 11.5 g
- Cholesterol 141 mg
- Sodium 153 mg
- Potassium 73 mg
- Protein 5.2 g

Quinoa Brussels Sprout Salad

Prep Time: 10 minutes; Cooking Time: 6 hours; Servings: 4
Ingredients:
- ½ cup of cabbage, diced
- ½ cup of quinoa, rinsed
- ½ carrot, peeled and shredded
- ¾ cup of water
- ¼ teaspoon of salt
- 1 cup of Brussels sprout, diced
- ½ cup of red onions, sliced
- 1 tablespoon of brown swerve
- 2 tablespoons, balsamic vinegar
- 1 tablespoon of vegetable oil
- 1 tablespoon of sunflower seeds
- 1 teaspoon of ginger, grated
- 1 garlic clove, minced
- Black pepper, to taste

Method:
1. Start by putting quinoa and water into the Crockpot.
2. Cover its lid and cook for 6 hours on Low setting.
3. Once done, remove its lid of the crockpot carefully.
4. Strain the cooked quinoa and add to a salad bowl.
5. Toss in all other Ingredients: and give it a stir.
6. Mix well and garnish as desired.
7. Serve warm.

Nutritional Information per Serving:
- Calories 195
- Total Fat 14.3 g
- Saturated Fat 10.5 g
- Cholesterol 175 mg
- Sodium 125 mg
- Potassium 83 mg
- Protein 3.2 g

Saucy Beans

Prep Time: 10 minutes; Cooking Time: 2 hours; Servings: 4
Ingredients:
- 1 cup of green beans
- ½ cup of bacon, diced
- ¼ medium onion, diced
- ½ teaspoon of salt
- ½ teaspoon of pepper
- ½ teaspoon of dry mustard
- ½ tablespoon of Worcestershire sauce
- ½ tablespoon of balsamic vinegar
- 1 tablespoon of tomato paste

- 3 tablespoons of dark brown swerve
- ½ cup of chicken stock
- ½ cup of water

Method:
1. Start by throwing all the Ingredients: into the Crockpot.
2. Cover its lid and cook for 2 hours on Low setting.
3. Once done, remove its lid of the crockpot carefully.
4. Mix well and garnish as desired.
5. Serve warm.

Nutritional Information per Serving:
- Calories 151
- Total Fat 14.7 g
- Saturated Fat 1.5 g
- Cholesterol 13 mg
- Sodium 53 mg
- Potassium 131 mg
- Protein 0.8 g

Cucumber Quinoa Salad

Prep Time: 10 minutes; Cooking Time: 6 hours; Servings: 8
Ingredients:
- ½ cup of quinoa, rinsed
- ¾ cup of water
- ¼ teaspoon of salt
- ½ carrot, peeled and shredded
- ½ cucumber, diced
- ½ cup of frozen edamame, thawed
- 3 green onions, diced
- 1 cup of shredded red cabbage
- ½ tablespoon of soy sauce
- 1 tablespoon of lime juice
- 2 tablespoons of swerve
- 1 tablespoon of vegetable oil
- 1 tablespoon of freshly grated ginger
- 1 tablespoon of sesame oil
- pinch of red pepper flakes
- ½ cup of peanuts, diced

Method:
1. Start by putting quinoa and water into the Crockpot.
2. Cover its lid and cook for 6 hours on Low setting.
3. Once done, remove its lid of the crockpot carefully.
4. Strain the cooked quinoa and add to a salad bowl.
5. Toss in all other Ingredients: and give it a stir.
6. Mix well and garnish as desired.
7. Serve warm.

Nutritional Information per Serving:
- Calories 261
- Total Fat 27.1 g
- Saturated Fat 23.4 g
- Cholesterol 0 mg
- Sodium 10 mg
- Potassium 57 mg
- Protein 1.8 g

Zucchini Spaghetti

Servings: 16; Prep Time: 30 minutes
Ingredients:
- 2 lbs. zucchini, spiralized
- 2 cups of water
- Cilantro to serve

Method:
1. Start by throwing all the Ingredients: except cilantro into the Crockpot.

2. Cover its lid and cook for 2 hours on Low setting.
3. Once done, remove its lid of the crockpot carefully.
4. Garnish this spaghetti with cilantro.
5. Serve warm.

Nutritional Information per Serving:
- Calories 139
- Total Fat 4.6 g
- Saturated Fat 0.5 g
- Cholesterol 1.2 mg
- Sodium 83 mg
- Protein 3.8 g

BBQ Smokies

Prep Time: 10 minutes; Cooking Time: 2 hours; Servings: 6
Ingredients:
- 1 (18 oz.) bottle barbeque sauce
- 1 cup of sugar-free tomato sauce
- 1 tablespoon of Worcestershire sauce
- 1/3 cup of diced onion
- 2 (16 ounce) packages little wieners

Method:
1. Start by throwing all the Ingredients: into the Crockpot.
2. Cover its lid and cook for 2 hours on Low setting.
3. Once done, remove its lid of the crockpot carefully.
4. Mix well and garnish as desired.
5. Serve warm.

Nutritional Information per Serving:
- Calories 251
- Total Fat 24.5 g
- Saturated Fat 14.7 g
- Cholesterol 165 mg
- Sodium 142 mg
- Potassium 80 mg
- Protein 51.9 g

Marinated Mushrooms

Prep Time: 10 minutes; Cooking Time: 12 hours; Servings: 12
Ingredients:
- 4 cubes chicken bouillon
- 4 cubes beef bouillon
- 2 cups of boiling water
- 1 cup of dry red wine
- 1 teaspoon of dill weed
- 1 teaspoon of Worcestershire sauce
- 1 teaspoon of garlic powder
- 4 lbs. fresh mushrooms
- 1/2 cup of butter, or more as needed

Method:
1. Start by throwing all the Ingredients: into the Crockpot.
2. Cover its lid and cook for 12 hours on Low setting.
3. Once done, remove its lid of the crockpot carefully.
4. Mix well and garnish as desired.
5. Serve warm.

Nutritional Information per Serving:
- Calories 159
- Total Fat 34 g
- Saturated Fat 10.3 g
- Cholesterol 112 mg
- Sodium 92 mg
- Protein 7.5 g

Cowboy Mexican Dip

Prep Time: 10 minutes; Cooking Time: 2 hours; Servings: 24
Ingredients:

- 12 beef tamales, husked and mashed
- 1 (15 oz.) can chili
- 1 (14.5 oz.) can tomatoes and green chilis
- 1 (1 lb.) loaf processed cheese, cubed

Method:
1. Start by throwing all the Ingredients: into the Crockpot.
2. Cover its lid and cook for 2 hours on Low setting.
3. Once done, remove its lid of the crockpot carefully.
4. Mix well and garnish as desired.
5. Serve warm.

Nutritional Information per Serving:

- Calories 107
- Total Fat 29 g
- Saturated Fat 14g
- Cholesterol 111 mg
- Sodium 122 mg
- Potassium 78 mg
- Protein 6 g

Glazed Spiced Carrots

Prep Time: 10 minutes; Cooking Time: 8 hours; Servings: 6
Ingredients:

- 2 lbs. small carrots
- 1/2 cup of peach preserves
- 1/2 cup of butter, melted
- 1/4 cup of packed brown swerve
- 1 teaspoon of vanilla extract
- 1/2 teaspoon of cinnamon, ground
- 1/4 teaspoon of salt
- 1/8 teaspoon of ground nutmeg
- 2 tablespoons of xanthan gum
- 2 tablespoons of water
- Toasted diced pecans, optional

Method:
1. Start by throwing all the Ingredients: into the Crockpot.
2. Cover its lid and cook for 8 hours on Low setting.
3. Once done, remove its lid of the crockpot carefully.
4. Mix well and garnish as desired.
5. Serve warm.

Nutritional Information per Serving:

- Calories 220
- Total Fat 20.1 g
- Saturated Fat 7.4 g
- Cholesterol 132 mg
- Sodium 157 mg
- Protein 6.1 g

Garlic Green Beans with Gorgonzola

Prep Time: 10 minutes; Cooking Time: 4 hours; Servings: 6
Ingredients:

- 2 lbs. fresh green beans, halved
- 1 can (8 oz.) sliced chestnuts, drained
- 4 green onions, diced
- 5 bacon strips, cooked and crumbled, divided
- 1/3 cup of white wine

- 2 tablespoons of minced fresh thyme
- 4 garlic cloves, minced
- 1 1/2 teaspoons of seasoned salt
- 1 cup of (8 oz.) sour cream
- 3/4 cup of crumbled Gorgonzola cheese

Method:
1. Start by throwing all the Ingredients: into the Crockpot except cheese and bacon.
2. Cover its lid and cook for 4 hours on Low setting.
3. Once done, remove its lid of the crockpot carefully.
4. Mix well and garnish with bacon and cheese.
5. Serve warm.

Nutritional Information per Serving:
- Calories 331
- Total Fat 32.9 g
- Saturated Fat 6.1 g
- Cholesterol 10 mg
- Sodium 18 mg
- Protein 4.4 g

Green Beans

Prep Time: 10 minutes; Cooking Time: 3 hours; Servings: 16
Ingredients:
- 16 cups of frozen French-style green beans, thawed
- 1/2 cup of butter, melted
- 1/2 cup of packed brown swerve
- 1 1/2 teaspoons of garlic salt
- 3/4 teaspoon of soy sauce

Method:
1. Start by throwing all the Ingredients: into the Crockpot.
2. Cover its lid and cook for 3 hours on Low setting.
3. Once done, remove its lid of the crockpot carefully.
4. Mix well and garnish as desired.
5. Serve warm.

Nutritional Information per Serving:
- Calories 237
- Total Fat 22 g
- Saturated Fat 9 g
- Cholesterol 35 mg
- Sodium 118 mg
- Protein 5 g

Party Sausages

Prep Time: 10 minutes; Cooking Time: 2 hours; Servings: 16
Ingredients:
- 2 lbs. smoked sausage links, sliced diagonally
- 1 bottle (8 oz.) Catalina salad dressing
- 1 bottle (8 oz.) Russian salad dressing
- 1/2 cup of packed brown swerve
- 1/2 cup of apple cider
- Sliced green onions, optional

Method:
1. Start by throwing all the Ingredients: into the Crockpot.
2. Cover its lid and cook for 2 hours on Low setting.
3. Once done, remove its lid of the crockpot carefully.
4. Mix well and garnish as desired.
5. Serve warm.

Nutritional Information per Serving:

- Calories 190
- Total Fat 17.25 g
- Saturated Fat 7.1 g
- Cholesterol 20 mg
- Sodium 28 mg
- Protein 23 g

Collard Greens

Prep Time: 10 minutes; Cooking Time: 10 hours; Servings: 6
Ingredients:
- 4 bunches collard greens, trimmed and diced
- 1 lb. ham shanks
- 4 pickled jalapeno peppers, diced
- 1/2 teaspoon of baking soda
- 1 teaspoon of olive oil
- black pepper to taste
- garlic powder to taste
- ¼ cup of vegetable stock

Method:
1. Start by throwing all the Ingredients: into the Crockpot.
2. Cover its lid and cook for 10 hours on Low setting.
3. Once done, remove its lid of the crockpot carefully.
4. Mix well and garnish as desired.
5. Serve warm.

Nutritional Information per Serving:
- Calories 121
- Total Fat 12.9 g
- Saturated Fat 5.1 g
- Cholesterol 17 mg
- Sugar 1.8 g
- Fiber 0.4 g
- Sodium 28 mg
- Protein 5.4 g

Garlic Chili Sprouts

Prep Time: 10 minutes; Cooking Time: 4 hours; Servings: 4
Ingredients:
- 1 lb. brussels sprouts halved
- 1 tablespoon of olive oil
- salt and black pepper, to taste
- ½ teaspoon of sesame oil
- 1 garlic clove, minced
- ¼ cup of coconut aminos
- ¼ cup of of water
- 1 teaspoon of apple cider vinegar
- ½ tablespoon of stevia
- 1 teaspoon of garlic chili sauce
- ½ pinch red pepper flakes

Method:
1. Start by throwing all the Ingredients: into the Crockpot.
2. Cover its lid and cook for 4 hours on Low setting.
3. Once done, remove its lid of the crockpot carefully.
4. Mix well and garnish as desired.
5. Serve warm.

Nutritional Information per Serving:
- Calories 236
- Total Fat 21.5 g
- Saturated Fat 15.2 g
- Cholesterol 54 mg
- Sugar 1.4 g
- Fiber 3.8 g
- Sodium 21 mg
- Protein 4.3 g

Garlicky Cauliflower Florets

Prep Time: 10 minutes; Cooking Time: 6 hours; Servings: 6

Ingredients:

- 3 tablespoon of Olive oil
- Juice of 1 lime
- 2 tablespoon of sweet chili sauce
- 1 pinch salt and black pepper
- 1 teaspoon of Cilantro, diced
- 3 Garlic cloves, minced
- 1 Cauliflower head, florets separated

Method:

1. Start by throwing all the Ingredients: into the Crockpot.
2. Cover its lid and cook for 6 hours on Low setting.
3. Once done, remove its lid of the crockpot carefully.
4. Mix well and garnish as desired.
5. Serve warm.

Nutritional Information per Serving:

- Calories 167
- Total Fat 35.1 g
- Saturated Fat 10.1 g
- Cholesterol 12 mg
- Sugar 3.8 g
- Fiber 2.1 g
- Sodium 48 mg
- Protein 6.3 g

Broccoli Cheese Florets

Prep Time: 10 minutes; Cooking Time: 4 hours; Servings: 4

Ingredients:

- 4 tablespoon of olive oil
- 2 broccoli heads, florets separated
- 4 garlic cloves, minced
- 1 cup of mozzarella, shredded
- ½ cup of parmesan, grated
- 1 cup of coconut cream
- 2 tablespoons of parsley, chopped

Method:

1. Start by throwing all the Ingredients: into the Crockpot.
2. Cover its lid and cook for 4 hours on Low setting.
3. Once done, remove its lid of the crockpot carefully.
4. Mix well and garnish as desired.
5. Serve warm.

Nutritional Information per Serving:

- Calories 175
- Total Fat 16 g
- Saturated Fat 2.1 g
- Cholesterol 0 mg
- Sugar 1.8 g
- Fiber 0.4 g
- Sodium 8 mg
- Protein 9 g

Brussels Sprouts

Prep Time: 10 minutes; Cooking Time: 4 hours; Servings: 6

Ingredients:

- 1 tablespoon of parsley, chopped
- 1 pinch salt and black pepper
- 2 teaspoons of sweet paprika
- 1 lb. Brussels sprouts halved
- 1 yellow onion, diced
- 2 tablespoons of stevia
- 7 bacon strips, diced
- 2 tablespoon of olive oil

Method:

1. Start by throwing all the Ingredients: into the Crockpot.
2. Cover its lid and cook for 4 hours on Low setting.
3. Once done, remove its lid of the crockpot carefully.

4. Mix well and garnish as desired.
5. Serve warm.

Nutritional Information per Serving:
- Calories 285
- Total Fat 27.3 g
- Saturated Fat 14.5 g
- Cholesterol 175 mg
- Sugar 0.4 g
- Fiber 0.9 g
- Sodium 165 mg
- Protein 7.2 g

Artichoke Spinach

Prep Time: 10 minutes; Cooking Time: 4 hours; Servings: 4

Ingredients:
- 7.5 oz. canned artichoke hearts, drained
- salt and black pepper to taste
- 1 cup of baby spinach
- 1 tablespoon of parsley, chopped
- ½ cup of mozzarella, shredded
- Juice of a ½ lemon
- 2/3 cup of coconut milk
- ¼ cup of chicken stock
- garlic clove, minced
- 1 tablespoon of butter, melted
- 1/2 pinch red pepper flakes

Method:
1. Start by throwing all the Ingredients: into the Crockpot.
2. Cover its lid and cook for 4 hours on Low setting.
3. Once done, remove its lid of the crockpot carefully.
4. Mix well and garnish as desired.
5. Serve warm.

Nutritional Information per Serving:
- Calories 215
- Total Fat 20 g
- Saturated Fat 7 g
- Cholesterol 38 mg
- Sugar 1 g
- Fiber 6 g
- Sodium 12 mg
- Protein 5 g

Cranberry Brussels Sprouts Mix

Prep Time: 10 minutes; Cooking Time: 3 hours; Servings: 8

Ingredients:
- 2 lbs. brussels sprouts halved
- 4 tablespoon of olive oil
- 2 teaspoons of rosemary, diced
- 2 tablespoons of balsamic vinegar
- 2 teaspoons of thyme, diced
- 1 cup of cranberries, dried

Method:
1. Start by throwing all the Ingredients: into the Crockpot.
2. Cover its lid and cook for 3 hours on Low setting.
3. Once done, remove its lid of the crockpot carefully.
4. Mix well and garnish as desired.
5. Serve warm.

Nutritional Information per Serving:
- Calories 198
- Total Fat 19.2 g
- Saturated Fat 11.5 g
- Cholesterol 123 mg
- Sugar 3.3 g
- Fiber 0.3 g
- Sodium 142 mg
- Protein 3.4 g

Cilantro Cauliflower Rice

Prep Time: 10 minutes; Cooking Time: 3 hours; Servings: 2
Ingredients:

- ½ tablespoon of butter, melted
- Juice of 1 lime
- salt and black pepper to taste
- ½ cup of cauliflower rice
- 2/3 cup of vegetable broth
- ½ tablespoon of cilantro, diced

Method:
1. Start by throwing all the Ingredients: into the Crockpot.
2. Cover its lid and cook for 2 3 hours on Low setting.
3. Once done, remove its lid of the crockpot carefully.
4. Mix well and garnish as desired.
5. Serve warm.

Nutritional Information per Serving:

- Calories 288
- Total Fat 25.3 g
- Saturated Fat 6.7 g
- Cholesterol 23 mg
- Sugar 0.1 g
- Fiber 3.8 g
- Sodium 74 mg
- Protein 7.6 g

Coconut Cauliflower Mash

Prep Time: 10 minutes; Cooking Time: 4 hours; Servings: 4
Ingredients:

- 1 cauliflower head, florets separated
- 1/6 cup of coconut cream
- 1/6 cup of coconut milk
- ½ tablespoon of chives, diced
- Salt and black pepper- to taste

Method:
1. Start by throwing all the Ingredients: into the Crockpot.
2. Cover its lid and cook for 4 hours on Low setting.
3. Once done, remove its lid of the crockpot carefully.
4. Puree the slow-cooked cauliflower using an immersion blender.
5. Mix well and garnish as desired.
6. Serve warm.

Nutritional Information per Serving:

- Calories 192
- Total Fat 17.44 g
- Saturated Fat 11.5 g
- Cholesterol 125 mg
- Sugar 1.4 g
- Fiber 2.1 g
- Sodium 135 mg
- Protein 4.7 g

Chapter 12: Desserts

Chocolate Fudge

Prep Time: 15 minutes; Cooking Time: 2 hours; Servings: 12

Ingredients:
- 2 1/2 cups of sugar-free chocolate chips
- 1/3 cup of almond milk
- 1 teaspoon of pure vanilla extract
- a dash of salt
- 2 teaspoons of swerve

Method:
1. Start by throwing all the Ingredients: into the Crockpot.
2. Cover its lid and cook for 2 hours on Low setting.
3. Once done, remove its lid of the crockpot carefully.
4. Now pour this mixture into a casserole dish lined with parchment paper.
5. Refrigerate this fudge for 30 minutes until it is set.
6. Slice and serve.

Nutritional Information per Serving:
- Calories 236
- Total Fat 13.5 g
- Saturated Fat 4.2 g
- Cholesterol 541 mg
- Sodium 21 mg
- Sugar 1.4 g
- Fiber 3.8 g
- Protein 4.3 g

Super Fudgy Brownies

Prep Time: 15 minutes; Cooking Time: 4 hours; Servings: 8

Ingredients:
- 1 (5 oz.) package Bok Choy, boiled
- 2 tablespoons of water
- 1/2 teaspoon of salt
- 1 cup of almond flour
- 1/2 cup of cocoa powder
- 1/2 cup of swerve
- 1 teaspoon of baking powder
- 1/2 teaspoon of espresso powder
- 2 large eggs
- 1/3 cup of coconut oil, melted
- 1 teaspoon of vanilla extract
- 1/3 cup of sugar-free chocolate chips

Method:
1. Blend bok choy with all the wet Ingredients: in a blender.
2. Gradually add the dry Ingredients: and mix well.
3. Fold in chocolate chips then spread this mixture in the Crockpot.
4. Cover its lid and cook for 4 hours on Low setting.
5. Once done, remove its lid of the crockpot carefully.
6. Slice and serve.

Nutritional Information per Serving:
- Calories 167
- Total Fat 5.1 g
- Saturated Fat 1.1 g
- Cholesterol 121 mg
- Sodium 48 mg
- Sugar 1.8 g
- Fiber 2.1 g
- Protein 6.3 g

Granola

Prep Time: 15 minutes; Cooking Time: 2 hours; Servings: 6

Ingredients:

- 1/3 cup of coconut oil
- 1 teaspoon of vanilla extract
- 1/2 cup of raw almonds
- 1/2 cup of walnuts
- 1/2 cup of pecans
- 1/2 cup of hazelnuts
- 1 cup of sunflower seeds
- 1 cup of pumpkin seeds
- 1 cup of shredded coconut
- 1/2 cup of Swerve
- 1 teaspoon of cinnamon, ground
- 1 teaspoon of salt
- 1 cup of whipped cream

Method:
1. Start by putting everything in the Crockpot and mix well.
2. Cover its lid and cook for 2 hours on Low setting.
3. Once done, remove its lid of the crockpot carefully.
4. Spread the mixture on a baking sheet and leave for 30 minutes.
5. Slice and serve.

Nutritional Information per Serving:
- Calories 175
- Total Fat 16 g
- Saturated Fat 2.1 g
- Cholesterol 0 mg
- Sodium 8 mg
- Sugar 1.8 g
- Fiber 0.4 g
- Protein 9 g

Maple Custard

Prep Time: 15 minutes; Cooking Time: 2 hours; Servings:
Ingredients:
- 2 eggs
- 1 cup of heavy cream horizon organic
- 1/2 cup of almond milk
- 1/4 cup of swerve
- 1 teaspoon of maple extract
- 1/4 teaspoon of salt
- 1/2 teaspoon of cinnamon

Method:
1. Start by blending all the Ingredients: together in a mixer.
2. Pour this mixture into a 4 oz. ramekin and place it in the Crockpot.
3. Cover its lid and cook for 2 hours on Low setting.
4. Once done, remove its lid of the crockpot carefully.
5. Allow it to cool and refrigerate for 1 hour.
6. Garnish as desired.
7. Serve.

Nutritional Information per Serving:
- Calories 215
- Total Fat 20 g
- Saturated Fat 7 g
- Cholesterol 38 mg
- Sodium 12 mg
- Sugar 1 g
- Fiber 6 g
- Protein 5 g

Pumpkin Pie Bars

Prep Time: 15 minutes; Cooking Time: 3 hours; Servings: 12
Ingredients:
Crust
- 3/4 cup of shredded coconut
- 1/4 cup of cocoa powder
- 1/2 cup of raw unsalted sunflower seeds
- 1/4 teaspoon of salt

- 1/4 cup of Swerve

Filling
- 1 29 oz. can pumpkin puree
- ¼ cup of swerve
- 1 cup of heavy cream
- 6 eggs

- 4 tablespoons of butter softened
- 1/2 teaspoon of salt
- 1 tablespoon of vanilla extract
- 1 tablespoon of pumpkin pie spice
- 1 teaspoon of cinnamon extract

Method:
1. Start by coarsely blending all the Ingredients: for the crust together in a blender.
2. Spread this crust in the greased based on your Crockpot.
3. Now separately blend the filling mixture in a blender until smooth.
4. Spread this filling the crust-lined in the crockpot.
5. Cover its lid and cook for 3 hours on Low setting.
6. Once done, remove its lid of the crockpot carefully.
7. Garnish as desired.
8. Slice into bars and serve.

Nutritional Information per Serving:
- Calories 198
- Total Fat 19.2 g
- Saturated Fat 11.5 g
- Cholesterol 123 mg
- Sodium 142 mg
- Sugar 3.3 g
- Fiber 0.3 g
- Protein 3.4 g

Raspberry Cake

Prep Time: 15 minutes; Cooking Time: 3 hours; Servings: 12
Ingredients:
Cake Batter
- 1 1/4 almond flour
- 1/2 cup of Swerve
- 1/4 cup of coconut flour
- 1/4 cup of Organic Valley Vanilla Fuel Protein Powder
- 1 1/2 teaspoons of baking powder

- 1/4 teaspoon of salt
- 3 large eggs
- 6 tablespoons of Organic Valley Pasture Butter melted
- 2/3 cup of water
- 1/2 teaspoon of vanilla extract

Filling
- 8 oz. Organic Valley cream cheese
- 1/3 cup of erythritol
- 1 large egg

- 2 tablespoons of Organic Valley whipping cream
- 1 1/2 cup of fresh raspberries

Method:
1. Separately blend the cake mixture and the filling in the mixer while reserving the berries.
2. Now spread the cake batter in the greased based on your crockpot.
3. Top it with the prepared filling evenly and spread the berries over it.
4. Cover its lid and cook for 3 hours on Low setting.
5. Once done, remove its lid of the crockpot carefully.
6. Allow it to cool and refrigerate for 1 hour.
7. Serve.

Nutritional Information per Serving:
- Calories 114
- Total Fat 9.6 g
- Saturated Fat 4.5 g
- Cholesterol 10 mg

- Sodium 155 mg
- Sugar 1.4 g
- Fiber 1.5 g
- Protein 3.5 g

Crockpot Chocolate Cake

Prep Time: 15 minutes; Cooking Time: 2.5 hours; Servings: 10
Ingredients:
- 1 cup of plus 2 tablespoons of almond flour
- 1/2 cup of Erythritol, Granular
- 1/2 cup of cocoa powder
- 3 tablespoons of unflavored whey protein powder
- 1 1/2 teaspoons of baking powder
- 1/4 teaspoon of salt
- 3 large eggs
- 6 tablespoons of butter, melted
- 2/3 cup of almond milk
- 3/4 teaspoon of vanilla extract
- 1/3 cup of sugar-free chocolate chips

Method:
1. Separately blend the wet and dry Ingredients: in the mixer.
2. Mix both the mixtures together in a bowl until smooth.
3. Now spread the cake batter in the greased based on your crockpot.
4. Cover its lid and cook for 2.5 hours on Low setting.
5. Once done, remove its lid of the crockpot carefully.
6. Allow it to cool and refrigerate for 1 hour.
7. Serve.

Nutritional Information per Serving:
- Calories 252
- Total Fat 17.3 g
- Saturated Fat 11.5 g
- Cholesterol 141 mg
- Sodium 153 mg
- Sugar 0.3 g
- Fiber 1.4 g
- Protein 5.2 g

Crockpot Lemon Custard

Prep Time: 15 minutes; Cooking Time: 2 hours; Servings: 4
Ingredients:
- 5 large egg yolks
- 1/4 cup of freshly squeezed lemon juice
- 1 tablespoon of lemon zest
- 1 teaspoon of vanilla extract
- ½ cup of erythritol
- 2 cups of whipping cream or coconut cream
- Lightly sweetened whipped cream

Method:
1. Start by blending all the Ingredients: together in a mixer.
2. Pour this mixture into 4 ramekins and place them in the Crockpot.
3. Cover its lid and cook for 2 hours on Low setting.
4. Once done, remove its lid of the crockpot carefully.
5. Allow it to cool and refrigerate for 1 hour.
6. Garnish as desired.
7. Serve.

Nutritional Information per Serving:
- Calories 195
- Total Fat 14.3 g
- Saturated Fat 10.5 g
- Cholesterol 175 mg
- Sodium 125 mg
- Sugar 0.5 g

- Fiber 0.3 g
- Protein 3.2 g

Slow-Cooked Cranberry Custard

Prep Time: 15 minutes; Cooking Time: 2 hours; Servings: 4

Ingredients:
- 1/4 cup of freshly squeezed lemon juice
- 1 tablespoon of lemon zest
- 5 large egg yolks
- 1 teaspoon of vanilla extract
- 2 cups of whipping cream or coconut cream
- 1/4 cup of cranberries
- ½ cup of erythritol

Method:
1. Start by blending all the Ingredients: together in a mixer.
2. Pour this mixture into 4 ramekins and place them in the Crockpot.
3. Cover its lid and cook for 2 hours on Low setting.
4. Once done, remove its lid of the crockpot carefully.
5. Allow it to cool and refrigerate for 1 hour.
6. Garnish as desired.
7. Serve.

Nutritional Information per Serving:
- Calories 151
- Total Fat 14.7 g
- Saturated Fat 1.5 g
- Cholesterol 13 mg
- Sodium 53 mg
- Sugar 0.3 g
- Fiber 0.1 g
- Protein 23.8 g

Cinnamon Almonds

Prep Time: 15 minutes; Cooking Time: 3 hours; Servings: 4

Ingredients:
- 1 cup of swerve
- 1 cup of brown swerve
- 3 tablespoons of cinnamon ground
- ⅛ teaspoon of salt
- 1 egg white
- 2 teaspoons of vanilla
- 3 cups of almonds
- ⅛ cup of water

Method:
1. Start putting all the Ingredients: into the Crockpot.
2. Cover its lid and cook for 3 hours on Low setting with occasional stirring
3. Once done, remove the pot's lid and give it a stir.
4. Serve fresh.

Nutritional Information per Serving:
- Calories 261
- Total Fat 7.1 g
- Saturated Fat 13.4 g
- Cholesterol 0.3 mg
- Sodium 10 mg
- Sugar 2.1 g
- Fiber 3.9 g
- Protein 1.8 g

Brown Fudge Cake

Prep Time: 15 minutes; Cooking Time: 3 hours; Servings: 8

Ingredients:
- ¼ cup of almond milk
- 2 tablespoons of extra-virgin olive oil

- 1 egg
- ¼ cup of almond flour
- ¼ cup of erythritol
- 1 tablespoon of cocoa powder
- ½ teaspoon of baking powder
- 2 teaspoons of fresh orange zest, grated finely
- Erythritol, as required
- 3 ramekins

Method:
1. Separately blend the wet and dry Ingredients: in the mixer while reserving the berries.
2. Mix both the mixtures together in a bowl until smooth.
3. Divide this batter into 3 ramekins and place them in the crockpot.
4. Cover its lid and cook for 3 hours on Low setting.
5. Once done, remove its lid of the crockpot carefully.
6. Allow them to cool and refrigerate for 1 hour.
7. Serve.

Nutritional Information per Serving:
- Calories 139
- Total Fat 4.6 g
- Saturated Fat 0.5 g
- Cholesterol 1.2 mg
- Sodium 83 mg
- Sugar 6.3 g
- Fiber 0.6 g
- Protein 3.8 g

Chocolate Cheese Cake

Prep Time: 15 minutes; Cooking Time: 4 hours; Servings: 8
Ingredients:
- ¼ cup of erythritol
- 3/4 tablespoon of cocoa powder
- 1 egg
- 8oz. cream cheese softened
- 1 tablespoon of powdered peanut butter
- ½ teaspoon of pure vanilla extract

Method:
1. Separately blend the wet and dry Ingredients: in the mixer while reserving the berries.
2. Mix both the mixtures together in a bowl until smooth.
3. Now spread the cake batter in a greased ramekin and place it in the Crockpot.
4. Cover its lid and cook for 3-4 hours on Low setting.
5. Once done, remove its lid of the crockpot carefully.
6. Allow it to cool and refrigerate for 1 hour.
7. Serve.

Nutritional Information per Serving:
- Calories 136
- Total Fat 10.7 g
- Saturated Fat 0.5 g
- Cholesterol 4 mg
- Sodium 45 mg
- Sugar 1.4 g
- Fiber 0.2 g
- Protein 3.4 g

Almond Cheese Cake

Prep Time: 15 minutes; Cooking Time: 4 hours; Servings: 8
Ingredients:
- ¼ cup of erythritol
- ¼ cup of almonds, sliced
- 1 egg
- 8oz. cream cheese softened

- 1 tablespoon of powdered peanut butter
- ½ teaspoon of pure vanilla extract

Method:
1. Separately blend the wet and dry Ingredients: in the mixer while reserving the berries.
2. Mix both the mixtures together in a bowl until smooth.
3. Now spread the cake batter in a greased ramekin and place it in the Crockpot.
4. Cover its lid and cook for 3-4 hours on Low setting.
5. Once done, remove its lid of the crockpot carefully.
6. Allow it to cool and refrigerate for 1 hour.
7. Serve.

Nutritional Information per Serving:
- Calories 276
- Total Fat 7.2 g
- Saturated Fat 6.4 g
- Cholesterol 134 mg
- Sodium 8 mg
- Sugar 31 g
- Fiber 0.7 g
- Protein 2.2 g

Nutmeg Raspberry Crisp

Prep Time: 15 minutes; Cooking Time: 3 hours; Servings: 6
Ingredients:
- 1 cup of raspberries
- 2 teaspoons of cinnamon ground
- ¼ teaspoon of ginger ground
- ¼ teaspoon of nutmeg ground
- 1 tablespoon of sugar-free maple syrup
- ½ cup of water
- ¾ cup of walnut meal
- ¼ cup of almond flour
- ¼ cup of brown swerve
- ¼ cup of unsalted butter, melted
- Pinch of salt

Method:
1. Start by tossing all the Ingredients: together in a suitable bowl.
2. Mix both the mixtures together in a bowl until smooth.
3. Now spread the mixture in a grease Crockpot.
4. Cover its lid and cook for 3 hours on Low setting.
5. Once done, remove its lid of the crockpot carefully.
6. Serve.

Nutritional Information per Serving:
- Calories 338
- Total Fat 28.8 g
- Saturated Fat 32 g
- Cholesterol 21 g
- Sodium 24 mg
- Fiber 3.4 g
- Sugar 1.3 g
- Protein 3.2 g

Blueberry Cheese Cake

Prep Time: 15 minutes; Cooking Time: 4 hours; Servings: 8
Ingredients:
- 8oz. cream cheese
- ½ cup of erythritol
- 2 eggs
- ¼ cup of sour cream
- 1 tablespoon of vanilla extract
- 2 cups of mixed nuts, crushed
- 2 tablespoons of unsalted butter, melted
- 2 tablespoons of erythritol
- ¼ cup of fresh blueberries pitted

Method:

1. Start by blending the Nuts with butter in the mixer.
2. Spread this Nuts mixture in the greased Crockpot firmly.
3. Now beat the remaining filling Ingredients: except berries in a blender until smooth.
4. Add this cream filling to the Nutty crust and spread evenly.
5. Cover its lid and cook for 3-4 hours on Low setting.
6. Once done, remove its lid of the crockpot carefully.
7. Allow it to cool and refrigerate for 1 hour.
8. Garnish with berries.
9. Serve.

Nutritional Information per Serving:

- Calories 371
- Total Fat 21.2 g
- Saturated Fat 0.5 g
- Cholesterol 5 mg
- Sodium 25 mg
- Fiber 8.2 g
- Sugar 1.6 g
- Protein 3.3 g

Tapioca Pudding

Prep Time: 15 minutes; Cooking Time: 4 hours; Servings: 2

Ingredients:

- 1½ cups of water
- ½ cup of small pearl tapioca
- ½ cup of erythritol
- Pinch of salt
- ½ cup of almond milk
- 2 egg yolks
- ½ teaspoon of vanilla extract
- ¼ cup of fresh raspberries

Method:

1. Start by throwing all the Ingredients: into the Crockpot except berries.
2. Cover its lid and cook for 3-4 hours on Low setting.
3. Once done, remove its lid of the crockpot carefully.
4. Allow it to cool and refrigerate for 1 hour.
5. Garnish with berries.
6. Serve.

Nutritional Information per Serving:

- Calories 320
- Total Fat 27.4 g
- Saturated Fat 9.9 g
- Cholesterol 0.5 mg
- Sodium 122 mg
- Fiber 7.3 g
- Sugar 1.2 g
- Protein 4.3 g

Cherry Cheese Cake

Prep Time: 15 minutes; Cooking Time: 6 hours; Servings: 8

Ingredients:

- 8oz. cream cheese
- 8oz. ricotta cheese
- ¼ cup of erythritol
- 2 eggs
- ¼ cup of sour cream
- 1 tablespoon of vanilla extract
- 2 cups of mixed nuts, crushed
- 2 tablespoons of unsalted butter, melted
- 2 tablespoons of erythritol
- ¼ cup of fresh cherries pitted

Method:

1. Start by blending the Nuts with butter in the mixer.
2. Spread this Nuts mixture in the greased Crockpot firmly.
3. Now beat the remaining filling Ingredients: except cherries in a blender until smooth.
4. Add this cream filling to the Nutty crust and spread evenly.
5. Cover its lid and cook for 6 hours on Low setting.
6. Once done, remove its lid of the crockpot carefully.
7. Allow it to cool and refrigerate for 1 hour.
8. Garnish with cherries.
9. Serve.

Nutritional Information per Serving:
- Calories 220
- Total Fat 2.8 g
- Saturated Fat 0.1 g
- Cholesterol 5 mg
- Sodium 177 mg
- Fiber 3 g
- Sugar 24.2 g
- Protein 3.7 g

Blueberry Pudding

Prep Time: 15 minutes; Cooking Time: 4 hours; Servings: 8
Ingredients:
- 1 cup of blueberries
- 1 cup of erythritol
- 2 eggs
- 1 tablespoon of vanilla
- 2 cups of almond flour
- 1 tablespoon of baking powder
- Topping:
- 1 stick butter
- 2 cups of brown swerve
- 1 cup of heavy cream

Method:
1. Separately blend the wet and dry Ingredients: in the mixer while reserving brown swerve and butter.
2. Mix both the mixtures together in a bowl until smooth.
3. Now spread the cake batter in a greased ramekin and place it in the Crockpot.
4. Cover its lid and cook for 3-4 hours on Low setting.
5. Once done, remove its lid of the crockpot carefully.
6. Allow it to cool and refrigerate for 1 hour.
7. Cook brown swerve with butter in a saucepan for 5 minutes.
8. Pour this mixture over the cooked pudding.
9. Serve.

Nutritional Information per Serving:
- Calories 193
- Total Fat 10 g
- Saturated Fat 13.2 g
- Cholesterol 120 mg
- Sodium 8 mg
- Sugar 1 g
- Fiber 0.7 g
- Protein 2.2 g

Orange Cheese Cake

Prep Time: 15 minutes; Cooking Time: 4 hours; Servings: 4
Ingredients:
- 8 oz. cream cheese
- ¼ cup of erythritol
- ½ teaspoon of almond flour
- ¼ teaspoon of vanilla
- 2 tablespoons of sour cream
- ½ tablespoon of lemon Juice

- zest of ¼ orange
- 1 ½ egg, room temp
- ½ jar Greek yogurt
- 3 raspberries
- 1 cup of water

Method:
1. Separately blend the wet and dry Ingredients: in the mixer.
2. Mix both the mixtures together in a bowl until smooth.
3. Now spread the cake batter in a greased ramekin and place it in the Crockpot.
4. Cover its lid and cook for 4 hours on Low setting.
5. Once done, remove its lid of the crockpot carefully.
6. Allow it to cool and refrigerate for 1 hour.
7. Serve.

Nutritional Information per Serving:
- Calories 173
- Total Fat 13 g
- Saturated Fat 10.1 g
- Cholesterol 12 mg
- Sodium 67 mg
- Sugar 1.2 g
- Fiber 0.6 g
- Protein 3.2 g

Lemon Cheese Cake

Prep Time: 15 minutes; Cooking Time: 6 hours; Servings: 4
Ingredients:
- 8 oz. cream cheese
- ¼ cup of erythritol
- ½ teaspoon of almond flour
- ¼ teaspoon of vanilla
- 2 tablespoons of sour cream
- ½ tablespoon of Lemon Juice
- zest of half lemon
- 1 ½ egg, room temp
- ½ jar lemon curd
- 3 raspberries
- 1 cup of water

Method:
1. Separately blend the wet and dry Ingredients: in the mixer while reserving the berries
2. Mix both the mixtures together in a bowl until smooth.
3. Now spread the cake batter in a greased ramekin and place it in the Crockpot.
4. Cover its lid and cook for 6 hours on Low setting.
5. Once done, remove its lid of the crockpot carefully.
6. Allow it to cool and refrigerate for 1 hour.
7. Garnish with the berries
8. Serve.

Nutritional Information per Serving:
- Calories 334
- Total Fat 28.9 g
- Saturated Fat 25 g
- Cholesterol 51 mg
- Sodium 30 mg
- Fiber 5.9 g
- Sugar 1.4 g
- Protein 4.3 g

Delicious Breakfast Cake

Prep Time: 15 minutes; Cooking Time: 6 hours; Servings: 6
Ingredients:
- 6 tablespoons of coconut flour
- 6 tablespoons of almond flour
- ¼ teaspoon of salt
- ½ teaspoon of baking soda

- ¼ teaspoon of baking powder
- 6 tablespoons of erythritol
- ¼ cup of berry compote
- 1 tablespoon of canola oil
- 1/2 cup of 2% vanilla yogurt
- 2 ½ eggs
- ¼ teaspoon of pure vanilla extract

Method:
1. Separately blend the wet and dry Ingredients: in the mixer.
2. Mix both the mixtures together in a bowl until smooth.
3. Now spread the cake batter in a greased ramekin and place it in the Crockpot.
4. Cover its lid and cook for 6 hours on Low setting.
5. Once done, remove its lid of the crockpot carefully.
6. Allow it to cool and refrigerate for 1 hour.
7. Serve.

Nutritional Information per Serving:
- Calories 107
- Total Fat 9.3 g
- Saturated Fat 4.8 g
- Cholesterol 77 mg
- Sodium 135 mg
- Fiber 0.8 g
- Sugar 9.9 g
- Protein 3.9 g

Traditional Egg Custard

Prep Time: 15 minutes; Cooking Time: 3 hours; Servings: 4
Ingredients:
- 4 cups of almond milk
- 6 eggs
- 3/4 cup of erythritol
- 1 teaspoon of vanilla extract
- 1 pinch salt
- ¼ teaspoon of cinnamon, ground
- Nutmeg, grated
- Fresh fruits, diced

Method:
1. Start by blending all the Ingredients: together in a mixer.
2. Pour this mixture into 4 ramekins and place them in the Crockpot.
3. Cover its lid and cook for 2-3 hours on Low setting.
4. Once done, remove its lid of the crockpot carefully.
5. Allow it to cool and refrigerate for 1 hour.
6. Garnish as desired.
7. Serve.

Nutritional Information per Serving:
- Calories 172
- Total Fat 10.7 g
- Saturated Fat 7.4 g
- Cholesterol 62 mg
- Sodium 121 mg
- Fiber 0.6 g
- Sugar 1.5 g
- Protein 12 g

Pineapple Cheese Cake

Prep Time: 15 minutes; Cooking Time: 6 hours; Servings: 8
Ingredients:
- 8oz. cream cheese
- 8oz. ricotta cheese
- 1 tablespoon of sugar-free pineapple extract
- ¼ cup of erythritol
- 2 eggs
- ¼ cup of sour cream
- 1 tablespoon of vanilla extract
- 2 cups of mixed nuts, crushed

- 2 tablespoons of unsalted butter, melted
- ¼ cup of raspberries

Method:
1. Start by blending the Nuts with butter in the mixer.
2. Spread this Nuts mixture in the greased Crockpot firmly.
3. Now beat the remaining filling Ingredients: except berries in a blender until smooth.
4. Add this cream filling to the Nutty crust and spread evenly.
5. Cover its lid and cook for 6 hours on Low setting.
6. Once done, remove its lid of the crockpot carefully.
7. Allow it to cool and refrigerate for 12 hours.
8. Garnish with berries.
9. Serve.

Nutritional Information per Serving:
- Calories 213
- Total Fat 19 g
- Saturated Fat 15.2 g
- Cholesterol 13 mg
- Sodium 52 mg
- Sugar 1.3 g
- Fiber 0.5 g
- Protein 6.1 g

Raspberry Custard Trifle

Prep Time: 15 minutes; Cooking Time: 3 hours; Servings: 4
Ingredients:
- 4 cups of almond milk
- 6 eggs
- 3/4 cup of erythritol
- 1 teaspoon of vanilla extract
- 1 pinch salt
- ¼ teaspoon of cinnamon, ground
- 4 tablespoons of brown swerve
- 2 tablespoons of water
- 1 cup of raspberries

Method:
1. Start by blending all the Ingredients: together in a mixer except raspberries, brown swerve, and water.
2. Pour this mixture into 4 ramekins and place them in the Crockpot.
3. Cover its lid and cook for 3 hours on Low setting.
4. Once done, remove its lid of the crockpot carefully.
5. Allow it to cool and refrigerate for 1 hour.
6. Meanwhile, boil brown swerve with water in a saucepan and cook until it is caramelized.
7. Garnish the custard with raspberries then pour the caramel mixture on top.
8. Serve.

Nutritional Information per Serving:
- Calories 197
- Total Fat 19.2 g
- Saturated Fat 10.1 g
- Cholesterol 11 mg
- Sodium 78 mg
- Sugar 1.2 g
- Fiber 0.8 g
- Protein 4.2 g

Fruity Custard Delight

Prep Time: 15 minutes; Cooking Time: 4 hours; Servings: 6
Ingredients:

- 4 cups of almond milk
- 6 eggs
- 3/4 cup of brown swerve

- 1 teaspoon of vanilla extract
- 1 pinch salt
- ¼ teaspoon of cinnamon, ground

To serve:
- 1 cup of whipped cream
- 1 lb. keto sponge cake, sliced

- Mix berries, sliced

Method:
1. Start by blending all the Ingredients: together in a mixer.
2. Pour this mixture into a steel pan and place it in the Crockpot.
3. Cover its lid and cook for 4 hours on Low setting.
4. Once done, remove its lid of the crockpot carefully.
5. Allow it to cool and refrigerate for 1 hour.
6. To serve, layer a casserole dish with sponge cake slices.
7. Top them with prepared custard and garnish with fresh fruits.
8. Refrigerate again for 4 hours or more.
9. Serve.

Nutritional Information per Serving:
- Calories 213
- Total Fat 19 g
- Saturated Fat 15.2 g
- Cholesterol 13 mg

- Sodium 52 mg
- Sugar 1.3 g
- Fiber 0.5 g
- Protein 6.1 g

Chocolate Cream Custard

Prep Time: 15 minutes; Cooking Time: 2 hours; Servings: 4

Ingredients:
- 4 cups of almond milk
- 6 eggs
- 3/4 cup of brown swerve
- 1 teaspoon of vanilla extract

- 1 teaspoon of cocoa powder
- ¼ teaspoon of cinnamon, ground
- Sugar-free chocolate, grated
- Whipped cream

Method:
1. Start by blending all the Ingredients: together in a mixer.
2. Pour this mixture into 4 ramekins and place them in the Crockpot.
3. Cover its lid and cook for 2 hours on Low setting.
4. Once done, remove its lid of the crockpot carefully.
5. Allow it to cool and refrigerate for 1 hour.
6. Garnish with chocolate and whipped cream.
7. Serve.

Nutritional Information per Serving:
- Calories 117
- Total Fat 21.2 g
- Saturated Fat 10.4 g
- Cholesterol 19.7 mg

- Sodium 104 mg
- Sugar 3.4 g
- Fiber 2 g
- Protein 8.1 g

Caramel Cheesecake

Prep Time: 15 minutes; Cooking Time: 6 hours; Servings: 6

Ingredients:
- 8oz. cream cheese

- ¼ cup of erythritol

- 2 eggs
- ¼ cup of sour cream
- 1 tablespoon of vanilla extract
- 2 cups of mixed nuts, crushed
- 2 tablespoons of unsalted butter, melted

Toppings:
- 10 caramels, unwrapped
- 2 tablespoons of heavy cream
- ¼ cup of melted sugar-free chocolate

Method:
1. Start by blending the Nuts with butter in the mixer.
2. Spread this Nuts mixture in the greased Crockpot firmly.
3. Now beat the remaining filling Ingredients: except berries in a blender until smooth.
4. Add this cream filling to the Nutty crust and spread evenly.
5. Cover its lid and cook for 6 hours on Low setting.
6. Once done, remove its lid of the crockpot carefully.
7. Allow it to cool and refrigerate for 1 hour.
8. Garnish with berries and other toppings.
9. Serve.

Nutritional Information per Serving:
- Calories 252
- Total Fat 17.3 g
- Saturated Fat 11.5 g
- Cholesterol 141 mg
- Sodium 153 mg
- Sugar 1.3 g
- Fiber 1.4 g
- Protein 5.2 g

Toffee Pudding

Prep Time: 15 minutes; Cooking Time: 4 hours; Servings: 4

Ingredients:
- 3/4 cup of diced pecans
- ¼ cup of sugar-free maple syrup
- ¼ cup of boiling water
- 3/4 cup of almond flour
- ½ teaspoon of baking powder
- 1 pinch salt
- 6 tablespoons of brown swerve
- 1/6 cup of unsalted butter
- ½ egg
- ½ teaspoon of vanilla extract

Method:
1. Start by blending all the Ingredients: together in a mixer.
2. Pour this mixture into 4 ramekins and place them in the Crockpot.
3. Cover its lid and cook for 4 hours on Low setting.
4. Once done, remove its lid of the crockpot carefully.
5. Allow it to cool and refrigerate for 1 hour.
6. Serve.

Nutritional Information per Serving:
- Calories 113
- Total Fat 9 g
- Saturated Fat 0.2 g
- Cholesterol 1.7 mg
- Sodium 134 mg
- Sugar 1.8 g
- Fiber 0.7 g
- Protein 7.5 g

Carrot Walnut Cake

Prep Time: 15 minutes; Cooking Time: 6 hours; Servings: 6
Ingredients:

- 1 ½ egg
- ½ cup of almond flour
- 1/3 cup of Brown swerve
- ½ teaspoon of baking powder
- 3/4 teaspoons of apple pie spice
- 2 tablespoons of coconut oil
- ¼ cup of heavy whipping cream
- ½ cup of carrots shredded
- ¼ cup of walnuts diced

Method:
1. Separately blend the wet and dry Ingredients: in the mixer.
2. Mix both the mixtures together in a bowl until smooth.
3. Now spread the cake batter in a greased ramekin and place it in the Crockpot.
4. Cover its lid and cook for 6 hours on Low setting.
5. Once done, remove its lid of the crockpot carefully.
6. Allow it to cool and refrigerate for 1 hour.
7. Serve.

Nutritional Information per Serving:
- Calories 101
- Total Fat 15.5 g
- Saturated Fat 4.5 g
- Cholesterol 12 mg
- Sodium 18 mg
- Sugar 1.2 g
- Fiber 0.3 g
- Protein 4.8 g

Pumpkin Custard

Prep Time: 15 minutes; Cooking Time: 4 hours; Servings: 4
Ingredients:
- 3 cups of almond milk
- 1 cup of pumpkin puree
- 6 eggs
- 3/4 cup of brown swerve
- 1 teaspoon of pumpkin spice
- 1 pinch salt
- ¼ teaspoon of cinnamon ground
- 1 cup of heavy cream
- Walnuts, to serve

Method:
1. Start by blending all the Ingredients: together in a mixer.
2. Pour this mixture into 4 ramekins and place them in the Crockpot.
3. Cover its lid and cook for 4 hours on Low setting.
4. Once done, remove its lid of the crockpot carefully.
5. Allow it to cool and refrigerate for 1 hour.
6. Garnish with walnuts and cream.
7. Serve.
8. 8. Serve.

Nutritional Information per Serving:
- Calories 174
- Total Fat 12.3 g
- Saturated Fat 4.8 g
- Cholesterol 32 mg
- Sodium 597 mg
- Fiber 0.6 g
- Sugar 1.9 g
- Protein 12 g

Low Carb Sweet Pecans

Prep Time: 15 minutes; Cooking Time: 3 hours; Servings: 4
Ingredients:
- 3 cups of pecans
- 1 cup of swerve
- 1 cup of brown swerve
- 3 tablespoons of cinnamon ground

- ⅛ teaspoon of salt
- 1 egg white
- 2 teaspoons of vanilla
- ⅛ cup of water

Method:
1. Start putting all the Ingredients: into the Crockpot.
2. Cover its lid and cook for 3 hours on Low setting with occasional stirring
3. Once done, remove the pot's lid and give it a stir.
4. Serve fresh.

Nutritional Information per Serving:
- Calories 266
- Total Fat 25.7 g
- Saturated Fat 1.2 g
- Cholesterol 41 mg
- Sodium 18 mg
- Protein 2.6 g

Peanut Butter Cake

Prep Time: 15 minutes; Cooking Time: 5 hours; Servings: 6

Ingredients:
- ½ cup of almond flour
- 1/3 cup of Swerve
- 1/2 teaspoon of baking powder
- 2 tablespoons of walnut, diced
- 2 tablespoons of cocoa powder
- 1 ½ egg
- 2 tablespoons of heavy cream
- 2 tablespoons of coconut oil
- ¼ cup of peanut butter

Method:
1. Separately blend the wet and dry Ingredients: in the mixer.
2. Mix both the mixtures together in a bowl until smooth.
3. Now spread the cake batter in a greased ramekin and place it in the Crockpot.
4. Cover its lid and cook for 5 hours on Low setting.
5. Once done, remove its lid of the crockpot carefully.
6. Allow it to cool and refrigerate for 1 hour.
7. Serve.

Nutritional Information per Serving:
- Calories 359
- Total Fat 34 g
- Saturated Fat 10.3 g
- Cholesterol 112 mg
- Sugar 2 g
- Protein 7.5 g

Delightful Crème Brule

Prep Time: 15 minutes; Cooking Time: 2 hours; Servings: 4

Ingredients:
- 4 ramekins
- 5 egg yolks
- 2 cups of heavy cream
- 1 tablespoon of vanilla extract
- ½ tablespoon of cocoa powder
- ½ cup of swerve
- ¼ cup of superfine swerve

Method:
1. Start by thoroughly blending all the Ingredients: in a blender until smooth.
2. Now divide the batter into 4 ramekins and place them in the Crockpot.
3. Cover its lid and cook for 2 hours on Low setting.
4. Once done, remove its lid of the crockpot carefully.
5. Allow it to cool and refrigerate for 1 hour.
6. Serve.

Nutritional Information per Serving:
- Calories 243
- Total Fat 21 g
- Saturated Fat 18.2 g
- Cholesterol 121 mg
- Sodium 34 mg
- Protein 4.3 g

Chocolate Crème Brule

Prep Time: 15 minutes; Cooking Time: 2 hours; Servings: 4
Ingredients:
- 4 ramekins
- 5 egg yolks
- 2 cups of heavy cream
- 1 tablespoon of vanilla extract
- ½ tablespoon of cocoa powder
- ½ cup of swerve
- ½ tablespoon of grated sugar-free chocolate

Method:
1. Start by thoroughly blending all the Ingredients: in a blender until smooth.
2. Now divide the batter into 4 ramekins and place them in the Crockpot.
3. Cover its lid and cook for 2 hours on Low setting.
4. Once done, remove its lid of the crockpot carefully.
5. Allow it to cool and refrigerate for 1 hour.
6. Serve.

Nutritional Information per Serving:
- Calories 183
- Total Fat 15 g
- Saturated Fat 12.1 g
- Cholesterol 11 mg
- Sodium 31 mg
- Protein 4.5 g

Lavender Crème Brule

Prep Time: 15 minutes; Cooking Time: 2 hours; Servings: 4
Ingredients:
- 4 ramekins
- 5 egg yolks
- 2 cups of heavy cream
- 1 tablespoon of vanilla extract
- ½ cup of swerve
- ½ tablespoon of lavender buds

Method:
1. Start by blending all the Ingredients: except lavender in a blender until smooth.
2. Now divide the batter into 4 ramekins and place them in the Crockpot.
3. Cover its lid and cook for 2 hours on Low setting.
4. Once done, remove its lid of the crockpot carefully.
5. Allow it to cool and refrigerate for 1 hour.
6. Garnish with lavender.
7. Serve.

Nutritional Information per Serving:
- Calories 188
- Total Fat 3 g
- Saturated Fat 2.2 g
- Cholesterol 101 mg
- Sodium 54 mg
- Protein 5 g

Pumpkin Cake

Prep Time: 15 minutes; Cooking Time: 4 hours; Servings: 6
Ingredients:
- 6 tablespoons of coconut flour

- 6 tablespoons of unbleached almond flour
- ¼ teaspoon of salt
- ½ teaspoon of baking soda
- ¼ teaspoon of baking powder
- ¼ teaspoon of pumpkin pie spice
- 6 tablespoons of swerve
- ½ medium banana mashed
- 1 tablespoon of canola oil
- ¼ cup of Greek yogurt
- ¼ (15 oz.) can pumpkin puree
- ½ egg
- ¼ teaspoon of pure vanilla extract
- ¼ cup of sugar-free chocolate chips

Method:
1. Separately blend the wet and dry Ingredients: in the mixer.
2. Mix both the mixtures together in a bowl until smooth.
3. Now spread the cake batter in a greased ramekin and place it in the Crockpot.
4. Cover its lid and cook for 4 hours on Low setting.
5. Once done, remove its lid of the crockpot carefully.
6. Allow it to cool and refrigerate for 1 hour.
7. Serve.

Nutritional Information per Serving:
- Calories 153
- Total Fat 13 g
- Saturated Fat 9.2 g
- Cholesterol 6.5 mg
- Sodium 81 mg
- Protein 5.8 g

Spiced Strawberry Pudding

Prep Time: 15 minutes; Cooking Time: 4 hours; Servings: 6
Ingredients:
- 1 cup of swerve
- 2 eggs
- 2 cups of strawberries, cored
- 1 tablespoon of vanilla
- 1 tablespoon of apple pie spice
- 2 cups of almond flour
- 1 tablespoon of baking powder

Topping:
- 1 stick butter
- 2 cups of brown swerve
- 1 cup of heavy cream

Method:
1. Separately blend the wet and dry Ingredients: in the mixer.
2. Mix both the mixtures together in a bowl until smooth.
3. Now spread the cake batter in a greased ramekin and place it in the Crockpot.
4. Cover its lid and cook for 4 hours on Low setting.
5. Once done, remove its lid of the crockpot carefully.
6. Allow it to cool and refrigerate for 1 hour.
7. Serve.

Nutritional Information per Serving:
- Calories 254
- Total Fat 09 g
- Saturated Fat 10.1 g
- Cholesterol 13 mg
- Sodium 179 mg
- Protein 7.5 g

Chapter 13: 30 Days Meal Plan

Week 01

Day 1

Breakfast: Leeks Parsley Quiche

Lunch: Cod & Peas with Sour Cream

Snack: Radish Spinach Medley

Dinner: Chicken Shrimp Curry

Dessert: Crockpot Chocolate Cake

Day 2

Breakfast: Long Beans, Egg Omelets

Lunch: Citrus Glazed Salmon

Snack: Herb Mixed Radish

Dinner: Garlic Butter Chicken with Cream Cheese Sauce

Dessert: Blueberry Pudding

Day 3

Breakfast: French Beans Omelets

Lunch: Rich Salmon Soup

Snack: Citrus rich Cabbage

Dinner: Chicken Dipped in tomatillo Sauce

Dessert: Lemon Cheese Cake

Day 4

Breakfast: Onion Spinach Frittata

Lunch: Seafood Stew

Snack: Creamy Mustard Asparagus

Dinner: Dijon Chicken

Dessert: Peanut Butter Cake

Day 5

Breakfast: Broccoli Egg Casserole

Lunch: Lemon Salmon

Snack: Savory Pine Nuts Cabbage

Dinner: Chunky Chicken Salsa

Dessert: Spiced Strawberry Pudding

Day 6

Breakfast: Italian Chicken Frittata

Lunch: Curried Shrimp

Snack: Nutmeg Fennel

Dinner: Chicken Roux Gumbo

Dessert: Pumpkin Cake

Day 7

Breakfast: Tofu Scramble

Lunch: Fish Curry

Snack: Herbed Cherry Tomatoes

Dinner: Saucy Duck

Dessert: Lavender Crème Brule

Week 02

Day 1

Breakfast: Cheesy Cauliflower Garlic Bread

Lunch: Lamb Leg with Thyme

Snack: Parmesan cream Green Beans

Dinner: Barbeque Chicken Wings

Dessert: Chocolate Crème Brule

Day 2

Breakfast: Zucchini Bread

Lunch: Vegetable Lamb Stew

Snack: Viennese Coffee

Dinner: Turkey Meatballs

Dessert: Low Carb Sweet Pecans

Day 3

Breakfast: Bell Pepper Hash

Lunch: Herbed Lamb Stew

Snack: Creamy Coconut Spinach

Dinner: Aromatic Jalapeno Wings

Dessert: Carrot Walnut Cake

Day 4

Breakfast: Ham Frittata

Lunch: Coconut Lamb Stew

Snack: White Mushrooms and Chard Mix

Dinner: Capers Eggplant Stew

Dessert: Chocolate Cream Custard

Day 5

Breakfast: Cheesy Sausage Quiche

Lunch: Dinner Lamb Shanks

Snack: Creamy Coconut Cauliflower

Dinner: Chard Chicken Soup

Week 03

Day 1

Breakfast: Mexican Casserole

Lunch: Prime Rib Luncheon

Snack: Paprika Zucchini

Dinner: Minced Beef Coriander Chili

Dessert: Blueberry Pudding

Day 2

Breakfast: Morning Quiche

Lunch: Red Beef Steak

Snack: Mushrooms Balsamic Mix

Dinner: Salsa Verde Soup

Dessert: Cherry Cheese Cake

Day 3

Breakfast: Sweet Pepper Hash

Lunch: Beef ramen

Snack: Nutty Green Beans with Avocado

Dinner: Minestrone Kale Soup

Dessert: Tapioca Pudding

Dessert: Raspberry Custard Trifle

Day 6

Breakfast: Mushroom Casserole

Lunch: Lamb Chops Curry

Snack: Spicy Rosemary Cauliflower

Dinner: Jalapeno Pork Tenderloin Soup

Dessert: Delicious Breakfast Cake

Day 7

Breakfast: Breakfast Frittata

Lunch: Smoked Lamb Chili

Snack: Celery and Broccoli Medley

Dinner: Meatball Spinach Soup

Dessert: Lemon Cheese Cake

Day 4

Breakfast: Grain-Free Granola with Orange Zest

Lunch: Ground beef and green beans

Snack: Mashed Broccoli

Dinner: Cream & Cheese Broccoli Soup

Dessert: Nutmeg Raspberry Crisp

Day 5

Breakfast: Egg Cauliflower Casserole

Lunch: Beef Fajita Stew

Snack: Rich Creamy Endives

Dinner: Vegetable Beef Soup

Dessert: Almond Cheese Cake

Day 6

Breakfast: Arugula Frittata

Lunch: Southwestern Pot Roast

Snack: Saffron Bell Peppers

Dinner: Low Carb Taco Soup

Dessert: Slow-Cooked Cranberry Custard

Day 7
Breakfast: Minced Turkey Egg Casserole
Lunch: Spicy Mexican Luncheon

Week 04

Day 1
Breakfast: Egg Hash Browns
Lunch: Vegetable Beef Stew
Snack: Broccoli Yogurt Dip
Dinner: Creamy Lemon Chicken Kale Soup
Dessert: Blueberry Lemon Custard Cake

Day 2
Breakfast: Mushroom Spinach Breakfast
Lunch: Beef Cabbage Casserole
Snack: Herbed Green Beans
Dinner: White Chicken Chili Soup
Dessert: Pumpkin Pie Bars

Day 3
Breakfast: Bacon Topped Hash Browns
Lunch: Pumpkin Beef Chili
Snack: Savory Pine Nuts Cabbage
Dinner: No Noodle Chicken Soup
Dessert: Blueberry Crisp

Day 4
Breakfast: Italian Chicken Frittata
Lunch: Beef Steaks with Peppercorn Sauce

Snack: Creamy Coconut Fennel
Dinner: Mexican Chicken Low Carb Soup
Dessert: Crockpot Chocolate Cake

Snack: Herb Mixed Radish
Dinner: Chicken Cordon Bleu Soup
Dessert: Maple Custard

Day 5
Breakfast: Creamy Egg and Ham Delight
Lunch: Beef Onion Stew
Snack: Parmesan cream Green Beans
Dinner: Pork Chops with Spice Rub
Dessert: Granola

Day 6
Breakfast: Kale with Eggs
Lunch: Mushroom Beef Goulash
Snack: Spicy Rosemary Cauliflower
Dinner: Homemade Thai Chicken Soup
Dessert: Super Fudgy Brownies

Day 7
Breakfast: Asparagus Parmesan Frittata
Lunch: Sweet Passata Dipped Steaks
Snack: Zucchini Eggplant Spread
Dinner: Cabbage Soup Recipe
Dessert: Chocolate Fudge

Conclusion

In the absence of carbohydrates, good fat can prove to be advantageous for our health, which is the real objective of a ketogenic diet. It is responsible for accelerating the body's natural metabolic process called Ketosis, by keeping the carb intake down to 50 grams per day or less. To harness its true benefits, it requires a good and deep understanding of the diet, its Dos and Don'ts just to get started with it, that is why the content of this cookbook will help you explore the basics of a ketogenic diet along with the recipes. These recipes are created with the consideration of the latest slow cooking innovation Crock-Pot so you can cook and enjoy with complete ease and convenience.

Made in the USA
Columbia, SC
01 October 2020